$12.98

Nazi Power at its Widest Extent

FINLAND

Helsinki

Leningrad

Sea

Tallinn
ESTONIA

Riga
LATVIA

Moscow

LITHUANIA
Kovno
Vilna

Tula

EAST
PRUSSIA

Minsk

SOVIET UNION

Warsaw

POLAND UNDER
GERMAN RULE

Kharkov

Stalingrad

Kiev

Cracow

Lvov

TRANSNISTRIA

UKRAINE

Rostov

...IA

Budapest

HUNGARY

Caspian Sea

...ANAT

RUMANIA

CRIMEA

Grozny

Belgrade
SERBIA

Bucharest

Black Sea

...ATRANIA

Sofia

BULGARIA

Istanbul

Ankara

GREECE

TURKEY

Athens

Crete

Cyprus

Sea

The German Reich

Areas under German Administration
and Occupation

German satellites

Italy and annexed areas

0   100   200   300

Miles

NEVER
TO FORGET

Books by Milton Meltzer

WORLD OF OUR FATHERS
The Jews of Eastern Europe

REMEMBER THE DAYS
A Short History of the Jewish American

BOUND FOR THE RIO GRANDE
The Mexican Struggle, 1845–1850

SLAVERY
From the Rise of Western Civilization to Today (2 volumes)

A PICTORIAL HISTORY OF BLACKAMERICANS
(with Langston Hughes and C. Eric Lincoln)

THE EYE OF CONSCIENCE
Photographers and Social Change

LANGSTON HUGHES
A Biography

UNDERGROUND MAN
A Novel

THE RIGHT TO REMAIN SILENT

NEVER
TO FORGET
The Jews
of the Holocaust

MILTON MELTZER

HARPER & ROW, PUBLISHERS
New York Hagerstown San Francisco London

ACKNOWLEDGMENTS

I gratefully acknowledge support from the Anti-Defamation League
of B'nai B'rith, which aided in my research for this book. I am also
indebted to the YIVO Institute for Jewish Research and its librarians,
Dina Abramowicz and Bella Weinberg, whose help was indispensable
to the writing of this book.

Acknowledgment is made for permission to quote from the following works:
Fromm, Bella, *Blood and Banquets*, copyright 1942 by Cooperation Publishing Co.,
Inc. Reprinted by permission of Harper & Row, Publishers, Inc. Shirer, William L., *Berlin Diary*, copyright 1941 by William L. Shirer. Reprinted by permission
of Alfred A. Knopf, Inc. Fackenheim, Emil L., "Torture Through Senseless
System," *Midstream*, April 1975. Letter by David Buffum from Henry Zieger,
The Case Against Adolf Eichmann, copyright © 1960 by Henry Zieger. Reprinted
by arrangement with The New American Library, Inc., New York, N.Y. Libau,
M. I., "That Bloody Day in November," *Congress Weekly*, vol. 9, no. 34, November 13, 1942. Dworzecki, Mark, "A Day in the Vilna Ghetto," *Jewish Frontier*,
May 1952. Passages by Levi Shalit, Shaye Gertner, Reuben Rosenberg, and
Stanislaw Kohn, and the record of a meeting held in February 1943 by the
Hechalutz, Bialystok Branch, all from *Anthology of Holocaust Literature*, edited
by Jacob Glatstein et al. Copyright © 1968 by The Jewish Publication Society of
America. Reprinted by permission of The Jewish Publication Society of
America. Ringelblum, Emmanuel, *Notes from the Warsaw Ghetto: The Journal of Emmanuel Ringelblum*, translated from the Yiddish and edited by Jacob Sloan, copyright © 1958. Used with permission of McGraw-Hill Book Company. Passages by
Georges Wellers, W. Szpilman, Johann Kremer, and Ludwik Hirszfeld from
Gerhard Schoenberner, *The Yellow Star: The Persecution of the Jews in Europe,
1933–1945*. Original German edition, *Der Gelbe Stern*, copyright © 1960 by Gerhard Schoenberner. Revised edition copyright © 1969 by Gerhard Schoenberner.
English translation copyright © 1969 by Transworld Publishers, Ltd. Reprinted by
permission of Bantam Books, Inc. Passage by Hans Baermann from Eugen Kogon,
*The Theory and Practice of Hell: The German Concentration Camps and the
System Behind Them*, copyright 1950 by Octagon Books. Reprinted by permission
of Farrar, Straus & Giroux, Inc. Kaplan, Chaim, *Scroll of Agony*, edited and
translated by Abraham Katsh, copyright © 1963 by Abraham Katsh. Reprinted by
permission of Macmillan Publishing Co., Inc. Passage by Jeanette Wolf from
We Survived, edited by Eric Boehm, copyright © 1966, Clio Press, Santa Barbara,
Calif. Reprinted by permission of Eric Boehm. Passages by Feigele Wladka and

In Memory of Max Hahn

CONTENTS

NEVER
TO FORGET

Why Remember?

I was fifteen years old when I first noticed the strange words "Nazi" and "Hitler" in the newspaper. I lived in Worcester, a city in the center of Massachusetts. It was September 1930, and I was just starting my junior year in high school. I used to read the papers, but not very thoroughly. Sports, the funnies, stories about local people, rarely any foreign news.

But on this day something caught my eye in a report datelined from Germany. A hundred-odd members of Adolf Hitler's Nazi party had just been elected to the German legislature—the Reichstag they called it—and they had shown up for the first session wearing brown uniforms and shouting, "*Deutschland erwache! Jude verrecke!*"

The paper obligingly explained what those foreign words meant: Germany awake! Jew perish!

Who was Hitler? What was a Nazi? Did the Germans take that slogan seriously—"Jew perish!"

It was those words that had leaped out at me from the small print. I wasn't looking for them; I didn't know they would be there. Still, I saw them as with a special sense, attuned to those three letters, J-E-W. The same sudden alarm would go off in a busy place—the school gym, the Y swimming pool, the corner hangout—if the word "Jew" were spoken by someone in the crowd. Through the confusion of noise the sound would arrow straight into my brain.

I was Jewish, of course, but a feeble kind of Jew, as I think of it now. I mean I had no religious training and almost no knowledge of Jewish life, history, or language. Our neighborhood was very mixed, and so were the schools I went to. I thought of myself as an American. If someone said yes, but what *kind* of American, then I'd say Jewish. Once on a Saturday morning an old Jewish widow who had just moved into the neighborhood saw me on the street and asked me to come into her house and light the stove. I wondered why she couldn't light it herself, but I did it, and she gave me a cookie. When I told my mother about it, she laughed and said, "She took you for a *Shabbos goy*." She explained that religious Jews could not light a fire on the Sabbath. If they needed it, they'd ask a non-Jew, a goy, to do it.

I thought it was funny, too.

Then why did my skin prickle when I saw those words in the newspaper? Whatever kind of Jew I was, I had somehow absorbed the knowledge that Jews lived under threat. I had heard of the Jews of Egypt, enslaved under Pharaoh, and of how Haman's plan to annihilate the Jews of Persia had been foiled by Queen Esther. I knew vaguely about the persecution of the Jews during the Crusades and that the Inquisition had driven the Jews from Spain. Somewhere I had seen the word "pogrom" in print, knew it meant bloody riots against the Jews, and linked it to the immigrants who, like my mother and father, had fled Eastern Europe. On the street I had heard Jewish boys called "kike" and seen them fling themselves upon their tormentors.

But for politicians to stand up now in public and shout that the Jews must die?

I shuddered. "That could never happen here, could it, Pa?" He looked up, then smiled to reassure me. "Don't worry about it," he said. "Hitler and those Nazis of his—they won't last long."

They didn't. Not in the long perspective of time. They took power in 1933; they lost power in 1945. Twelve years. It's the length of time most of us spend in grade school and high school. That's only about a sixth of the average life span.

But how do you measure the cost of those dozen years of Nazi rule over Germany and most of Europe? By the time Hitler's power was smashed, 29 million people were dead. They were from many different countries, including Hitler's Germany and our United States.

Among the myriad slaughtered were the Jews. Six million of them. Two out of every three in Europe. One-third of the world's Jews. Statistics. But each was a man, a woman, or a child. Each had a name. Each suffered his or her own death.

Historians now speak of Hitler's extermination of the Jews as the Holocaust. The word derives from the word *olah* in the Hebrew Bible. It had the religious meaning of a burnt sacrifice. In the Greek translation of the Old Testament the word became *holokauston*. The English definition made it "an offering wholly consumed by fire." In our century it has acquired the secular meaning of a general disaster. But what Hitler did added another meaning to the dictionary definition: "a complete or thorough sacrifice or destruction, especially by fire, as of large numbers of human beings." (The Hebrew noun the Israelis use for it is *Shoa*. In Yiddish the word is *Khurbn*.)

The Holocaust was one of innumerable crimes committed by the Nazis. Then why single out the extermination of the Jews? Is it necessary to remember? Is it good? Can it even be understood by those who have come after?

No one would claim that the Nazi extermination of the Jews was greater or more tragic than what has been done to other persecuted peoples. Such comparisons are unfeeling and fruitless. What is historically significant is its uniqueness. There is no precedent for it in Jewish history. Nor in the history of any other people.

Civilians in the past have been massacred for what men called "reasonable" goals, utilitarian goals—to extend power, to acquire wealth, to increase territory, to stamp out opposition, to force conversion. What some power conceived to be in its self-interest was the reason behind the persecution.

But Hitler and the Nazis wanted to murder all Jews *because* they were Jews. Not because of their faith, not despite their faith. But because of what Hitler called their "race." He did not believe this "inferior" people had any right to share the earth with their "superiors," the Germans. So Jews—religious and unreligious—were exterminated. They were killed even when their deaths proved harmful, militarily or economically, to the Nazis. It was a crime against all humanity, committed upon the body of the Jewish people. That the Jews were the victim this time derives from the long history of anti-Semitism.

How could it have happened?

It did not occur in a vacuum. It was the logical outcome of certain conditions of life. Given the antihuman nature of Nazi beliefs, the crime of the Holocaust could be expected. We see that now. That it happened once, unbelievable as it seems, means it could happen again. Hitler made it a possibility for anyone. Neither the Jews nor any other group on earth can feel safe from that crime in the future.

I do not believe that the world of Hitler was totally alien to the world we know. Still, before we can compare Hitler's Germany to anything else, we need to find out what it was like and how it came to be. And just as important, we need to expand our knowledge of our own human nature to understand why people were infected by Nazism, how the poison spread, and what its effects were. The question has to do with good and evil, with our inner being, with our power to make moral choices.

No one of us can know the whole truth. It is not made up merely of facts and figures. We have an abundance of that kind of evidence now, for the hell of Nazi Europe has become one of the most fully documented crimes in history. One can read the cold record for endless hours. The better path to the truth is through the eyewitness accounts—the letters, diaries, journals, and memoirs of those who experienced the terror and grief. This book will rely upon them. However inadequate words are, human language is all we have to reach across barriers to understanding.

BOOK ONE

History of
Hatred

Not Citizens, Only Subjects

Jude verrecke . . . Jew perish . . .

How did it come to that? And why in Germany?

Germany is the country where modern anti-Semitism of the racist kind began. The term itself, "anti-Semitism," was first used only a few years before Hitler was born. But the roots of anti-Semitism go much farther back in history. The religious basis for it in the Christian world is the accusation (it appears in the Gospels) that the Jews were to blame for the crucifixion of Jesus. "Christ-killer" became a synonym for Jew. The anti-Semites took that charge as sanction for the persecution of the Jews.

In the early fourth century, Constantine the Great made Christianity the state religion of the Byzantine Empire. The Church insisted that Christianity was the true religion, the only religion, and demanded the conversion of the Jews. When the Jews would not easily give up their faith, the Church used the power of the State to make them outcasts. They were denied citizenship and its rights. By the end of the century, Jews were viewed as devils, cursed by God.

A popular and enduring hatred of the Jews built up. If Jews suffered misfortune, it was only divine punishment for Christ's crucifixion. But the punishment was not left to God alone. Both Church and State took legislative steps—later imitated in Hitler's edicts—to ensure Jewish misery. Among them were decrees that made it impossible for Jews to farm the land or to engage in the crafts. Trade was almost the only choice left, and many Jews became merchants, working with and through other Jews scattered throughout the world.

As the economy of the medieval world developed, the Church lifted the restrictions it had placed on commercial activity, and Christians replaced Jews. The Church still forbade Christians to receive interest on loans, so the Jews provided the service of banking. But when banking profits became attractive, the Church eased its restrictions, and Christians then competed with Jews in finance, too. Yet, even as Christians took over the same financial functions, they libeled the Jews as avaricious and heartless—the image perpetuated by Shakespeare's Shylock.

The launching of the Crusades in 1096 marked the beginning of an oppression that for duration and intensity would be unmatched until Hitler's time. The hordes of nobles, knights, monks, and peasants who set off to free the Holy Land from the Moslem infidels began their bloody work with "the infidels at home"—the Jews. Offering the choice of baptism or death, the Crusaders slaughtered Jews on a stunning scale. Those Jews who refused baptism and sacrificed themselves "to sanctify the Name of God" became martyrs who set an example of heroism for centuries to come. What had been done in the name of Christianity made very few in the Church feel regret when the fury ended. Nested in the popular mind was the conviction that such atrocities must have been deserved. Piety became a convenient excuse for plunder.

To make the Jew an ever easier target for mobs hunting down the "Christ-killer," the Church's Fourth Lateran Council in 1215 required Jews to wear a distinctive badge on their clothing. Now no Jews could escape humiliation. As public pariahs, they were blamed for everything that went wrong. "The guilty Jews"—the words were inseparable. Expulsion or extermination seemed to be the Jews' fate. What delayed their elimination was their usefulness. While their money could be diverted into the treasuries of king and noble, they were tolerated. When that value was gone, they were expelled. In England it happened in 1290, in France in 1306, in Spain in 1492.

It was in these centuries that Europe began moving from the medieval into the modern world. Epochal changes were taking place in economic, political, cultural, and religious life. But the mass of Jews remained cut off from the mainstream and isolated. They were compelled to live behind ghetto walls. A new humanism induced more tolerance, but not for the Jews. Persecution continued, followed often by expulsion.

The Jews of Spain and Portugal fled into Turkey, the Balkans, Palestine, northern Italy, and Holland. Some migrated to the New World, settling in Brazil and the West Indies, and soon in North America, too. The Jews of Germany made new homes in Eastern Europe. The Polish rulers welcomed them because they needed Jewish enterprise. Jews were allowed to become traders and financiers.

The flow east was heightened by the founding of Martin Luther's new faith in the sixteenth century. In his youth, Luther had been a champion of the Jews. When he failed to win them to Protestantism, he raged at them in a language that exceeded even Hitler's for violence. He renewed all the old charges—the Jews were poisoners, ritual murderers, usurers, parasites, devils. He called for the burning of their synagogues, the seizure of their books, and their expulsion from all of Germany. (Centuries later, Hitler would find it helpful to circulate Luther's anti-Jewish writings in mass editions.)

Even as Catholics warred with Protestants, a few brave souls dared to argue for toleration. The Dutch scholar Erasmus suggested that toleration among all Christians would mean a more humane faith. He could even conceive of being a friend to a Jew. New ideas about the rights of the common man emerged later, as the Industrial Revolution developed in Western Europe. A struggle for civil emancipation began. By then there were numbers of middle-class Jews eager to break free of the ghetto and to share in the civil rights promised by the movement for Enlightenment.

It was Germany's Jews who were the first to be touched by the Enlightenment. Frederick the Great, a despotic ruler and no lover of the Jews, realized that his Prussia could prosper by encouraging enterprising Jews to found new industries and build up commerce. Many Jews seized the opportunity offered and rose to prominence as manufacturers, merchants, and bankers. In dealing with Prussia's chief customer, France, the German Jews absorbed the ideas of the French Enlightenment and circulated them at home.

Young Jews, especially, responded to the promise of liberty, equality, and fraternity. But their elders feared that Christian Enlightenment would lead to the desertion of Judaism. Moses Mendelssohn sought to work out a compromise between loyalty to his Jewish faith and participation in the broader culture. A brilliant thinker, he had left the poverty of the Dessau ghetto at fourteen and gone to Berlin to master secular learning. While working as a bookkeeper in the silk business of a wealthy Jew, he won acclaim in Berlin society for his critical essays in philosophy. Soon he was Europe's most celebrated Jew. Through the printed word and the founding of Jewish schools combining religious and secular education, he and his disciples spread the Enlightenment to the Jews of Europe.

Inspired by his example, young Jews devoted themselves to modern education so that they could make a mark in Western culture. Cracks appeared in the ghetto walls even before the French Revolution of 1789, and Napoleon's armies finished the job, bearing the banners of freedom wherever they marched. They defeated the Prussians in 1806; and in 1812 Prussia issued the Edict of Emancipation, which made Jews citizens. Jews were to have all the rights of the dominant majority. But not for long. Napoleon's downfall brought powerful reaction in its wake. Emancipation was undone in many places. The ideals of the Enlightenment were drowned in a wave of German nationalism. To be a patriot now meant to be a product of German culture and a Christian. Again the Jew was defined as an outsider. He was viewed as a parasite feeding upon the German body, which could never absorb him. His political rights were cut down or taken away altogether. An endless stream of anti-Semitic books and pamphlets polluted the culture of Germany. Some of the most distinguished intellectuals contributed to it. Feeling against the

Jews mounted to the point of violence. The old cry, "Hep, hep, death to the Jews!" echoed again in Germany's streets.

Popular writing dropped all distinctions between the "good" Jew and the "bad" Jew. Even the baptized and assimilated Jew was not spared, for the anti-Semite now condemned *all* Jews. No longer was it a question of religion. It was the Jew's "race," his "blood," that damned him. A Jewish stereotype took shape in widely read novels. The Jew was depicted as puny and cowardly. The ugly features given the Jewish villain were said to be the outward sign of an evil soul.

The Germans built hatred of the Jews into what they considered to be an unchallengeable scientific system. A "theory" of anti-Semitism was created to lend scientific justification to their prejudice. Wilhelm Marr based his theory of anti-Semitism on racial identity. He said that Jews, or Semites, had an inborn character that made them a "slave race," while the Germans, or Aryans, were the "master race." The Jews couldn't help being morally and physically inferior because Nature had predetermined that. The lucky Aryans (he meant the Teutonic or Nordic peoples, such as the Germans, Austrians, Scandinavians, Dutch, English, and French) were by the same token born to be superior. The Aryans were the jewel of the world. Everything great and good was said to be the creation of this "master race."

Such nonsense, fed to the ignorant and unthinking, infuriated some scientists of that time. Max Müller, the noted German philologist and orientalist, said:

> It is but too easily forgotten that if we speak of Aryan and Semitic families, the ground of that classification is language and language only. There are Aryan and Semitic languages, but it is against all rules of logic to speak . . . of an Aryan race, of Aryan blood, or Aryan skulls, and to attempt ethnological classification on purely linguistic grounds.

The smashing victory over the French in the Franco-Prussian War in 1870 made many Germans feel they truly belonged to a "master race." And when Otto von Bismarck's policy of "blood and iron" succeeded in molding the petty states into the German Empire in 1871, it intensified that feeling of superiority. Chancellor Bismarck proclaimed the State's highest duty was to increase its own power. Germany's destiny was to conquer the world; "lesser" peoples had to be subdued.

Militarism and the doctrine of "blood and iron" became the dominant forces in German life. Under Bismarck's leadership, the educated classes turned away from rationalism and liberalism. A new kind of pseudo-scholarship, useful to politicians who prosper on myths, held sway. Two foreign writers, the Frenchman Arthur de Gobineau and the Englishman Houston Stewart Chamberlain, contributed props for the myth of racial superiority. De Gobineau held that the Jews were a "mongrel race." Chamberlain wrote that "The Jewish race is altogether bastardized, and its existence is a crime against the holy laws of life." Both men won vast audiences in Germany by singing the praises of the "Aryan race."

Politicians began to draw upon the power of anti-Semitism for their propaganda arsenal. In 1878 speakers for a Christian Social Workers' party fired up mass meetings by blaming Jews for business failures and profiteering. The party leader, Dr. Adolf Stöcker (court preacher to the Kaiser), coined the slogan "Deutschland erwache!"; Hitler would borrow it later. And as Hitler would, Stöcker directed his appeal to the lower middle classes—artisans, shopkeepers, clerks, petty officials—who yearned for better incomes and higher social status. In 1879 Wilhelm Marr founded the League of Anti-Semitism "to save the German fatherland from complete Judaization." A year later the anti-Semites were able to secure 300,000 signatures to a petition demanding that the government bar the Jews from all schools and universities and from holding public office.

By 1893 candidates of anti-Semitic political parties were able to muster 400,000 votes and elect many deputies to the Reichstag. A new slogan—"The Jews Are Our Misfortune"—appeared in print and on banners. Another philosopher, the anarchist Eugen Dühring, stepped forth to sound the final note in anti-Semitism. The Jews, he wrote, are "inferior and depraved. . . . The duty of the Nordic peoples is to exterminate such parasitic races as we exterminate snakes and beasts of prey."

His was a paranoid image of the Jew as the universal enemy. Entrenched as an article of German faith, it would have the destructive power of an atomic arsenal when Hitler triggered it.

2

Hitler's Magic Formula

Adolf Hitler was born in 1889 in an Austrian village across the border from German Bavaria. His father was a minor customs official who retired when Hitler was six and began moving about restlessly. The boy attended many schools in different towns. At eleven he was sent to a high school in Linz to study for the civil service. But he did not want to follow his father's course; he desired to become an artist. His grades fell off and he dropped out. His father died in 1903, leaving his widow Klara a tiny pension on which to support Adolf and his sister.

Adolf would not find a job to help his mother out. For three years he roved the countryside. By sixteen, he showed an interest in politics as well as a hatred for all the non-German subject peoples who lived within the Austro-Hungarian Empire. In 1907 he was rejected by an art school in Vienna because he showed no promise. That same year his mother died.

Homeless and penniless, Hitler spent four despairing years in Vienna. He lived in flophouses and ate in charity kitchens. Vienna was thriving then, and he could have earned a living if he had wished. Instead, he gave all his time to voracious reading, mostly German history and mythology. The ideas of Fichte, Hegel, de Gobineau, and Houston Stewart Chamberlain, soaked up in his youth, became the stuff of his later writings and speeches. But how this young man became the demonic figure whose incredible willpower and hypnotic influence led to the greatest crimes in history has never been explained. The circumstances of his childhood and youth—are these enough to account for it? Why Hitler, then, and not the many others whose early lives paralleled his?

In 1913, Hitler left Vienna for Germany. He wanted to escape military service in the Austrian army because he refused to bear arms with Jews, Czechs, and Slavs. The longer he lived in Vienna, he wrote, "the more my hatred grew for the foreign mixture of peoples which had begun to corrode the old site of German culture."

At the age of twenty-four, he came to Munich. A year later the First World War exploded, and Hitler wrote that "[I] sank down on my knees, thanked heaven out of the fullness of my heart for giving me the good fortune to be permitted to live in such a time." Now he could shoulder arms for his adopted Fatherland in a war that would destroy untold millions.

The huge German armies swept through Belgium and northern France, but the swift total conquest planned by the German General Staff did not occur. The two-front war—against Russia in the east and France, Britain, and finally the United States in the west—bogged down in seas of mud and blood. As German victory failed to come, the tensions the Bismarck system had suppressed boiled up to the surface. The German economy was in ruins and people faced starvation. Political leaders asked why the masses should make all the sacrifices for an autocratic regime. The Emperor made promises of reform, but they came too late. The radical parties were calling not only for an end to the war but for a democratic socialist republic. The German fleet mutinied, and troops on the western front refused to fight anymore. Antiwar strikes and demonstrations broke out all over Germany. With defeat in the field and support melting away at home, the General Staff entered negotiations with the Allies and accepted their peace terms. Kaiser Wilhelm II abdicated and fled to Holland. Bismarck's German Empire was in ruins.

To Corporal Hitler, who had fought in many battles throughout the long war and earned the Iron Cross for bravery, the news of final defeat was a shocking blow. He, like countless other

Germans fed on the myth of German invincibility, could not believe his beloved army had lost. Germany's defeat must have been caused by betrayal at home. The liberals, the democrats, the radicals, the Jews—they were to blame for this incredible calamity.

The Treaty of Versailles reflected the fact of German defeat. Its terms included the return of territories seized by Germany from others, the reduction of the army and navy to small forces, the outlawing of the General Staff, and payment for war costs and damages. In signing, Germany was forced to admit it had been the aggressor in this war.

All the German parties joined in bitterly denouncing the Versailles treaty, forgetting it was not as harsh as the Treaty of Brest Litovsk, which the Germans had imposed on the Russians in this same war. Unfortunately, instead of placing the responsibility for disaster where it belonged, on the General Staff and the Empire's rulers, the German people turned against the new republic struggling to rise from the ashes of defeat. The legend grew that the German army had not lost on the battlefield but had been "stabbed in the back" by evil forces behind the lines—speculators, radicals, politicians, and Jews.

The democratic constitution which Germany adopted in 1919 at the old cultural center of Weimar was one of the most advanced in political history. But it was only a piece of paper. The social cement needed to make it effective was missing. Germany was a fiercely divided society, torn between extremes of radical and right-wing thought and separated by rigid class, regional, and religious lines. Whoever governed Germany would have to meet mountainous problems.

The Weimar Constitution turned out to have many weaknesses. Its democratic provisions were almost destroyed by Article 48. This allowed the President to scrap the entire bill of rights in emergencies and to rule by decree. Thus, upon the whim of whoever held the office, the Constitution could be invalidated and dictatorship take over.

The Weimar Republic, as it was called, staggered from the beginning under the humiliating weight of defeat and the Versailles treaty. The German people were badly prepared for any form of democracy. Even as great an artist as the novelist Thomas Mann could write in 1918, "Away with the foreign and repulsive slogan 'democratic.' The mechanical democratic political institutions of the West will never take root here."

In the four years immediately following the war, Germany's economy was shattered, and the middle class almost destroyed. As unemployment and misery spread, the German people listened to voices that promised a quick end to their troubles. Radical sections of the working class wanted to follow the example of Russia, where the Communist, or Bolshevik, party had seized power and set up a dictatorship. But the German Socialists followed a moderate policy, and from them came the republic's most solid support. Still, many Germans held the Weimar Republic in contempt because it was not curing economic ills and because it had not restored Germany to the status of a great power.

Politics was ridiculed as a hypocritical and dirty business good people must shun. So the vital decisions were left to governmental authorities. Politics degenerated into brutal and bloody street battles for power. There were hundreds of political assassinations in those years, few of the guilty punished. Extremists of the right wing got away with literal murder, while liberals were sentenced to long prison terms on trumped-up charges of "treason."

After the war Hitler found a job with a Munich regiment, propagandizing the soldiers against democracy and socialism. He also served the army by informing on "subversive" groups. That was how he encountered the German Workers' party (suspected of being subversive because of that word "worker") at a meeting in a beer cellar. Seeing that the tiny group shared his ideas about racism and anti-Semitism and espoused his militant nationalism, he joined its executive committee.

At once Hitler showed his enormous talent as an orator. It is hard to understand his effectiveness when one listens today to recordings of his radio speeches. His voice is shrill, hysterical, coarse. His speeches seem only a string of slogans. And his physical appearance was unimpressive, too. Pictures show him as short and flabby, and that little toothbrush mustache is ridiculous. Many who knew him have said that his mind was mediocre. He liked nothing better than to eat sweets and talk about his loyal dogs and his war record. Movie musicals were his favorite entertainment.

Whatever it was, something about Hitler persuaded people, even in these early 1920s, to regard him as their messiah. His magnetism became one of his greatest weapons in building a political party that would carry him to power. He soon renamed it the National Socialist German Workers' party, or Nazi party. He organized strong-arm squads to guard his own meetings from hecklers and to break up rival meetings. These squads, known as the SA, or Storm Troopers, were built up over the years into a huge private army. Hitler chose the party symbol, the swastika. This ancient hooked cross was emblazoned on Nazi uniforms, arm bands, posters, flags, and banners. Eventually it decorated even dog collars, bed sheets, matchbooks, and water glasses.

Within two years Hitler was sole master of the Nazi party, the leader whose wish and word were absolute law to his followers. Party membership grew slowly at first. Funds came from collections and meetings and from party dues—probably, too, from secret army contributions. Soon the movement had its own newspaper, the *People's Guardian*, to spread its propaganda more widely.

When inflation made German currency worthless in 1923, the buying power of wages and salaries was reduced to nothing. The hungry, desperate Germans blamed the government and democracy itself for the disaster. Amid the chaos, Hitler saw his chance to make a bid for power. With General Ludendorff, he engineered the "beer-hall putsch" in Munich in November 1923. This attempt to overthrow the government was quickly stopped by the German army. The Nazi party was suppressed, and Hitler was tried for treason. During his three-week trial he spoke out boldly and made himself a national figure through the press. He declared he was only trying to crush the Communists and Socialists—the Marxism that had caused the ruin of Germany. "I feel myself not a traitor," he told the court, "but a German who wished the best for his people." He was treated lightly, and served only nine months in a comfortable cell.

In prison Hitler wrote much of his book, *Mein Kampf* (*My Struggle*). It told the story of his early struggles and outlined what he meant to do to create a new Germany. He did not conceal his aims. He wanted to reunite Germany and Austria on the racial principle that "people of the same blood should be in the same Reich." If the reunited people should lack *Lebensraum* (living space), "then can the moral right arise, from the need of the people, to acquire foreign territory. The plough is then the sword; and the tears of war will produce the daily bread for generations to come."

To carry out his life's work, he said, "every possible means should be employed." He meant just that: every possible means.

In his book Hitler speaks of the Jews as parasites on the bodies of other peoples, conspiring to achieve a world dictatorship. Through financial manipulation the Jews were gaining economic control of Germany; through Marxism they were controlling the socialist parties and the trade unions. The Nazis, said Hitler, aimed to eradicate this alien race.

In the program Hitler's party had announced in 1920, 7 of the 25 points dealt with the Jews. The program called for the denial of citizenship and public office to Jews, the expulsion of Jews who had immigrated, and the exclusion of Jews from the press. All German Jews were categorized as "foreigners" and "guests" of the nation.

Hitler used anti-Semitism brilliantly, if insanely, to reconcile all contradictions and oppositions. It was the force which cemented together such disparate elements as workers and industrialists, land barons and peasants, fools and intellectuals, socialists and capitalists, radicals and conservatives, atheists and preachers, young and old. It was a magic formula to solve all social problems. It was a weapon against all opposition. Anyone who differed with Hitler was a Jew or a stooge of the Jews.

The Catholic historian of anti-Semitism, Father Edward H. Flannery, points out how this brand of anti-Semitism differed from earlier forms:

Hitlerian or Nazi anti-Semitism was something beyond the older kind. . . . This radical and nihilistic Jew-hatred preached with a boundless fury and coarseness was essentially new. No longer was the Jew a mere scapegoat or member of an inferior race, but the cause of every problem, the destroyer, the poisoner of Aryan blood, the epitome of evil. And he was all this inherently and uneradicably; neither baptism nor renunciation of Judaism could redeem him. The solution to the Jewish problem was also new and simple, and concisely summarized in the Nazi slogan, "Jude verrecke!"

But did it really differ? Or was it only the last step in a progression that had begun with the early Christian saints? Raul Hilberg, an historian of the Holocaust, has outlined the steps:

The missionaries of Christianity had said in effect: You have no right to live among us as Jews. The secular rulers who followed had proclaimed: You have no right to live among us. The German Nazis at last decreed: You have no right to live.

Hitler had learned a great lesson from the failure of the Munich uprising in 1923. No longer would he call for an open physical attack on the citadel of power. Mounting the barricades was romantic foolishness in the age of the machine gun. It was suicidal to smash head-on into the army and the rulers of the state. He would use trickery instead. "Democracy," he said, "must be defeated with the weapons of democracy." He would have his revolution, but after, not before, he came to power.

Hitler had no new or original ideas. Neither in *Mein Kampf* nor in the Nazi party program is there any coherent ideology. He mouthed what all the other reactionary politicians were saying. His call for *Lebensraum* and for the expulsion of the Jews was the common stock-in-trade of all the right-wing parties. Several recent studies of Nazi history conclude that Hitler had no blueprint for a totalitarian state. He improvised hastily to meet each crisis, both in his rise to power and in his exercise of that power once he attained it.

16

While never letting up on his rabid anti-Semitism, Hitler offered something for everybody except, of course, the Jews. To workers he promised jobs; to employers, fatter profits and freedom from union restraints; to the lower middle class, status and self-respect; to the generals, a glorious army; to Germany, world supremacy; to the nations abroad, peace. He was the master demagogue; he understood crowd psychology; he knew how to manipulate issues, to mobilize the disaffected. The mass of his followers came from the poor, the youth, the small tradesmen, and the handicraftsmen.

Promising everything to everybody means promising nothing to anybody. But in the hot pursuit of power, it did not matter. Hitler himself, not the program, was the sole unifying force. Despair with things as they were united his followers with their mystical leader. No one stopped to discuss what would be done once power was attained.

In the last half of the 1920s, the German economy had a striking recovery, financed largely by foreign funds. German industry was rebuilt. The government followed the traditional policy of paternalism in industry, housing, agriculture, and labor. These more normal times were lean years for the Nazis. Hitler seemed unimportant and his party was powerless. Still, the membership hung on, growing slowly, and the lieutenants Hitler needed stayed with him.

Then the worldwide depression that began in 1929 hit Germany with devastating force. Again the people were plunged into despair. In the Reichstag election of 1930, the Nazi vote shot up from about a million to over six million; the number of Nazi deputies, from 12 to 107. The Nazis were no longer a fringe party but the second largest party. This was a clear sign that the German people hungered for new leadership.

But why did they turn to Hitler? Why to the Nazis and not the other right-wing nationalist parties who advocated much the same program? One answer seems to be Hitler's greater credibility. The German masses believed he, and not the others, could deliver what he promised. They recognized him as one of them. He too had been a common soldier; he too had known life's failures. He talked their language, and he spoke with passionate conviction. He made them believe that his will, and his will alone, could solve all their problems and save Germany.

Marching along the streets to take their seats in the Reichstag, the new Nazi deputies threw rocks into Jewish store windows. In the parliamentary chamber they chanted, "Germany awake! Jew perish!" A fourth of the population had not enough to eat. Millions were on relief. Hitler seemed, to many, a Siegfried returned to earth to avenge the defeat of 1918 and lead the Germans to prosperity. He renewed his savage propaganda against the paralyzed government. "Democracy," he sneered, "is a rule by crazy brains. The German Republic is a monstrosity."

By 1932 there were 6 million jobless in Germany. The deepening crisis pushed the Nazi party ahead. That year its vote went up to nearly 14 million, and 230 Nazi Brownshirts were seated in the Reichstag. The Nazis were now the largest party in Germany but still unable to win a·clear majority. They stood on the threshold of power. The right-wing clique around the senile President Hindenburg (in his mid-eighties now) speculated that Hitler's mass support might be the means of shoring up the crumbling government. Hitler sat down for talks with them.

He might have been stopped even now if the other German parties—the Social Democrats, the Communists, the Nationalists, the Catholic Center—had united against him. After all, he had never won more than 37 percent of the popular vote. But the other parties' leaders failed to see that their political differences were nothing compared to the terrible menace of Nazism. When the other leaders remained hopelessly divided, Hitler was able to make the political bargains that won him the post of Chancellor.

On January 30, 1933, Nazism had its miracle. Scarcely a dozen years before, with a handful of other unknown men, Hitler had founded the Nazi party. Now, on this historic night, in the flickering light of thousands of torches, endless columns of Brownshirts, flanked by cheering crowds, paraded through the streets of Berlin.

At the chancellery window stood the delighted Hitler, arm outstretched in the Nazi salute. "No power on earth," he vowed that night, "shall bring me out of here alive."

3

Ein Volk,
Ein Reich, Ein Führer!

Hitler's first aim in office was to consolidate his power. He moved at once to fulfill the Nazi slogan: *EIN VOLK, EIN REICH, EIN FÜHRER!** (*ONE PEOPLE, ONE GOVERNMENT, ONE LEADER!*) First, he imposed a universal ban on demonstrations. His right-hand man, Hermann Goering, took control of the regular police and the Nazi secret police, the Gestapo. Goering, a fighter pilot in World War I, was a beefy blusterer with great energy who helped Hitler capture power. "My measures will not be hindered by any legal considerations or bureaucracy whatsoever," he said. "It is not justice that I have to carry out but annihilation and extermination."

In February 1933 the Reichstag building was set on fire by secret order of Joseph Goebbels, Hitler's propaganda chief. The crime was called a Communist plot. The next day, Hitler persuaded President Hindenburg to sign an "emergency" decree empowering the government to suspend all civil rights. Now Hitler could arrest and even execute any suspicious person. Thousands of Communists, Socialists, liberals, and trade unionists were dragged off to jails or to abandoned warehouses and factory basements. Many of them were beaten or tortured to death. The non-Nazi press was banned. Under these conditions of hysteria and fear, a national election was held on March 5. The Nazis got 17

* Führer is the German spelling. Except in German quotations, the English spelling Fuehrer is used throughout this book.

million votes, still not a clear majority. Nevertheless, by throwing the elected Communist deputies out of their seats and joining with the Nationalists and the Catholic Center, the Nazis succeeded in obtaining the two-thirds majority vote in the Reichstag needed to make Hitler legal dictator. (It was the last meaningful act of the German parliament. From then on it was nothing but a cheering section for Hitler's speeches.) Next, Hitler abolished every political party but his own; he dissolved the trade unions, seized their funds and headquarters, and jailed their leaders. Labor in Germany became slavery in all but name. With the abolition of the unions went the right to strike, to collective bargaining, even to shift jobs. The National Labor Front made all the decisions. Wages sank while profits rose. Despite their Socialist or Communist tradition, the workers accepted the brutal discipline, perhaps because Hitler had wiped out unemployment through his vast public works and rearmament programs and by drafting youth into the armed forces.

Having reduced German labor to serfdom, Hitler turned to capital. All the financial institutions were taken over by the state, and industry was mobilized for rearmament. Total control of newspapers, magazines, books, radio, and film was given to the Ministry of Propaganda and Popular Enlightenment, headed by Joseph Goebbels.

Goebbels was a tiny figure, scarcely five feet tall and weighing under a hundred pounds, with a bad limp from childhood polio. He had a degree from the University of Heidelberg and aspired to become one of Germany's literary greats. But his true talent lay in creating not art but propaganda. He understood the power of propaganda. It had nothing to do with truth, he said. "The propaganda which produces the desired results is good and all other propaganda is bad. Therefore, it is beside the point to say your propaganda is too crude, too mean, too brutal, or too unfair, for all this does not matter. . . . Propaganda is always a means to an end."

As Hitler's chief "enlightener," Goebbels banned all democratic literature. On May 10, 1933, gangs of Nazi youths ripped out of the libraries the works of all authors on Goebbels' blacklist. By the truckload, they took what was best in German and non-German literature to the Berlin square where the opera house faced the university, and set the books on fire as thousands of students cheered. One among those whose books they burned—the poet Heinrich Heine—once wrote, "When they burn books, in the end it is man that they burn."

The only obstacle still in Hitler's way was the left wing of his own party, headed by Ernst Roehm. Roehm wanted a "Second Revolution" to take over big business and the landed estates. Had not Hitler made such radical promises in his climb to power? But now the Fuehrer wanted to use those forces, not alienate them. Fearing that the SA, headed by Roehm and over 2-million strong, might get out of control, Hitler arranged for the Gestapo to murder Roehm. Added to the death list were many other political, as well as personal, enemies. Over 1,000 men and women fell victim to the blood purge that took place on June 30, 1934.

When President Hindenburg died in August, Hitler was able to toss away the last scrap of constitutionalism. He immediately united the offices of President and Chancellor and proclaimed himself Supreme Head of State and Commander-in-Chief of the Armed Forces. He demanded and received from the army and all servants of the state a "sacred oath" of "unconditional obedience." Then he asked the German people to approve by plebiscite; 90 percent voted "Yes." He was master now. Germany was under the personal rule of one man, Adolf Hitler. Every time Germans exchanged the greeting—"*Heil Hitler!*"—it was a recognition of that fact. His supremacy was felt in every sphere of political and personal life.

Although the Nazi apparatus had swelled enormously, the Party alone was not enough to carry out Hitler's goals. Nazis penetrated the most crucial organizations, making deals or concessions to gain full cooperation. The big institutions were let alone, as long as they followed governmental policy. Hitler preferred not to disturb the army, industry, or the civil service. Kept intact, they could be made to carry out his aims.

Alongside these existing institutions was the Party's political and social machinery. Its leaders built up their own personal empires until there were at least four major power complexes: economic development, centering on Goering; labor, on Robert Ley; the police, on Heinrich Himmler; and propaganda, on Goebbels. The four men acted with considerable independence, because Hitler hated the details of administration. Complicated by personal rivalries and jealousies, the system nevertheless worked with astonishing success. In just six years the productive and military power of Germany was developed to the point where Hitler was ready to challenge the world.

Party membership, a million when Hitler began his rule, was carefully regulated. The only basic Party rules, said Hitler, were "blind discipline and the absolute recognition of authority." Goering expressed what that meant: "I have no personal conscience; Adolf Hitler is my only conscience." At its peak the Party included nearly 7 million members. For most positions of authority in Germany, Nazi party membership was essential. Expulsion was therefore a serious matter. The Party was organized by region and reached down into the neighborhood. Every block had its Nazi agent to spy on the people's thoughts and behavior. Everyone in Germany—child, youth, or adult—was touched somehow by the vast Party network.

The Nazis sought to mold the young, from infancy, into a race of "true" Germans. "It is my duty," Hitler said, "to make use of every means of training the German people to cruelty, and to prepare them for war. . . . A violently active, dominating, intrepid, brutal youth—that is what I am after. Youth must be all this. It must be indifferent to pain. There must be no weakness or tenderness in it." There were separate organizations for very young boys and girls; and at fourteen, the boys joined the Hitler Youth. An exciting life of marching, singing, saluting, camping, physical training, and sports captured youths' loyalty early. At eighteen, the young men began six months' compulsory-labor service in a camp (women also did labor service), followed by two years of military service.

Children quickly responded to the poisonous Nazi propaganda. Bella Fromm was a prominent Berlin journalist with many friends in high places. Perhaps that was why, although Jewish, she was still allowed to work. One evening she was having dinner with old non-Jewish friends. At the table were Ilse and Otto Kapp, and Ilse's brother, with his two daughters. The young girls were fond of "Aunt Bella." These passages from the Fromm diary for October 1935 are a token of the vicious spying and informing that had become common in Germany:

Inge and Lolo, the two little girls, sat at table with us. Inge had not come to see me for weeks. I asked her why, though I had a feeling that I knew the answer.

Inge looked at me as though trying to visualize me all over again. "Aunt Bella," she said, "you don't really seem so—so fiendish."

Her father reprimanded her with a stern glance. "Don't blame the child," I interceded for her. "I know what they teach her in school."

Relieved, the little one chatted on without inhibition. "I told Herr Runge, that's our teacher, that you weren't like that, Aunt Bella. So he said we didn't understand how wicked you really were. Then for the rest of the lesson, he read to us out of a book about Jews . . . that they are evil . . . they look like devils . . . they should all be killed. He said we should spit at them whenever we see them."

Blond, delicate, sweet Inge! The words, though not her own, came strangely from her lips.

"On our way home," Inge continued, "Ursel and I saw an old woman. She looked very poor, and we thought she might be Jewish. Ursel said we should spit at her. So we ran up to her and Ursel spat on her coat. . . . it was an old coat . . . torn. . . . I didn't spit, Aunt Bella. I thought it was disgusting. Ursel yelled at her: 'Old Jew witch!' She says that tomorrow she will tell the teacher I wouldn't spit, too."

We sat there in silence for a moment or two. Then I said: "Inge, darling, you are intelligent enough to know that evil has nothing to do with the race a person is born into. It is God who decides whether you are to be a Jew or a Christian. There are nasty people everywhere, but most people are the same, whether they are Catholic, Protestant, or Jewish. All worship the same God . . . the God of Love."

"I won't do it," said Inge quietly. "I won't do it. Even if they punish me."

"That's right," said her father. "I wouldn't want you to. If you could do it, I would never want to see you again."

Five days later, Ilse Kapp, pale and disturbed, came to see Bella Fromm:

"I did not come before everything was settled. The day after our talk with Inge, Herr Runge [the teacher] discussed the Jewish question again. 'Inge,' he said, 'do you admit that all Jews are damnable and vile?'

" 'No,' insisted Inge.

"Herr Runge became increasingly aggressive. Inge ever more frightened. 'Daddy says I am right,' she said.

"That same night the Gestapo came to take my brother away. We did everything in our power. He escaped with a severe warning, and some horrible scars on his body. I have just been to his house to see him."

It was not only children who responded to Nazi propaganda. Each September at Nuremberg, the week-long Party rally demonstrated "the most frenzied adulation for a public figure" the American reporter William L. Shirer said he had ever seen. Watching it in 1934, Shirer observed:

Like a Roman emperor Hitler rode into this medieval town at sundown today past solid phalanxes of wildly cheering Nazis. . . . Tens of thousands of Swastika flags blot out the Gothic beauty of the place. . . . The streets are a sea of brown and black uniforms. . . . I got caught in a mob of ten thousand hysterics who jammed the moat in front of Hitler's hotel, shouting: "We want our Fuehrer!" I was a little shocked at the faces, especially those of the women, when Hitler finally appeared on the balcony for a moment. . . . They looked up

at him as if he was a Messiah, their faces transformed into something positively inhuman. . . . He is restoring pageantry, color
and mysticism to the drab lives of the twentieth century
Germans. . . .

Shirer attended the mass rally in a great hall:

Hitler's arrival was dramatic. The band stopped playing.
There was a hush over the thirty thousand people packed in
the hall. Then the band struck up the "Badenweiler March," a
very catchy tune and used only when Hitler makes his big
entries. Hitler appeared in the back of the auditorium, and
followed by his aides, Goering, Goebbels, Hess, Himmler, and
the others, he strode slowly down the long center aisle while
thirty thousand hands were raised in salute. . . . Then an
immense symphony orchestra played Beethoven's Egmont
Overture. Great Klieg lights played on the stage, where Hitler
sat surrounded by a hundred party officials and officers of the
army and navy. Behind them the "blood flag," the one carried
down the streets of Munich in the ill-fated putsch. Behind
this, four or five hundred SA standards. When the music was
over, Rudolf Hess, Hitler's closest confidant, rose and slowly
read the names of the Nazi "martyrs"—Brownshirts who had
been killed in the struggle for power—a rollcall of the dead, and
the thirty thousand seemed very moved.
    In such an atmosphere no wonder, then, that every word
dropped by Hitler seemed like an inspired Word from on
high . . . and every lie pronounced is accepted as high truth
itself.
    Later in the rally an immense chanting chorus of 50,000
youths from the Labor Corps, shiny spades on their shoulders,
broke into a perfect goose-step and with one voice intoned,
WE WANT ONE LEADER! NOTHING FOR US!
EVERYTHING FOR GERMANY! HEIL HITLER!

Women were relegated by Hitler to the function of breeding
machines. Their duty was to present the Fatherland with as many

soldiers as possible. Under Nazism, antifeminism was a kind of secondary racism. Women were considered naturally inferior, like non-Germans and non-Aryans. Motherhood was the prime patriotic, as well as moral, virtue. When women were not busy in that role, then they must do the work women were "naturally" inclined to: farm labor, domestic service, sales help. The one place, especially, women did not belong was in politics. From the beginning, women were kept out of leadership in the Party. But even within the Party's *Frauenschaft* (Women's Organization), a feminist countermovement surfaced which dared to criticize male domination. Such voices were soon silenced.

To gain control of the army, Hitler Nazified it at the top, putting in generals devoted to his regime. He drew both the civil service and business more directly under Party and state influence. The machinery of power carried on the routine of government while it advanced the aims of Nazism. But Hitler also had at his command a huge apparatus for coercion—secret police, imprisonment, concentration camps, execution. The chief instruments for coercion penetrated every corner of German life. Nazi agents spied on everyday behavior, policed the performance of Party and state tasks, ran concentration camps, and later carried out mass killings. To squirm out of the reach of this vast network, this police state, was almost impossible.

The Gestapo (*Geheime Staatspolizei*), organized by Goering, was not concerned with ordinary crime. Its mission was to suppress independent thought and to eliminate all opposition.

The SS (*Schutzstaffel*) was the Blackshirted security service led by Himmler. It started out in the 1920s as a special guard for Hitler, and developed into an elite of Nazi fanatics. Its men were recruited from the aristocracy, the intelligentsia, and the middle class. Chosen for physique and devotion to the Fuehrer's goals, members of the SS were trained to consider themselves the "super race." The SS had its own courts, its own press, and finally its own military branch, the *Waffen-SS*. It built a reputation as the most merciless instrument of terror. By 1936 Himmler's fanatical efficiency won him supreme command not only of the SS but of the Gestapo and the criminal police.

Himmler, the son of a Bavarian schoolmaster, was brought up as a devout Catholic. He served in the army briefly at the end of World War I, then bought a small chicken farm and became a fertilizer salesman. He was a veteran of the Munich putsch and the most dogged disciple of Hitler's racism. He turned easily from breeding chickens to planning the breeding of a "master race." Short, pudgy, stupid-faced, he did not resemble his ideal Aryan. He was an ignorant and bloodless man, indifferent to cruelty. When he heard objections to what went on in his torture chambers, he would say that his victims were only "animals" or "criminals." He was the type of man ready to sacrifice humanity for an abstract ideal. The horrors done in the name of safeguarding the "master race" never disturbed his complacency.

As boss of all the security forces, Himmler also held the strings of the third major instrument of terror, the SD (*Sicherheitsdienst*). It was designed as a security service for the SS and kept small. Its 3,000 operatives controlled 100,000 informers, who spied on the private lives of the German people, including Party members.

The SD's chief was Reinhard Heydrich. A blond giant of a man, he took Himmler's fancy as the ideal Aryan. In 1932, at the age of twenty-eight, Heydrich began organizing his intelligence network. Brilliant and coldhearted, he had a keen eye for the ambitions and weaknesses of the Nazi leadership. He played them against one another to his own advantage.

Concentration camps were created in the earliest days of the Hitler regime as places to hold people in "protective custody." A decree allowed the Gestapo to send anyone to a concentration camp for as long a time as the Gestapo pleased, without trial or conviction, even if a court had already absolved the person of guilt or if the person had already served his sentence in prison. The law—a joke to call it that!—let the Gestapo do with people whatever it wished. This meant mass control by terror. The true function of the concentration camps was to eliminate every form of active or potential opposition.

By the end of 1933, there were at least 50 camps spread throughout Germany. These early camps were the forerunners of the later labor camps and the death camps. In the beginning, many victims were given a bad beating and then ransomed to family or friends. It was intimidation combined with blackmail. Sometimes the prisoners were murdered, because they were considered too dangerous, or out of sheer sadism. At first the camps were controlled by the Gestapo.

By mid-1934, however, Hitler gave the SS control of the camps. As leaders of the "master race," the SS had no qualms about treating camp inmates any way they liked. The terror began with segregation and humiliation and went on to torture and murder. They beat, flayed, strangled, shot, and gassed their victims. Their goal was to exterminate enemies. Any means would serve the purpose. At first, some Germans thought the camps would disappear when opposition faded, especially after the Roehm purge. But instead, their number grew steadily. By 1936, camps were being planned for permanence. The designers worked out camp quarters for the prisoners, barracks for the guards, and housing projects for the SS officers, all as a unit. In the years before World War II, the camps whose names conjured up the greatest fear were Dachau near Munich, Buchenwald near Weimar, Sachsenhausen near Berlin, and Ravensbruck near Mecklenburg.

The camps held three types of prisoners. The "politicals" were the Communists, Social Democrats, Jehovah's Witnesses, opposition clergymen, people who talked against the regime, and purged Nazis. The second group were the "asocials," primarily habitual criminals and sex offenders. The last group were members of "inferior races," the Jews and the Gypsies. Children too, by the tens of thousands, were imprisoned in the concentration camps, with or without their parents. About 15 percent were under the age of twelve; the others were between twelve and eighteen.

The Nazis did not arrest all German Jews during this period. Sometimes there were mass roundups which put many Jews into camps. Or individual Jews were picked up because they were "politicals" or fitted into some other category. But in whatever camp they were placed, the Jews stayed in segregated barracks and were given the most menial tasks.

All prisoners wore prescribed markings on their clothes to indicate their category. These were a serial number and colored triangles, both sewn on the left shirt breast and the right trouser leg. The triangles pointed down. Red denoted politicals; green, criminals; purple, Jehovah's Witnesses; black, "shiftless elements"; pink, homosexuals. The classification triangle for Jews was yellow. It had to be sewn on point-up, so that if a Jew were placed in another category as well, the two triangles would form a six-pointed Star of David. Non-Jews of various categories were mixed together within the individual camps, on the principle of divide-and-rule.

The Nazis used a deliberately senseless system in the camps to rob prisoners of their dignity and humanity. Emil Fackenheim, twenty-two, was one of those sent to the Sachsenhausen camp. The prisoners worked daily in a tile factory outside the camp. The work seemed like ordinary labor directed to a purpose. But then, he says:

> . . . Many a day we spent carrying sand—always on the double! —from place A to place B, only in order to be ordered the next day to carry it back from place B to place A. The senselessness of this labor was so obvious that everyone understood it. . . . We kept our morale through humor. We knew that this system had no purpose. Hence we also knew that its only purpose could be torture for torture's sake—to break us down. And aware of this purpose, we resisted it.
>
> I recall an incident early in our imprisonment (when we were still quite naive) when a well-known Berlin rabbi and I lined up outside the medical barrack for treatment for a sore or infected leg (I forget which). After a while the Nazi medical officer came out, kicked us with his jackboots and shouted, "Run, Jews!" As we were running, the rabbi turned to me and asked, "Are you still sick?"

Another inmate of Sachsenhausen, sent there at the same time, was Dr. K. J. Ball-Kaduri. A favorite amusement of the Nazi guards, he recalls, was to stand him up and force him to bellow again and again this "poem":

Dear old Moses, come again,
Lead your Jewish fellowmen
Once more to their promised land.
Split once more for them the sea,
Two huge columns let it be
Fixed as firmly as two walls.
When the Jews are all inside
On their pathway, long and wide,
Shut the trap, Lord, do your best!
Give us the world its lasting rest!

Fackenheim notes that this "poem" was not the creation of Nazi anti-Semitism, but something handed down from the 1880s, from Dr. Adolf Stöcker's Christian anti-Semitism. "It was simply humanly impossible," he says, "first for German Jews, then for European Jews, to recognize that the enemies were so many and so vicious. Hence, on the Jewish side, wishful thinking, and on the Nazi side, its systematic exploitation."

"The Protection of German Blood and German Honor"

With his hand on the lever of power, Hitler began a progressive terror against the Jews.

How many Jews did Germany contain? In 1933, there were half a million—less than 1 percent of the population. But ignoring how few they were, the Nazis had charged day in and day out that the Jews dominated industry, finance, and government.

Did they? Not one of the most powerful German industries—Krupp, Klöckner, Siemens, Stinnes, I. G. Farben, Hugenberg, Vereinigte Stahlwerke, Hapag, Stumm, Nordlloyd—was in Jewish hands. And the international cartels which German industries were part of—oil, iron, potash, chemicals, shipping—Jews had no influence in them, either as owners or directors. Tick off the most powerful families in the country: not one was Jewish.

It was true that many Jews had achieved prominence and prosperity in Germany. In 1871, when the Jews had acquired full civil emancipation, and therefore equal opportunity, under the laws, they began entering many new fields of endeavor. It was in the same period that Germany's great industrial and commercial expansion began. Jews, like other Germans, found a ready outlet for their talents. Many became rich or famed as merchants, bankers, manufacturers, publishers, scientists, physicians, lawyers, engineers, musicians, artists, writers. The sudden rise in status made many anti-Semites envious and resentful of the Jews.

A great many German Jews, up until the First World War, felt they were "more German than Jewish." They were confident that cultural assimilation had made them true equals. Jewish liberation, they thought, would last forever. Their contributions to German life were great, but as the historian Peter Gay has noted, "in many respects . . . Germany's Jews remained outsiders. There were still social clubs that would not admit them, private industries that would not employ them, public bodies that would not appoint them. There were fanatics who would not leave them alone."

Jews who converted to Christianity did so for a number of reasons. Whatever the motive, says Professor Gay, "Jews generally despised their baptized brethren as renegades, Christians despised them as opportunists. Converts, seeking to win by moving from one camp to another, lost in both." When Jews refused to assimilate, they were attacked by anti-Semites for being unassimilable. When Jews tried to assimilate, they were accused of debasing or corrupting someone else's culture.

Another charge made by the Nazis was that the German government had been "riddled" with Jews. But in the 19 cabinets of the Weimar Republic, up to 1932, of a total of 237 ministers, only 3 had been Jews; 4 more were described as "of Jewish descent." The last few governments preceding Hitler's had no Jewish ministers. In the federal states the picture was the same.

Documentations of such "innocence" were published by organizations combating anti-Semitism. But it was like trying to stem the cataracts of Niagara with one's hand. Facts were drowned in the ceaseless torrent of anti-Semitic lies.

The truth was the opposite of what Hitler said it was. Rather than an all-powerful threat, the Jews of Europe were the weakest enemy Hitler could have chosen. They had no land of their own, no government, no central authority, no allies, no political weight. They were divided in every possible way. In faith they ranged from devout believers to atheists or converts to Christianity; in income they were rich, poor, and in-between; in politics they included conservatives, liberals, and radicals. If they had been united and highly organized the way the Nazis said they were, then millions more of them might have been saved.

32

The campaign against the Jews began with a pretense of legality. Hitler's measures were introduced one by one. There seems to have been no anti-Jewish program mapped carefully in advance to move from the early step of discrimination to the final step of annihilation. Because the actions taken were sporadic, the effect was to deceive and confuse the Jews. By gradually weakening and demoralizing them, the Nazis were able to reduce resistance and prepare the way for the next, and invariably more terrible, steps. Not until the Holocaust was all over did it become clear that the unbelievable had actually happened. And then people began to say the whole process of destruction had been inevitable from the beginning. They looked back at the steps taken down the long road to death and asked, How could anyone have overlooked the signs?

With the advantage of hindsight, it is not hard to ask that question. But the Jews living through the experience could behave only on the basis of what they knew *then*. The German Jews, the first in Europe to fall victim to Hitler, could reach no real agreement on the nature and extent of the danger threatening them. Nor could they agree on what to do about it. We must realize that there was no historical precedent for the Holocaust. It was a *new* event in world history; the mechanical mass-murder system of an Auschwitz had never happened before. Like any person anywhere, each Jew thought and acted on the basis of his own level of understanding, his own degree of courage, his own moral judgment. For us to evaluate the Jews' actions requires of us that we be able to reconstruct accurately the historical situation which confronted them.

When it was all over, a pattern became clear, of course. First, the Jews were defined and separated from all others; next, everything they owned was stripped from them; then, they were concentrated in ghettos; and finally—extermination.

Nazi propaganda, which had always been fiercely and unrelentingly anti-Semitic, prepared the way for dividing the Jews from the rest of the population. With his party in power, Minister of Propaganda Goebbels had the means to barrage the public daily with complaints and threats against the Jews. The next step was open terror. For a whole week in March 1933, "*Jude verrecke!*" rang through the streets while Storm Troopers beat, robbed, and murdered Jews at will. The police, on orders, stood by and watched. At railway stations, SA bullies met each train, shouting in cadence, "To hell with the Jews!" Nazi thugs stormed into hospitals and courts, ousting Jewish doctors, lawyers, and judges. Then, on April 1, the Nazis sprang the first official governmental act against the Jews—a boycott. SS and SA men picketed Jewish stores, factories, and shops—keeping people from entering. Across shop windows was smeared the word "*Jude.*" The Nazi intent was to cut off Jewish enterprises from their customers and suppliers, and thus force the owners to transfer their businesses—cheaply— to non-Jews.

Terror reached into the small towns, too. On Boycott Day in Tienen on the upper Rhine, Storm Troopers paraded through the streets behind a brass band. They set up a firing range—the targets were ugly caricatures of local citizens, labeled "Jew"—and invited the people to practice shooting. At night young men and women caroused in the tavern, bawling out the party anthem, the "*Horst Wessel Lied*":

> . . . *When Jewish blood spurts from the knife,*
> *Then everything will be fine!* . . .

Driving through the countryside, one could see anti-Jewish posters adorning the entrances and exits of the villages. Shopkeepers posted warnings in their windows: WE DON'T DEAL WITH JEWS.

A week after the boycott, a new law eliminated all "non-Aryans" from civil service and public employment. A "non-Aryan" was any person who had a Jewish parent or Jewish grandparents. In Germany the civil service also included all teaching positions, from the elementary school through university; and most branches of the entertainment industry, including radio, theater, opera, and concerts. About 5,000 Jews lost their jobs. Then came decrees removing all Jews from newspaper staffs and ousting Jews from the guilds which controlled the arts. For a time, Jews holding important jobs in business felt safe, thinking their contracts and their usefulness would save them. But they too were fired. At first, it was by unofficial pressure for "Aryanization"; then, by decree.

Many Jews decided it was time to leave Germany. By the end of the year, over 37,000, about 7 percent of the German Jewish population, had gone abroad to begin new lives.

Still, 1933 was only the beginning. Many Jews (and non-Jews, too) could not believe this barbarism was real. They lived with the illusion that such extreme cruelty could not last much longer —perhaps because it began almost casually, as Maurice Meier describes it. Meier was a Jewish farmer living with his wife Martha and son Ernst near the Swiss border.

> Toward the end of May [1933] Ernst and his schoolmates were looking forward to and making plans for the great day of the school picnic. On the morning of the appointed day Ernst shouldered his rucksack, stuck a spray of blossoms in his hat, and went marching off to school, whistling and full of happy anticipation. About an hour later somebody came and told us that Ernst was standing alone and forlorn on the school grounds. I found him with bloody hands and face, his clothing torn, the contents of the rucksack scattered and trampled in the dust. As he walked home with me he sobbed out his story.
>
> The teacher had read off the names of the pupils who were to go on the picnic, omitting Ernst's name. At the end of the rollcall he looked at Ernst and said, "Jews are not wanted at our picnic." Ernst stepped out of the line and started to walk away, but the teacher shouted to the children, "Boys, get him and knock out of him any ideas he may have about coming to our school anymore." Several rowdies thereupon attacked him, and soon the whole class was scratching, kicking and beating him with the teacher gleefully shouting his encouragement.

The next day Mr. Meier called on the teacher:

> After I had made my complaint he launched into a tirade against the Jews. I then went to the principal. He listened

sympathetically and said, "I am truly sorry for you and for Ernst, but I cannot do a thing because Ernst's teacher is a party member."

"Then what can I do to save the child from such painful experiences?" I asked.

"The only advice I can give you, Herr Meier, is to take Ernst out of school."

This we did, and gave him his lessons at home ourselves.

"Racial science" and "racial culture," as taught in the schools, deeply scarred the young German mind. Erna Listing, a schoolgirl in Gelsenkirchen, was so proud of her essay on the assigned theme, "The Jews Are Our Misfortune," that she sent it to Der Stürmer, one of the most violently anti-Semitic newspapers. Appearing in January 1935, it read in part:

Unfortunately many people today still say, "God created the Jews too. That is why you must respect them also." We say, however, "Vermin are also animals, but we still destroy them." The Jew is a half-caste. He has inherited characteristics of Aryans, Asiatics, Negroes and Mongols. In a half-caste, the worst characteristics predominate. The only good thing about him is his white color. . . .

The Jews have a wicked book of laws. It is called the Talmud. The Jews look on us as animals as well and treat us accordingly. They use cunning tricks to take away our wealth. . . . The Jews have plotted revolts and incited war. They have led Russia into misery. In Germany they gave the Communist Party money and paid their thugs. We were at death's door. Then Adolf Hitler came. Now the Jews are abroad and stir up trouble against us. But we do not waver and we follow the Fuehrer. We do not buy anything from the Jews. Every penny we give them kills one of our own people.

Heil Hitler!

Not until 1935 did Hitler make anti-Semitism part of Germany's basic legal code. On September 15, he introduced the

Nuremberg Laws. They dealt with "Citizenship" and the "Protection of German Blood and German Honor." Under these laws the Jews were deprived of their political rights. They were no longer citizens; they were reduced to subjects. Mixed marriages and extramarital sex relations between Jews and Aryans were made criminal offenses. The Nazis simply legalized the terror that had preceded the laws and went ahead to erect, on the foundation of the Nuremberg Laws, a structure of new decrees which robbed the Jews of their last remaining rights.

A quota system had already reduced the number of Jews in higher education to the proportion of Jews in the population. Now came a decree expelling all Jews from German schools. (Jews could then attend Jewish schools only.) The segregation of Jews extended to sleepers and dining cars on all railway lines, then to waiting rooms and rest rooms in all railway stations. Special shopping hours for Jews were introduced, limiting them to one or two hours a day. Beaches, resorts, and public baths were declared off limits to Jews. Jews could not have their hair cut in Aryan barbershops or get medical care in Aryan hospitals. A curfew was ordered: all Jews had to be off the streets after 8:00 P.M. Jews could not use trolleys and buses in rush hours and could sit only when there were no Aryan standees. Non-Aryan cars were assigned "Jew numbers" for their license plates. Private telephones were ripped out of Jewish apartments, and Jews were denied the use of public phones. Even before ghetto districts were set up, there was a period when Jews could live only in those houses marked for Jews.

The Nuremberg Laws and their thirteen supplementary decrees were nothing new, the German government claimed. Hitler was simply restoring the conditions of the era before Emancipation. As one Nazi spokesman put it, "It will henceforth and for all future times be impossible for the Jews to mix with the German people and to meddle in the political, economic, and cultural management of the Reich."

These restrictions—so like the old slave codes and Jim Crow laws that afflicted Black Americans for centuries—were reinforced by identification measures. As in any police state, identification documents were vital. Jews had to carry ID cards and to show them in all dealings with Party and government offices. German passports held by Jews were stamped with a big, red capital "J." When rationing began, the same "J" was printed on the ration cards of Jews. Even a Jew's name could no longer be his or her own choice. Jews who had taken German names had to go back to their old names. In addition, Jewish men had to use the middle name "Israel"; and Jewish women, the middle name "Sarah." The imposed names had to be recorded on all birth and marriage certificates.

Then came the stamping of Jewish identification on the person and the home. Jews six years of age or over were ordered to wear a Jewish star in public. It had to be a black star on a yellow background, big as the palm of the hand and sewn over the left breast of the clothing. In the center of every star, the word "Jude." Later, Jews were ordered to paste a paper star on their doors, too.

The labeling of Jews was a viciously effective weapon. It helped the Nazis monitor residence and movement. It made it easy for the police to pick up Jews anywhere at any time. And it had a crippling effect on the victims. Jews felt naked before their enemies. The whole world was watching them. To hide, to escape, to resist meant ridding oneself of badge, middle name, ID papers. But to do that was a serious crime, and there were spies and informers everywhere to recognize and denounce a Jew. Yet to go on wearing the star—what could it mean but disaster, death?

In the beginning, the Jews of Germany had no central organization to turn to for help. Each city had its own Jewish administrative group, which took care of Jewish schools, hospitals, and synagogues. A few months after Nazism took over, these groups began planning a national organization. Called the Representative Council of Jews in Germany, it began work late in 1933, under the chairmanship of Rabbi Leo Baeck of Berlin. Its original purpose was political, not financial. It sought open debate with the Nazis on anti-Semitism and the future of Germany's Jews. But Hitler listened to no one else's opinion. And so, the organization found it more and more essential to provide relief, care for the sick, schooling for the children, and opportunities for emigration.

The anti-Semitic program proved useful in mobilizing the country for total war. While ridding Germany of Jews, Hitler was training the Germans in the brutality needed to gain domination over all of Europe. The violence and corruption typical of the Nazis before they came to power now became endemic to Germany. It was known that Count Helldorf, head of Berlin's police force, had developed an enormously profitable racket out of the Jews' desperate desire to escape abroad. He would seize their passports, then sell them back at the highest possible price. They paid it. No price was too high if it was liberty one was buying. Bribery became so highly organized, it seemed legal to everyone.

As for violence, the German people became so accustomed to it that even the children practiced it casually. Bella Fromm, the Berlin journalist, jotted down this scene in her diary for June 1, 1938:

> Driving out to Potsdam, I came across a group of youngsters, dressed in the Hitler Youth outfit, beating up a skinny, under-sized, fair boy. I stopped.
> "Aren't you ashamed, eight big strong fellows like you, jumping on a six-year-old?"
> The oldest of the gang explained. "We discovered that this dirty swine was nothing but a Jewish bastard. He refused to answer the Heil Hitler salute, and said he was Jewish. So we took his pants off to find out whether he is circumcised."

On June 28, Fromm was alerted by a friend in the Foreign Office that a pogrom had been organized for that day in Berlin. She went out on the streets to observe:

> The entire Kurfürstendamm was plastered with scrawls and cartoons. "Jew" was smeared all over the doors, windows and walls in waterproof colors. It grew worse as we came to the part of town where poor little Jewish retail shops were to be

found. The SA had created havoc. Everywhere were revolting and bloodthirsty pictures of Jews beheaded, hanged, tortured, and maimed, accompanied by obscene inscriptions. Windows were smashed, and loot from the miserable little shops was strewn over the sidewalk and floating in the gutter.

We were just about to enter a tiny jewelry shop when a gang of ten youngsters in Hitler Youth uniforms smashed the show window and stormed into the shop, brandishing butcher knives and yelling: "To hell with the Jewish rabble! Room for the Sudeten Germans!"

The smallest boy of the mob climbed inside the window and started his work of destruction by flinging everything he could grab right into the streets. Inside, the other boys broke glass shelves and counters, hurling alarm clocks, cheap silverware, and trifles to their accomplices outside. A tiny shrimp of a boy crouched in a corner of the window, putting dozens of rings on his fingers and stuffing his pockets with wristwatches and bracelets. His uniform bulging with loot, he turned around, spat squarely into the shopkeeper's face, and dashed off.

The little old Jew kept his poise and tried to reassure us. "I am only glad that my wife died ten days ago. God spared her this ordeal. We have been starving for a long time. Business was dead. The law prevents us from getting out of a lease or dismissing an employee as long as a penny can be squeezed out."

Bella Fromm was worried about two old friends whom she had helped with money and food during the last two years. They had lost their two sons—killed for Germany!—during the First World War. She went to find out whether they had suffered:

Their shop was in ruins. Their goods, paper and stationery, trampled into the gutter. Three SA men, roaring with obscene laughter, forced the trembling old man to pick up the broken glass with hands that were covered with blood. We stood there, choking with rage, trembling in horror, impotent and helpless.

The next day, when we returned to bring them food and see what else we could do to help them, we found two coffins *surrounded by silent neighbors. The faces of the old couple seemed peaceful and serene amid the broken glass and destruction. As we put down our baskets and stood there wretchedly, a young woman spoke to me. "It is better for them. They took poison last night."*

Making what would be her last trip through Germany before emigrating to America, Bella Fromm came across a sight that crystallized everything she had experienced in these first six years of Hitlerism. In Frankfurt they had changed the *Paul Ehrlich Strasse* into *Heinrich Himmler Strasse*. "The man who saved humanity by his cure for syphilis," she wrote, "has been replaced by a sadistic butcher."

Flight—to Nowhere

Stripped of citizenship, rights, work, property, dignity, the Jews of Germany had only one hope: emigration. By the end of 1937, nearly 130,000 Jews had taken that course. But three-quarters of Germany's Jews still remained inside Hitler's borders. As they scrambled frantically to find a way out, the Jewish leader Chaim Weizmann spoke prophetically of the fate of all of Europe's Jews:

> *Today almost six million Jews are doomed to be pent up*
> *in places where they are not wanted, and for whom the world*
> *is divided into places where they cannot live, and places into*
> *which they cannot enter.*

Hitler did not want the Jews. Get rid of them, he told his officials. His policy still seemed to be expulsion, not extermination. But as he moved closer to war, the possibility of flight for the Jews narrowed. And the possibility of extermination widened.

Late in 1937 Hitler confided to a few trusted military and political leaders that he planned to take over Austria and then Czechoslovakia. If it took war to achieve his goals, Germany must be ready for it. His successes at home and abroad had given him a monumental confidence in his own infallibility. In the spring of 1936 he had remilitarized the Rhineland, illegally, and no one had acted to stop him. That summer of 1936 he had played host to the world at the Olympic Games in Berlin, and no one had refused to take part. For two years now his troops and planes had been helping Franco to destroy the Spanish Republic, and the West had stayed "neutral."

Now in March 1938, he took over Austria while everyone watched and no one interfered. The Nazis set up a Jewish emigration center in Vienna in April. And Adolf Eichmann, one of Heydrich's civil servants, was put in charge. Eichmann had joined the Nazi party in 1932, after a short career as a traveling salesman for an oil company. As a young Nazi hopeful, he behaved like the typical bureaucrat, doing exactly what he was told and getting little recognition for it. Until he saw, in this movement powered by a raging anti-Semitism, his chance to advance by becoming an "expert" on Jewish affairs. By 1938 he was head of the SD unit called "Jewry." And now he had his first big job in Vienna.

In one year, by combining terror and blackmail with the threat of concentration camps, he deported 100,000 Jews, almost half the total number in Austria. He saw himself as a disciplined technician, providing an "objective" solution to the Jewish problem. "Each of us," he said later, "as an individual had no wish to harm the Jews individually."

But what could Eichmann do with the hundreds of thousands of Jews still in Germany and Austria? The refugee problem came to a head, for as the cry for help swelled, the chance to escape grew slimmer. A High Commission for Refugees from Germany had been established by the League of Nations. But so little willingness to help was displayed by the member nations that the commissioner, James MacDonald, resigned in protest.

In July 1938, at the request of President Franklin D. Roosevelt, 32 nations met at Evian, France, to see what refuge they could offer to the persecuted Jews. Just before the conference, on Hitler's orders, the synagogues of Munich, Nuremberg, and Dortmund were destroyed, and mass arrests of Jews were made. The delegations came up with no proposals, nor did they even show any indignation over Nazi policy. In a week the conference closed. No country was willing to change its policy for the Jews.

That September at Munich, Hitler frightened England and

France into signing a pact that sacrificed Czechoslovakia. That Republic, created by peace treaties after the First World War, was made up of several nationalities, among them the Germans of the Sudetenland region. Concealing his true aim—to destroy the Czech state and grab its territory and people for the Third Reich —Hitler threatened war unless his outrageous claim upon the Sudetenland was satisfied. He assured the British and French, who had pledged to defend Czechoslovakia from attack, that the Sudetenland was his final territorial demand in Europe. The gullible British Prime Minister, Neville Chamberlain, took Hitler's word. Czechoslovakia, deserted by her allies, fell into Hitler's hands. Such futile attempts to appease an insatiable appetite for power and territory came to be known as the "Munich spirit." People everywhere foolishly gave thanks that "peace in our time" was assured.

When the Western powers failed to support Czechoslovakia against Hitler, Heydrich took it as a signal that he could dump Jews upon the smaller nations without fear of reprisals. Toward the end of October, thousands of Polish Jews living in Germany were served deportation notices. Roused from their beds at night, 12,000 Jews, taking only what they could carry, were bundled into freight cars, forced across the Polish border, and dumped into a freezing no-man's-land. Many of the old and sick died of exposure. The others, through the efforts of the American Joint Distribution Committee (JDC), were finally quartered in Polish towns.

By the end of 1938, it was clear to Hitler that emigration alone would not solve his "Jewish problem." There were still too many Jews in Reich territory. A Foreign Office memo complained that "almost every state in the world has . . . hermetically sealed its borders against these parasitical Jewish intruders. . . ."

Eichmann, however, kept trying to get rid of Jews. In July 1939 he set up another emigration center in Prague, and announced that 70,000 Jews would be deported within a year. The Jewish Community Council of the city was told to provide daily quotas of Jews and the funds to pay for their emigration. Jews were ordered to leave the Czech provinces and to gather in Prague. But once there, where could they be deported? Those with property negotiated their own exits with the Gestapo; the poorer Jews were stranded.

What was the rest of the world doing to help the desperate Jews? The United States let in about 100,000 Jewish refugees until 1939, the outbreak of the Second World War. (It was less than 2 percent of America's small Jewish population.) Few as they were, their entrance was resisted by many Americans. It was hard for Europe's beleaguered Jews to understand why. They had thought of President Roosevelt as their friend. His New Deal government was certainly humane. But though he spoke often and sympathetically of the plight of the persecuted Jews, his administration did little to help them. Some people argued that to bring in more refugees during the Great Depression would add to the nation's problems. Others claimed it would be taken as interference with another nation's internal affairs. Some said it would force changes in the immigration quota system, which they did not want to make. And, when the war came, some said, it would hurt the defense effort.

The terrible truth was that in ten crucial years, 1933–1943, there were over 400,000 unfilled places within United States immigration quotas for refugees from countries under Hitler's rule. Each place unfilled was a sentence of death for a European Jew.

The non-Nazi countries of Europe took about 150,000 refugees. England accepted the largest number, 80,000; France, about 25,000; Holland, 22,000; Belgium, 13,000; Switzerland, 9,000.

About 40,000 refugees found homes in Latin America. Half went to Argentina, and the remainder dispersed to other countries in South and Central America and the West Indies. But by the end of 1938, Latin America banged the door shut. In 1939 Japanese-occupied Shanghai, China, became the haven for 10,000 Jews. It was a free port that put up no bar to refugees, except that they could not move into the interior of China.

Other than the United States, Palestine was the most practical goal of emigrating Jews, but it, too, put up entry restrictions. The policy of the British, who controlled the Middle East, was concerned with Arabs as well as Jews. If war with Hitler should come, the support of the Jews was inevitable. But not that of the Arabs. So the British Mandate for Palestine, which provided for facilitating Jewish emigration "under suitable conditions," was interpreted to suit imperial, not humane, policies. The British allowed entry to Jews with a certain amount of money, but all others were restricted. Then, in its White Paper of May 1939, the British Colonial Office took steps to end Jewish entry into Palestine. It was to be permitted for only another five years, at the rate of 10,000 per year. To help meet the immediate crisis, an additional 25,000 people were to be allowed in if their maintenance could be guaranteed. The result was that only about 70,000 refugees entered Palestine up until 1941. All hope of escape was denied to the millions of Jews the war would trap in Eastern Europe.

(The Arabs, it should be noted, failed to defend British interests during World War II. Instead, they allied themselves with Hitler. The Jews of Palestine—what other choice did they have?—fought alongside the British wherever they could.)

How could Jews leave Hitler's Reich if there was no place for them to go? By this time Jews would pay any price and undergo any danger to escape Nazism. A new "travel trade" sprang up, a racket that police and ministry officials manipulated. The market for exporting Jews was lively, and Nazis (and many others) could make fat profits at every stage of the deadly game. As the pressure increased, the number who could find a route of escape diminished to a lucky few. One of those routes was via water. It was an enormously complex task to organize a rescue by ship. An available vessel had to be located; money raised to buy it and put a crew aboard; smugglers paid to sneak refugees to the port; and officials bribed to close their eyes to illegalities. To finance the steamship fares, dollars were almost always demanded, a transaction the American Joint Distribution Committee (JDC) organized through a special bureau.

And after all this, there was never any guarantee that the ship would sail, or if it did, that it would reach a safe harbor.

The story of the voyage of the *St. Louis* is but one such

episode. The ship left Hamburg, Germany, in May 1939, bound for Havana, Cuba. Aboard were 937 Jewish passengers, all with American quota permits and special permits to wait in Cuba while their American visas were being processed. But when they reached Havana, a presidential decree had made their permits worthless. The ship cruised aimlessly in the Atlantic, waiting for some government to save the despairing passengers. Finally, after thirty-five days at sea, England, France, Holland, and Belgium agreed to share the human cargo. But many other ships were ordered back when country after country refused to accept refugees.

The *Struma*, a broken-down cattle boat, carried 769 Rumanian Jews to Istanbul, Turkey, where they were to be given visas for Palestine. But the Turks sent them back; the ship suddenly sank in the Black Sea; and all the refugees but one drowned.

The ancient paddle-wheel steamer, the *Pentcho*, took aboard 511 Jews fleeing from Central Europe, hoping to reach Palestine. Down the Danube they sailed on the rickety, leaking boat, past one country after another which refused to let them come in for food and water. After weeks aboard, the refugees were filthy and starving. Many jumped overboard to swim ashore, but they were forced back. It took almost five months to reach the Black Sea. With no lifeboats, no life preservers, and no radio, the ship began a wild, aimless journey among the Greek Islands. Then one day the boiler exploded, and the engine stopped. Bunk sheets were gathered, and the women sewed them up into sails. A storm drove the *Pentcho* onto the rocks of an uninhabited island in the Aegean Sea. The passengers managed to scramble ashore and watched the ship break into pieces and sink. Scouring the island for food, they could find no birds, no animals, and no fresh water. Eleven terrible days passed. Then an Italian warship rescued them, only to put them into a concentration camp on the island of Rhodes. There they stayed for a year and a half, until finally they were sent to Italy, only, once more, to be penned up in a concentration camp.

BOOK TWO

*Destruction
of the Jews*

6

The Night
of Broken Glass

On November 7, 1938, a seventeen-year-old boy, Herschel Grynszpan, walked up to the German embassy in Paris and shot to death one of its minor staff, Ernst vom Rath.

Young Herschel was the son of one of the 12,000 Jews of Polish origin who a few days earlier had been deported from Germany to Poland. Herschel's father had lived in Germany for twenty-seven years. Like many such immigrants, he had never bothered to seek naturalization. Now, overnight, his life had been senselessly smashed.

When Herschel, in Paris visiting an uncle, got a postcard telling of his father's deportation, the act of murder followed. Exactly why the boy did it or what he hoped to achieve by it has never been clear. But the consequences were catastrophic.

The assassination triggered a nationwide pogrom (massacre) in Germany on the night of November 9, the *Kristallnacht* (Night of Broken Glass), which foreshadowed the extermination of the Jews. The assault had been planned by Heydrich and Goebbels at the first news of the shooting of vom Rath. Nazi regional chiefs were instructed by teletype to destroy Jewish shops, synagogues, businesses, and homes. The police were not to interfere, except to protect Aryan life and property. Jews, especially rich ones, were to be arrested and confined in concentration camps.

The Party carried out its orders. The torch was set to most of Germany's synagogues; 7,500 shops were ransacked and many destroyed; and hundreds of homes were looted and wrecked. Damage to property, equipment, and stock was estimated at several hundred million marks. At least 1,000 Jews were murdered, and 26,000 were flung into concentration camps.

An American eyewitness described what he saw in Leipzig that night:

> Jewish dwellings were smashed into and the contents demolished or looted. In one of the Jewish sections, an eighteen-year-old boy was hurled from a three-story window to land with both legs broken on a street littered with burning beds and other household furniture. . . . Jewish shop windows by the hundreds were systematically and wantonly smashed throughout the city at a loss estimated at several millions of marks. . . . The main streets of the city were a positive litter of shattered plate glass. . . . The debacle was executed by SS men and Storm Troopers, not in uniform, each group having been provided with hammers, axes, crowbars and incendiary bombs. . . .

A fourteen-year-old boy, M. I. Libau, had gone to bed that night in his home in Berlin. Suddenly, at six o'clock in the morning, the doorbell rang, waking him up. His mother went to the door and opened it. He told what happened then:

> I heard the shrill, barking, yelling voices of men. It seemed to me there were at least twenty.
> "Are here Gojim or Iwrim [Gentiles or Jews]?" Then I heard my mother's calm voice. "Please speak German. I understand it very well, but if you wish to know whether we are Christians or Jews, we are Jews!"
> "Where are the Jews? Where are they?" they yelled. I heard noises of falling furniture and breaking glass. I could not imagine what was happening. I stood behind my bed when one Nazi in full uniform entered the room. He stepped back a fraction of a second when he saw me; then he began to yell, "I'll do nothing to you. I won't do any harm to you."

Now he stood near me, his face sweating. A smell of bad alcohol came out of his mouth. He took another glaring look at me and began to destroy everything within reach. While he was breaking the closet door, my mother came into the room. He commanded her to hold the clothes for him so that he would be able to tear them better. Desperately my mother called out, "Those are all our clothes! What shall we wear?"

"You wear? Nothing!" he shouted. "You don't need any more clothes! You can go naked now."

It almost broke my heart when I saw him take my father's best suit. "This is my father's best suit," I called out. "Don't tear it! Don't!"

. . . We watched the men destroy the whole apartment of five rooms. All the things for which my parents had worked for eighteen long years were destroyed in less than ten minutes. Piles of valuable glasses, expensive furniture, linens—in short, everything was destroyed; nothing was left untouched. After those ten minutes, the apartment was a heap of ruins.

My mother and I looked at everything without shedding a tear. We felt as if we had lost our minds. The Nazis left us, yelling, "Don't try to leave this house! We'll soon be back again and take you to concentration camp to be shot."

But the Nazis did not come back—then. Mr. Libau, who had been working nights as a forced laborer on the railroad, came home and went into hiding in the cellar of a Christian friend. Many of the family's friends committed suicide that night, some went insane, and some were murdered.

In cold, precise detail, like a bookkeeper's account, the leader of the SS in the town of Geldern reported the action taken locally on orders he had received by telephone:

The first measure was the setting on fire of the synagogue in Geldern at about 4 A.M. By 9 A.M. this was burned down to the foundations. Some bibles in Hebrew characters were taken into safekeeping. Simultaneously the interior fittings of the synagogue in Xanten (a private house) were completely destroyed.

There existed two Jewish shops in the Sturm district, the fittings and small stock of which were likewise completely destroyed.

The furnishings of the remainder of the Jews, former cattle-Jews and now earning their living by private means, were totally demolished and rendered unusable, the windows and windowpanes first having been broken in. . . .

By about 11 hours [11 A.M.] all the male Jews fifteen to seventy years of age were arrested by the police and kept temporarily in the local guardhouses. . . . The population took a passive attitude to the demonstrators. . . .

Making a secret report on Nazi party members who had murdered Jews that night, the chief Party judge, Major Walter Buch, revealed how justice had disappeared in Hitler's Germany:

In the following cases of killing Jews, proceedings were suspended or minor punishments were pronounced: Party Member Fruehling, August, because of shooting of the Jewish couple Goldberg and because of shooting of the Jew Simasohm . . . Party Members Behring, Willi and Heike, Josef, because of shooting of the Jew Rosenbaum and the Jewess Zwienicki . . . Party Members Schmidt, Heinrich, and Meckler, Ernst, because of drowning of the Jew Ilsoffer . . . etc. etc. etc.

Why the Kristallnacht pogroms at this moment? Earlier, if they had wished, the Nazis could have invented any pretext to commit the same barbarism. But not until now did Hitler feel secure enough to dare a crime of this magnitude. He had learned he need fear no opposition from Germans or from the world outside.

Kristallnacht was still another measure of how far Hitler would go. Coming immediately after his successful intimidation of the major powers at Munich, it tested the German spirit. If his people could swallow this, they could swallow anything. Was any voice raised in protest? Neither the Catholic nor the Protestant

Church offered sanctuary to the stricken Jews. Hitler could smile comfortably and say, "My Germans are united behind me."

There were notable exceptions. One Catholic churchman, Bernard Lichtenberg, Provost of Saint Hedwig's Cathedral in Berlin, spoke out from the pulpit the morning after the pogrom:

> What took place yesterday, we know; what will be tomorrow, we do not know; but what happens today, that we have witnessed; outside, the synagogue is burning, and that, also, is a house of God. . . .
>
> In a number of Berlin homes, an anonymous inflammatory rag against the Jews is being distributed. It says that any German who, from allegedly false sentimentality, helps the Jews, commits treason against his own people. Do not let yourself be led astray by such unChristian thoughts, but act according to the clear command of Christ: "Thou shalt love thy neighbor as thyself."

Because Father Lichtenberg spoke, he served two years in prison. Released, he was seized by the Gestapo and sent to Dachau. He died on the way.

Far more true to the feelings of German Christians at the time was the action of *Landesbischof* Weidemann of Bremen; on November 28, shortly after the burning, pillaging, imprisonment, and murder of the Jews throughout Germany, the state bishop sent this telegram:

TO: THE FUEHRER AND REICHSCHANCELLOR ADOLF HITLER
THE THREE CHURCHES OF GRATITUDE IN BREMEN HAVE BEEN INAUGURATED. THEY BEAR YOUR NAME, MEIN FÜHRER, IN GRATITUDE TO GOD FOR THE MIRACULOUS REDEMPTION OF OUR NATION AT YOUR HANDS FROM THE ABYSS OF JEWISH-MATERIALISTIC BOLSHEVISM. I THANK YOU FOR HAVING ENABLED US TO EXPRESS IN THESE NEW CHURCHES WHAT IS A DEEP CONFESSION FOR US WHO ARE FULLY CONSCIOUS CHRISTIAN NATIONAL SOCIALISTS.

HEIL, MEIN FÜHRER!

The pogroms of *Kristallnacht* were the unofficial penalty for the death of vom Rath. The next day, Hitler decided to demand the collective punishment of all the Jews. The Fuehrer told Goering that the "Jewish question" must be "coordinated and solved, now, once and for all, in one way or another."

The German bureaucracy swung into action. Measures against the Jews would be planned in an orderly, legal, and systematic way. Pogroms were too messy. The mob turned loose could not always be controlled: *Kristallnacht* had done harm to non-Jewish property and had cost the state some losses. No more. The experts would confer; decisions would be scientifically made; the proper directives would be issued; the necessary reports made out and filed.

When casual violence on the streets stopped, many Jews were fooled into believing the worst was over. But it was not; terror simply took another form. Goering imposed the huge fine of 1 billion marks on the Jews; it was the value of 20 percent of all their remaining property. Two billion marks had already been taken from the Jews. The government had collected this "Atonement Payment" and poured it into the rearmament program. Compulsory Aryanization of Jewish businesses moved ahead rapidly. By the year's end, what was left of Jewish business and self-employment was wiped out. It is worth noting that such steps taken "for the good of the German people" at first benefited only one class—the owners of Aryan enterprises. Later the state pocketed a part of the loot.

Before the time of *Kristallnacht*, about a quarter of the Jewish population of Germany had emigrated. A year later, more than half the Jews were gone. Three-quarters of those who remained were older people—their businesses, savings, professions, jobs, all gone. They were a dependent community badly in need of relief. It was now that the SD took over the Representative Council of Jews, converted it into the Reich Association of Jews in Germany, and made membership for all "racial" Jews compulsory. It was the equivalent of a Nazi-controlled ghetto. Public relief was denied the Jews. Unemployed Jews were put to hard labor on construction and reclamation projects, or in arms plants. Jewish wages were slashed, and what was left, taxed. It was slave labor.

"But," said Heydrich, "in spite of the elimination of the Jews from economic life, the main problem remains, namely, to kick the Jew out of Germany."

7

A Prophecy

*Today I will once more be a prophet! If the international
Jewish financiers inside and outside Europe should again
succeed in plunging the nations into a world war, the result
will be not the bolshevization of the earth and thus the victory
of Jewry, but the annihilation of the Jewish race throughout
Europe.*

This was Hitler's voice, speaking to the Reichstag on January
30, 1939. His prophecy of annihilation for the Jews came only
seven months before he himself would plunge the nations into
the war of conquest he had been planning from the day he took
power.

Did he predict annihilation because he knew his policy of mass
deportation was coming to an end? Through "voluntary" emigration he had already driven out half the Jews of Germany, and
brought the remainder to mass destitution. On September 1,
1939, he took the step which would lead to the destruction of the
Jews of Europe. Germany attacked Poland.

The blame for starting World War II rests solely on Nazi
Germany. It would be hard to find a historian who disagrees. The
deeper roots of that war may be tangled and hard to trace, but
one cause was Hitler's desire to see his "superior" Germans rule
mankind. More important, argues historian Lucy Dawidowicz,

was Hitler's conception of the war as a means to reach the Jews of Europe and annihilate them.

Back in November 1937, Hitler had secretly told his military leaders of his plans for the war. The only question for Germany, he said, is where the greatest possible conquest could be made at lowest cost. By a policy of international blackmail, and without firing a shot, he had already taken the Rhineland, Austria, and Czechoslovakia. When he sent his armies smashing through Poland, he scrapped the pact he had made at Munich assuring the West that Germany's territorial ambitions were satisfied. "In starting and making a war," he said, "it is not right that matters, but victory."

He began the war with the brute desire to exploit the people and the resources of the territories he would conquer. Everything that could be used by the German war economy was to be ripped away from Poland, and the Poles were to be made the "slaves of the Greater German World Empire." He had no plans to remake Poland, only to destroy it.

In scarcely three weeks most of the fighting was over. The new German army moved with a speed, efficiency, and ruthlessness that astonished and terrified the world. (Six months later Hitler conquered Denmark and Norway. Then Holland, Belgium, and France fell to the German army's *Blitzkrieg* [onslaught]. Only Britain was left in the West.)

The German soldiers entering Poland saw themselves as heroes of the "master race"; their victims, the Poles, were *Untermenschen*, subhumans. And the Jews among them were an even lower category—bacilli. In 1939 there were 3.3 million Jews in Poland—10 percent of the total population. About a third lived in the countryside, and two-thirds, in towns and cities. Two million Jews fell directly into Hitler's hands in the invasion. The others came under Russian control when Stalin (under the pact he had signed with Hitler in August 1939) invaded Poland from the other side. The two powers divided the country between themselves, and Poland, as a state, ceased to exist.

On September 21, Heydrich issued his plan for Poland's Jews.

First, they would be concentrated in ghettos. Jews would be removed from the countryside and its villages, and forced into ghettos in the larger cities. Councils of Jewish Elders would be set up to administer the segregated communities. Later, it would turn out that the ghettos were way stations to the death camps, and the Councils were not the traditional councils of Jewish self-government but Nazi instruments for extermination.

Who were the Jews of Eastern Europe? There were 7 million of them living in that huge territory bounded by Germany on the west, the Dnieper River on the east, the Baltic Sea on the north, and the Black Sea on the south. Their settlement in Eastern Europe had started in the thirteenth century, with people from Bohemia and Germany. The Jews expelled from the West during the next centuries headed in many directions, but large numbers of them settled in the East. They were welcomed by the Polish rulers for the help they could give in the crucial task of building the country's economy. By 1500, the center of the Jewish world had moved east of the Rhine. Their lot in the Middle Ages, contrasted with the horrors of Western Europe, was not unbearable.

But the good life did not last long. Soon the epidemic of religious hatred and violence reached into the East too, and the effect was catastrophic. Living conditions became as intolerable for Jews in Poland, Lithuania, the Ukraine, and Galicia as they were in the other Christian countries. Church laws forced Jews into ghettos and branded them with the yellow badge. In the seventeenth century, a Ukrainian uprising wiped out hundreds of Jewish communities, and hundreds of thousands—a third of the Jewish population—died by the sword, famine, and pestilence. Repeated pogroms left deep wounds in the consciousness of East European Jews, wounds which succeeding generations never healed.

When Poland was swallowed up by Russia, Prussia, and Austria after the defeat of Napoleon, a huge mass of Jews came under czarist rule. To keep the Jews out of the interior, the czar mapped out a region all Jews were forced to live in—the Pale of Settlement. The Jews were allowed their traditional right of self-government in religious affairs, but the state restricted every other aspect of life. Hundreds of anti-Jewish laws and regulations were applied mercilessly. No matter what czar sat on the throne, the persecution of the Jews continued. Anti-Semitism was like an official faith, observed and respected everywhere in the Russian Empire.

In the 1870s, pogroms engineered by the government began to break out. Within a decade, new anti-Jewish restrictions and disabilities were piled upon the old. Under these crushing blows, 1⅓ million Jews fled the Empire between 1881 and 1918. Most settled in the United States, but many went to Western Europe and elsewhere. More would have escaped if they had had the means. But the mass of East European Jews were desperately poor. Most were factory workers, artisans, and petty tradespeople who worked fifteen and more hours a day and lived on a diet of potatoes and herring.

They lived largely in the shtetls of Eastern Europe, the thousands of small towns scattered throughout the Pale of Settlement. The shtetls were essentially marketplaces for trading goods and services. The little towns were islands in a sea of poor, illiterate peasants. The Jews lived a separate life as a minority within the culture of the majority. During World War I, the Jews fell victim to both sides as the fighting moved back and forth. They were arrested, tortured, deported, massacred. Out of that war came the birth of Poland as an independent state. But it did not bring the Jews a better life. Not even to the small number of assimilationist Jews, who came from the wealthy families. These "Poles of Mosaic faith," as they called themselves, stressed their deep bonds with the Polish nation and their distinctness from the Orthodox Jews. In their own eyes they were really Poles, not Jews. (Didn't the assimilationist Jews of Germany think the same way?) But the Poles didn't believe the Jews were Poles. Poland, like Nazi Germany, defined the Jews as a race. The Poles thought of the Jews as a strange people, a foreign people, a hostile people. And the very fact that assimilationist Jews were especially prominent among the leading scientists, artists, and writers made them highly suspect to the Poles. No matter how they talked, looked, or behaved—no matter what medals they wore or what contributions they made to Polish culture—Jews they were and Jews they would remain. Only, unlike the other Jews, *these* were enemies in disguise.

The assimilationist Jews did not join political movements which offered nationalist solutions to the problems of anti-Semitism. They rejected both the Zionists and the Bundists, who fought for the right of Jews to live as a distinct people. The Zionists, with whose aims perhaps 40 percent of the Polish Jews sympathized, saw the goal as a return to the national homeland in Palestine. The Bund, which was the socialist organization to which most of the Jewish workers belonged, believed a revolution in Poland would give the Jews freedom and national equality. Only some 20 percent of all Polish Jews were "still dominated by a religious mentality" at this time, according to the historian Reuben Ainsztein.

The great majority of Jews supported Polish freedom, hoping for recognition as a national minority and for equal rights. But most Polish political parties opposed those demands. Pogroms broke out the very day Polish independence was proclaimed. And from that time on, robberies, beatings, and murders of Jews were everyday events. Poland earned a worldwide reputation as a state where national minorities were oppressed and persecuted. Although Jewish deputies were elected to the Polish parliament, they never succeeded in winning enough support to protect Jewish interests. The ancient anti-Semitism continued, fueled now by the rise of new fascist parties and anti-Jewish groups.

In the depression of the 1930s, anti-Semitic violence raged through the universities and the provincial towns. A new slogan appeared everywhere: "There is no place for Jews in Poland." The government-supported press was peppered with articles treating the Jews as an inevitable evil. In despair, the Jewish press forecast a "catastrophe for Polish Jewry." In 1935 a new Polish constitution abolished parliamentary democracy and replaced it with a fascist system. Nazi racial theories and practices were adopted. Plans were made to force mass Jewish emigration.

But most countries discriminated against Jewish immigrants. Only 117,000 Jews were able to leave Poland in the years between 1931 and 1938. Anti-Jewish riots broke out in many cities and towns. Jewish people were attacked, stores looted, tradespeople barred from markets and fairs. When a delegation of Polish Jews called on the head of the government's Nationalities Department to ask that steps be taken against anti-Semitic propaganda, he replied:

> Nowadays everybody in Poland is anti-Semitic. We cannot assign police to protect every single Jew. We do not intend, moreover, to hang young people just for being anti-Semitic.

Knowing that the government would not protect Jews, the Bund, as early as 1920, had organized its own self-defense force. The small but permanent militia guarded not only the Bund, its members, headquarters, and street demonstrations, but Jews in general. It countered violence with violence.

Although the use of physical force had been regarded by many as alien to Jewish character and tradition, the Bund concluded that self-defense was not only necessary now, but honorable and heroic. And when violence had to be used, the Bund—through the trained and armed militia of both its adult and youth groups —used it to good effect. During a general strike called to protest a pogrom of 1936, a Bund leader, Z. Artur, declared:

> Today the Jewish working class is saying to the fascist and anti-Semitic hooligans: the time has passed when Jews could be subjected to pogroms with impunity. There exists a mass of workers raised in the Bund tradition of struggle and self-defense. With them one can wage war, but not pogroms that remain unpunished.

One day the Polish Foreign Minister announced that Poland had room for barely half a million Jews. The rest of them, he said, had better get out.

By 1938 the Polish government was coordinating its policy

with Nazi Germany's. But that confidence in Hitler as an ally was terribly misplaced. It led to a catastrophe for Poland itself, as well as for the Jews.

From the first day of Hitler's invasion, the massacre began. The *Einsatzgruppen*—the "mobile killing units" of the SS, under the command of Reinhard Heydrich—moved into Poland with the regular armored columns. Their instructions were to kill as many civilians as possible, especially Jews. Masses of Jews were now condemned to death, although at this point it was not yet clear that Hitler planned total extermination. He would use three basic methods for his "Final Solution of the Jewish Question": starvation, shooting, and, in the end, gassing. The *Einsatzgruppen's* weapon was the gun. (Later it became the gas van.) The troops were drafted from the Armed SS, and their commanders were chosen by Heydrich from the SS elite having academic degrees. Most were professional men—teachers, artists, lawyers, a physician, even a clergyman—and most were in their thirties. No one was asked to volunteer, but once chosen, they did their job of mass murder with zeal and skill.

There were four of these mobile killing units, each of battalion size, totaling about 3,000 men. Operating in different zones of Eastern Europe, they worked closely with the regular armed forces, which handed over captured Jews and often lent their own men to assist in the massacres. In addition, the killing units were aided by more than 200,000 eager collaborators from the local populations. Historian Raul Hilberg estimates they murdered 1.4 million Jews by the end of the war. One officer alone, Dr. Otto Bradfisch, handled the killing of at least 15,000 people. Another, Dr. Otto Ohlendorf, a research economist, directed the killing of 90,000 Jews.

Death did not always come swiftly at the hands of the killing squads. Before the bullet there was often barbarous cruelty, details of which the SS liked to photograph and send home. In town after town—Bielsko, Kalisz, Wloclawek, Mielec, Wieruszow, Zgierz, Aleksandrovsk, Piotrkow, Lukow—the horrors mounted. The conquest was rapid and ruthless; the torture, slow and bestial. The goal, in Heydrich's aseptic words, was "the housecleaning of Jews, intelligentsia, clergy, and the nobility."

One high army officer, General Johannes Blaskowitz, wrote a letter of complaint:

> The unlimited brutalization and moral depravity . . . will spread like an epidemic through the most valuable German human material. If the high officials and SS continue to call for violence and brutality, brutal men will soon reign supreme. With disconcerting speed depraved birds of a feather find one another out and band together in order to satisfy their pathological and bestial instincts—as they are now doing in Poland. They can be barely kept in hand; for they have good reason to feel that they have official sanction to commit the most horrible of acts.

But neither he nor the other German generals made any effective attempt to stop the atrocities. The High Command knew of Hitler's war plans before the war started, and they did their best to carry them out.

When Hitler broke his pact with Stalin and invaded Russia in June 1941, the frenzied killing was renewed. Five million Jews were living under the Soviet flag, four million of them in territories the Germans would overrun. About a million and a half of these fled or were evacuated before the Nazi troops arrived. The slaughter of those who remained was enormous. The mobile killing squads murdered 7,000 in Lvov, 2,500 in Zhitomir, 11,000 in Dnepropetrovsk, 15,000 in Rovno, 14,000 in Kharkov. . . . In Kiev, 35,000 Jews were marched to the Babi Yar ravine and shot. All in just two days, a tribute to German efficiency. A few months later, another 15,000 Jews were murdered in Kiev.

In the town of Zagrodski, in the Pinsk district, lived some 500 Jewish families. A killing squad arrived in mid-August 1942. The Jews were ordered to leave everything in their houses, take only their children, and come out to the square for a rollcall. Trucks rolled up, and the Jews were jammed aboard. There wasn't room for everyone, so the rest were ordered to run after the trucks. A young mother, Rivka Yosselevscka, was among them. After the war, she told a court what happened:

Q: And you ran with your daughter?
A: I had my daughter in my arms and ran after the truck. There were mothers who had two or three children and held them in their arms—running after the truck. We ran all the way. There were those who fell—we were not allowed to help them rise. They were shot—right there—wherever they fell. . . . When we reached the destination, the people from the truck were already down and they were undressed—all lined up. All my family was there. . . .
Q: Where was that?
A: This was some 3 kilometers from our village. . . . There was a kind of hillock. At the foot of this little hill, there was a dugout. We were ordered to stand at the top of the hillock and the four devils shot us—each one of us separately.
Q: Now these four—to what German unit did they belong?
A: They were SS men—the four of them. They were armed to the teeth. They were real messengers of the Devil and the Angel of Death.
Q: Please go on—what did you see?
A: When I came [to] the place—we saw people naked lined up. But we were still hoping that this was only torture. Maybe there is hope—hope of living. One could not leave the line, but I wished to see—what are they doing on the hillock? Is there anyone down below? I turned my head and saw that some three or four rows were already killed—on the ground. There were some twelve people amongst the dead. I also want to mention that my child said while we were lined up in the ghetto, she said, "Mother, why did you make me wear the Shabbat dress; we are being taken to be shot"; and when we stood near the dugout, near the grave, she said, "Mother, why are we waiting, let us run!" Some of the young people tried to run, but they were caught immediately, and they were shot right there. It was difficult to hold on to the children. We took all children not ours, and we carried—we were

anxious to get it all over—the suffering of the children was
difficult; we all trudged along to come nearer to the place
and to come nearer to the end of the torture of the children.
The children were taking leave of their parents, and parents,
of their elder people.

PRESIDING JUDGE: How did you survive through all this?

ATTORNEY-GENERAL: She will relate it.

PRESIDING JUDGE: Please will you direct the witness.

WITNESS: We were driven; we were already undressed; the clothes
were removed and taken away; our father did not want to
undress; he remained in his underwear. We were driven up
to the grave, this shallow. . . .

ATTORNEY-GENERAL: And these garments were torn off his body,
weren't they?

A: When it came to our turn, our father was beaten. We prayed,
we begged with my father to undress, but he would not
undress; he wanted to keep his underclothes. He did not
want to stand naked.

Q: And then they tore them off?

A: Then they tore the clothing off the old man and he was
shot. I saw it with my own eyes. And then they took my
mother and shot her too; and then there was my grandmother,
my father's mother, standing there; she was eighty years old
and she had two children in her arms. And then there was my
father's sister. She also had children in her arms and she was
shot on the spot with the babies in her arms.

Q: And finally it was your turn.

A: And finally my turn came. There was my younger sister, and
she wanted to leave; she prayed with the Germans; she asked
to run, naked; she went up to the Germans with one of her
friends; they were embracing each other; and she asked to be
spared, standing there naked. He looked into her eyes and
shot the two of them. They fell together in their embrace,
the two young girls, my sister and her young friend. Then my
second sister was shot and then my turn did come.

Q: Were you asked anything?

A: We turned towards the grave and then he turned around and asked, "Whom shall I shoot first?" We were already facing the grave. The Germans asked, "Who do you want me to shoot first?" I did not answer. I felt him take the child from my arms. The child cried out and was shot immediately. And then he aimed at me. First he held on to my hair and turned my head around; I stayed standing; I heard a shot, but I continued to stand and then he turned my head again and he aimed the revolver at me and ordered me to watch and then turned my head around and shot at me. Then I fell to the ground into the pit amongst the bodies, but I felt nothing. The moment I did feel, I felt a sort of heaviness and then I thought—maybe I am not alive anymore, but I feel something after I died. I thought I was dead, that this was the feeling which comes after death. Then I felt that I was choking; people falling over me. I tried to move and felt that I was alive and that I could rise. I was strangling. I heard the shots and I was praying for another bullet to put an end to my suffering, but I continued to move about. I felt that I was choking, strangling, but I tried to save myself, to find some air to breathe, and then I felt that I was climbing towards the top of the grave above the bodies. I rose, and I felt bodies pulling at me with their hands, biting at my legs, pulling me down, down. And yet with my last strength I came up on top of the grave, and when I did, I did not know the place, so many bodies were lying all over, dead people; I wanted to see the end of this stretch of dead bodies but I could not. It was impossible. They were lying, all dying; suffering; not all of them dead, but in their last sufferings; naked; shot, but not dead. Children crying "Mother," "Father"; I could not stand on my feet.

PRESIDING JUDGE: Were the Germans still around?

WITNESS: No, the Germans were gone. There was nobody there. No one standing up.

ATTORNEY-GENERAL: And you were undressed and covered with blood?

WITNESS: I was naked, covered with blood, dirty from the other bodies, with the excrement from other bodies, which was poured on me.

Q: What did you have in your head?

A: When I was shot, I was wounded in the head.

Q: Was it in the back of the head?

A: I have a scar to this day from the shot by the Germans; and yet, somehow I did come out of the grave. This was something I thought I would never live to recount. I was searching among the dead for my little girl, and I cried for her—Merkele was her name—"Merkele!" There were children crying "Mother!" "Father!"—but they were all smeared with blood and one could not recognize the children. I cried for my daughter. From afar I saw two women standing. I went up to them. They did not know me. I did not know them, and then I said who I was, and then they said, "So you survived." And there was another woman crying, "Pull me out from amongst the corpses, I am alive, help!" We were thinking how could we escape from the place. The cries of the woman, "Help, pull me out from the corpses!" We pulled her out. Her name was Mikla Rosenberg. We removed the corpses and the dying people who held on to her and continued to bite. She asked us to take her out, to free her, but we did not have the strength.

ATTORNEY-GENERAL: It is very difficult to relate, I am sure, it is difficult to listen to, but we must proceed. Please tell us now: after that you hid?

A: And thus we were there all night, fighting for our lives, listening to the cries and the screams, and all of a sudden we saw Germans, mounted Germans. We did not notice them coming in because of the screamings and the shoutings from the bodies around us.

Q: And then they rounded up the children and the others who had got out of the pit and shot them again?

A: The Germans ordered that all the corpses be heaped together into one big heap and with shovels they were heaped together, all the corpses, amongst them many still alive, children running about the place. I saw them. I saw the children. They were running after me, hanging on to me. Then I sat down in the field and remained sitting with the children around me. The children who got up from the heap of corpses.

Q: Then the Germans came again and rounded up the children?

A: Then Germans came and were going around the place. We were ordered to collect all the children, but they did not approach me, and I sat there watching how they collected the children. They gave a few shots and the children were dead. They did not need many shots. The children were almost dead, and this Rosenberg woman pleaded with the Germans to be spared, but they shot her.

ATTORNEY-GENERAL: Mrs. Yosselevscka, after they left the place, you went right next to the grave, didn't you?

A: They all left—the Germans and the non-Jews from around the place. They removed the machine guns and they took the trucks. I saw that they all left, and the four of us, we went onto the grave, praying to fall into the grave, even alive, envying those who were dead already and thinking what to do now. I was praying for death to come. I was praying for the grave to be opened and to swallow me alive. Blood was spurting from the grave in many places, like a well of water, and whenever I pass a spring now, I remember the blood which spurted from the ground, from that grave. I was digging with my fingernails, trying to join the dead in that grave. I dug with my fingernails, but the grave would not open. I did not have enough strength. I cried out to my mother, to my father, "Why did they not kill me? What was my sin? I have no one to go to." I saw them all being killed. Why was I spared? Why was I not killed?

And I remained there, stretched out on the grave, three days and three nights.

While the mobile killing units were at work in the Ukraine, a German civilian, serving as a construction engineer, happened to be on the scene when the ghetto in Dubno was wiped out. After the war, Hermann Graebe testified to what he had seen:

On October 5, 1942, when I visited the building office at Dubno, my foreman Hubert Moennikes told me that in the vicinity of the site, Jews from Dubno had been shot in three large pits, each about 30 meters long and 3 meters deep. About 1,500 persons had been killed daily. All of the 5,000 Jews who had been living in Dubno before the pogrom were to be liquidated. As the shootings had taken place in his presence, he was still much upset. . . .

Moennikes and I went directly to the pits. Nobody bothered us. Now I heard rifle shots in quick succession, from behind one of the earth mounds. The people who had got off the trucks—men, women and children of all ages—had to undress upon the order of an SS man who carried a riding or dog whip. They had to put down their clothes in fixed places, sorted according to shoes, top clothing, and underclothing. I saw a heap of shoes of about 800 to 1,000 pairs, great piles of underlinen and cloth-ing. Without screaming or weeping these people undressed, stood around in family groups, kissed each other, said farewells and waited for a sign from another SS man, who stood near the pit, also with a whip in his hand.

During the fifteen minutes that I stood near the pit, I heard no complaint or plea for mercy. I watched a family of about eight persons, a man and woman, both about fifty, with their children of about one, eight and ten, and two grown-up daughters of about twenty and twenty-four. An old woman with snow-white hair was holding the one-year-old child in her arms and singing to it and tickling it. The child was cooing with delight. The couple were looking on with tears in their eyes. The father was holding the hand of a boy about ten years old and speaking to him softly; the boy was fighting his tears. The father pointed toward the sky, stroked his head, and seemed to explain something to him. At that moment the SS man at the pit shouted something to his comrade. The latter counted off about twenty persons and instructed them to go behind the earth mound. Among them was the family which I have mentioned.

I well remember a girl, slim and with black hair, who, as she passed close to me, pointed to herself and said, "Twenty-three!" I walked around the mound, and found myself confronted by a tremendous grave. People were closely wedged together and lying on top of each other so that only their heads were visible. Nearly all had blood running over their shoulders from their heads. Some of the people shot were still moving. Some were lifting their arms and turning their heads to show that they were still alive. The pit was already two-thirds full. I estimated that it already contained about a thousand people.

I looked for the man who did the shooting. He was an SS man, who sat at the edge of the narrow end of the pit, his feet dangling into the pit. He had a tommy gun on his knees and he was smoking a cigarette. The people, completely naked, went down some steps which were cut in the clay wall of the pit and clambered over the heads of the people lying there, to the place where the SS man directed them. They lay down in front of the dead or injured people; some caressed those who were still alive and spoke to them in a low voice. Then I heard a series of shots.

I looked into the pit and saw that the bodies were twitching or the heads lying already motionless on top of the bodies that lay before them. Blood was running from their necks. I was surprised that I was not ordered away, but I saw that there were two or three postmen in uniform nearby. The next batch was approaching already. They went down into the pit, lined themselves up against the previous victims and were shot.

When I walked back, around the mound, I noticed another truckload of people which had just arrived. This time it included sick and infirm people. An old, very thin woman with terribly thin legs was undressed by others who were already naked, while two people held her up. The woman appeared to be paralyzed. The naked people carried the woman around the mound. I left with Moennikes and drove in my car back to Dubno.

On the morning of the next day when I again visited the site, I saw about thirty naked people lying near the pit—about 30 to 50 meters away from it. Some of them were still alive; they looked straight in front of them with a fixed stare and *seemed to notice neither the chilliness of the morning nor the workers of my firm who stood around. A girl of about twenty spoke to me and asked me to give her clothes and help her escape. At that moment we heard a fast car approach and I noticed that it was an SS detail. I moved away to my site. Ten minutes later we heard shots from the vicinity of the pit. The Jews still alive had been ordered to throw the corpses into the pit—then they themselves had to lie down in this to be shot in the neck.*

By the end of the winter of 1941–42, more than 90 percent of the Jews trapped by the Germans east of the Soviet border were dead. The extermination of men, women, and children did not disturb Hitler. "Nature is cruel," he said. "Therefore, we, too, may be cruel. If I don't mind sending the pick of the German people into the hell of war without regret for the shedding of valuable German blood, then I have naturally the right to destroy millions of men of inferior races who increase like vermin."

OUR TOWN IS BURNING (es brent)
By Mordecai Gebirtig

Translated from the Yiddish by Joseph Leftwich

Our town is burning, brothers, burning,
Our poor little town is burning.
Angry winds are fanning higher
The leaping tongues of flame and fire,
The evil winds are roaring!
Our whole town burns!

(Refrain)
And you stand looking on with folded arms,
And shake your heads.
You stand looking on with folded arms
While the fire spreads!

Our town is burning, brothers, burning,
Our poor little town is burning.
Tongues of flame are leaping,
The fire through our town goes sweeping,
Through roofs and windows pouring.
All around us burns.   (Repeat refrain.)

Our town is burning, brothers, burning.
Any moment the fire may
Sweep the whole of our town away,
And leave only ashes, black and gray,
Like after a battle, where dead walls stand,
Broken and ruined in a desolate land.   (Repeat refrain.)

Our town is burning, brothers, burning.
All now depends on you.
Our only help is what you do.
You can still put out the fire
With your blood, if you desire.

Don't look on with folded arms,
And shake your heads.
Don't look on with folded arms
While the fire spreads!

ES BRENT

8

Phantoms in the Ghetto

Soon Heydrich, Goering, Himmler, and other Nazi leaders began referring to the "Final Solution of the Jewish Question" whenever they meant the extermination of the Jews. The innocent-sounding abstraction may have spared such sensitive souls the pain of thinking about what they really meant to do. More likely, they wanted to conceal from others their murderous intentions.

Early in the Polish campaign, Hitler, Himmler, and Heydrich decided that the next stage in the Final Solution was to concentrate the Jews in a small area. They meant not only the Polish Jews but all the Jews of Germany, Austria, Czechoslovakia, and whatever other countries the Nazis might take over. In the orders Heydrich sent to the officers of the *Einsatzgruppen* in September 1939, he said they must distinguish between the "final aim, whose attainment will take some time," and the "steps necessary for reaching it, which can be applied more or less at once."

The interior of occupied Poland was set aside as the place to concentrate Jews whom the killing squads had not reached. Instead of sending the killers to the victims, the victims were now to be brought to the killers.

The region chosen contained several cities—Warsaw, Cracow, Lodz, Lvov, Lublin, Radom—with large numbers of Jews. Warsaw alone now held half a million Jews, the largest Jewish population of any city in the world 'except New York. All Jewish communities of less than 500 were herded into the nearest concentration city.

At the head of this administrative region, called the General Government, Hitler placed Dr. Hans Frank. A Munich lawyer, he had been convicted several times of embezzlement in the Weimar days, and had murdered a lawyer who once prosecuted him. He prided himself on his love of good books and music. At the end of his first year in office, he told his co-workers in Poland, "I could not eliminate all lice and Jews in only one year. But in the course of time, and if you will help me, this end will be attained."

Once the Jews were concentrated, and the central machinery was set up, the closing-in of the ghettos began. It was in April 1940 that the first ghetto was created, in Lodz. The steps taken were gradual. Warsaw came next, in October; then Cracow in March 1941; Lublin and Radom in April; and Lvov in December. By the end of 1941 the ghettoizing process was almost complete.

The methods used were essentially the same everywhere. Never was the ghetto meant to be permanent. As Friedrich Uebelhoer, one Nazi chief working on the problem, put it: "The creation of the ghetto is, of course, only a transition measure. I shall determine at what time and with what means the ghetto—and thereby also the city of Lodz—will be cleansed of Jews. In the end, at any rate, we must burn out this bubonic plague."

To carry out their instructions, the Nazis set up a Jewish Council (called a *Judenrat* in German) in each ghetto. Its functions were typically dual and opposite: to take charge of survival—health, welfare, supplies; and to take charge of destruction—registration, records, police. Some who served on them thought the Councils would run the internal affairs of the ghetto in the prewar tradition of Jewish self-government, and speak for the Jews before the Nazi authorities controlling the ghetto. The Nazis, of course, were offering this pretense of self-government as a device to get the Jews to cooperate in their own extermination. It was a fiendishly clever idea to put the blame for their degradation and destruction upon the Jews themselves. The intention was to paralyze the Jews in the ghetto while they waited, consciously or unconsciously, for the Final Solution.

The ghettos were placed in the poorest part of each city. Jews who lived outside the ghetto areas were driven from their homes, robbed of their possessions, and jammed into cramped quarters with many other families. The Jews of surrounding towns were herded into the cities and thrown into the ghettos. Stone, brick, wood, and barbed wire sealed each ghetto off from the outside world. To be caught outside meant death.

In Czernowitz the Nazis mapped out a ghetto and ordered 50,000 Jews to move into it within eight hours. The mayor of the city, Traian Popovicz, recorded what happened:

> I looked out the window of my bedroom and amidst the flying flakes of the early snow I saw a scene which was incredible. In the streets was a vast crowd of wandering people. The aged were helped by children, there were women with infants in their arms, cripples dragging their lame frames. All had bundles in their hands or were pushing small carriages loaded with boxes. Some carried their burden on their backs: luggage, bundles of linen, cushions, blankets, clothing, rags. They were beginning their mute pilgrimage to their vale of tears, the Ghetto.
>
> Only one who knows the topography of Czernowitz can grasp how inadequate was the space reserved for the Ghetto. . . . This section that could hardly have accommodated 10,000 people had to house 50,000 Jews plus the Christian population which lived there. . . . Many were forced to live in corridors, cellars, garages, under bridges, anywhere to find shelter against snow and rain. Of the hygienic conditions I don't even speak. No sanitary water to drink . . . the pungent smell of sweat, urine, and excrement, of loathsome humidity . . . exactly like the smell of a flock of sheep in the field.

Lublin became the concentration point for Jews from western Poland, Bohemia, and Austria. Before the war the town held

72,000 Gentiles and 40,000 Jews. Now many times that number of Jews were penned into the ghetto. A journalist, S. Moldawer, described what he saw on the streets:

> Lublin is a vale of sorrow. No human beings are they who walk its streets; all are phantoms, shadows, haunting a world that is no longer in evidence. Nobody speaks in Lublin; nobody exchanges greetings. They have even ceased to weep. . . . The congestion, the stench, the poverty, the disease and the chaos which reign in Lublin cannot be paralleled anywhere on earth. Men live in the streets, in cattle stalls, in cellars, in carts and in the debris of devastated houses.
>
> Men die like flies in the thoroughfares, their bodies strewn on the roadway like old cinders. Shrouds are no longer used for the dead because none can be bought. . . . The whole city is girt with barbed wire fences, and the Nazis allow no traffic to pass through it. The water has turned foul and cannot be drunk. All the wells have become polluted. Cholera and typhus were already rampant when we reached Lublin. . . . The communal soup kitchen can actually serve nothing but potato broth and stale, black bread. Hundreds have not slept for weeks, cramped and confined in noisy freight cars. They wander about sad-eyed and distraught, like mourners at funerals. . . . One thing is as clear as the day: the devil himself could not have devised such hell. . . .

But even in the hell of such ghettos, people struggled to live the normal lives they once knew. Mark Dworzecki, a young physician of Vilna, continued to practice medicine there after the Nazis turned it into a huge prison for the Jews. From his diary of a day in the ghetto comes this entry, headed EIGHT P.M.:

> The young people are taking their evening stroll in twos and threes. The streets are very crowded.
>
> Youngsters laugh and joke, exchange glances, flirt, forgetting for the moment the grim squalor and the ever-present sense of dread that pervades the ghetto.

80

Thronged main streets. Rudnitzka, Shavelska, Strashun Streets look almost festive. The ghetto café offers black, unsweetened coffee-roasted bran extract.

Romantic couples stroll to the yard of the Judenrat. There stands a tree—the only tree in the ghetto—giving the illusion of a park.

The lumberyard at 6 Strashun Street is the tryst for young lovers. Perched on the heaps of timber they hold hands and sing the sad, stirring Russian songs. Refrains are caught up, voices blend:

> *We shall meet again*
> *At the cannon's breech . . .*

There is a performance at the ghetto theater. In the ghetto café people crowd around the little tables, recounting the hardships and horrors of the day. The evening prayers are recited in the synagogue. Committees of the Underground hold their consultations. The ghetto choirs sing Hebrew and Yiddish songs.

News bulletins of the Partisan Organization circulate from hand to hand.

Starving the Jews to death was cheaper than shooting them. The Nazis looted the occupied countries of food and sent it to Germany. They left barely enough to keep the Poles alive and less for the ghetto Jews. Once the barbed wire went up, the Jews were cut off from the open market. The Judenrat alone could buy and distribute food. Theft, bribery, and favoritism had full play. Under the grave shortages, black markets and smuggling sprang up. Smugglers made it possible for some to survive a bit longer. If they managed to retain something of value, they would swap it for food. Jews who were allowed some liberty of movement outsmarted the police and the SS who guarded the ghetto. Levi Shalit observed how one woman, called Baylke, did it:

More than once Baylke has come face to face with death. More than once bullets have grazed her as she leaps over the barbed wire fence. But now that she has the task of transporting excrement out of the city, there is much less risk.

Actually her husband was assigned to the job, but Baylke, who is more capable and more daring, seizes the reins in her chunky hands and drives the horse herself. The cart filled with feces trundles on two huge wheels through all the remote streets of the town to the public toilets, which the city council has ordered to be cleaned. After they are emptied, the waste is deposited outside the city.

Baylke is everywhere, constantly in touch with her Christian neighbors in the surrounding villages; she sells them everything the ghetto gives her in exchange for produce. Her hiding place is safe—inside the sealed tin box in the cart of excrement.

Twice a day, at noon and in the evening, she rides into the ghetto, takes the hidden box from the wagon and removes from it bread, butter, fat and meat.

Everyone in the ghetto knows where Baylke takes the merchandise but nobody objects. On the contrary—they plead with her to take something to sell or exchange. They know their things won't get lost or confiscated. Not from Baylke's hiding place.

The two largest ghettos were in Warsaw and Lodz. In Warsaw, half a million Jews were forced within the walls. A third of the city's total population was sardined into 1.3 percent of the city's total area. Lodz had the most elaborate Judenrat imposed on its 160,000 Jews.

In some places, the Councils were made up of the men who had been the community leaders before the occupation. Or the local Nazi chief simply told the nearest rabbi to make up a Judenrat list on the spot. There were Jews who volunteered to serve, and others who were forced. If everyone refused to volunteer, as happened in one little town near Vilna, the community had to gather and draw lots for the Judenrat. The Councils consisted mostly of people with higher education or in the professions. There were few workers or artisans among them.

Whatever the method of selection, the Councils were caught

in the Nazi trap. At first, their functions embraced chiefly welfare: food rationing, job allocation, health and sanitation, housing, schooling, even policing. But then came the duty of providing forced-labor contingents for the Nazis. And as food supplies shrank and hunger increased, the Councils had to choose which categories of Jew should get food enough to stay alive (children? women? men? the old? the sick? the healthy? the rich? the poor?). Later, when the call came for what the Nazis deceptively called "resettlement" selection, the Councils were ordered to identify and register the victims, confiscate their posessions, and round them up for deportation to what, in fact, were death camps.

The Councils, their staffs, and their police forces became agents of the Nazi killing machine and instruments of their own execution. Can they be condemned outright and wholesale? Could they have done anything else but carry out the functions dictated by the Nazis? As with any manifestation of human behavior, the answer is not simple. Every Council member was a unique person, a complex of qualities: brave, cowardly, honest, corrupt, docile, aggressive, strong, weak, intelligent, stupid. And as a body, each Council performed in its own unique way. How estimate the role played by the Councils? Isaiah Trunk asks that question in the last chapter of his massive study of the Judenrat. And he says, "No historian of the catastrophe era can escape raising the question: Did the Councils in their strategy toward the Germans really exercise some justifiable policy that warranted, at least in their own minds, the hope of a delay or amelioration of the ominous end?" Trunk himself does not give a direct answer. But in his and many other studies there is ample evidence now of what the Councils did. Some followed the desperate principle of "Rescue Through Work." In Bialystok, Poland, the Council president was an engineer, Ephraim Barash. He tried to prove to the Nazis that the 50,000 Jews of his ghetto were so useful as workers that they were worthy of preservation. For a time Bialystok was treated as a peaceful "show ghetto." But inevitably the Nazis destroyed this ghetto, like all the others, and with the help of Barash's treachery. He ended up dishonored, an enemy of his people.

The Jewish police in the ghettos were patterned after the Nazi police. They wore black caps with blue Stars of David on them. Like the Nazi police, they had no justice department standing above to see that human and legal rights were being protected. No matter what an individual Jewish policeman might have desired to do, he could only be a tool of Nazi policy. The police themselves were the law, subject in this case, of course, to Nazi orders handed down through the Judenrat.

In Warsaw, the Judenrat recruited 2,000 men between the ages of thirty and thirty-five for the Jewish police force. Their commander was Sherinsky, a Jew converted to Christianity who had once been a Warsaw police captain. He had a notorious record as a Jew-hater, but it had not saved him from being locked into the ghetto with his "racial brothers." Later he was killed by the underground.

Ghetto life under the Nazis has been likened by some historians to Black slavery in the United States. One teacher and scholar who lived inside the Warsaw ghetto made the same analysis, except that he saw it as even worse in important respects. He was Emmanuel Ringelblum, who founded the Oneg Shabbat, the secret archives of the Warsaw ghetto. With the help of others, he collected documents and wrote his own notes on day-to-day events from January 1940 to early 1943. With his family, he was murdered by the Nazis, but his notes were found later in the ruins of the ghetto. This passage from them was headed "The Signs of Modern Slaves":

1. *Numbered and stamped.*
2. *Live in barracks—without their wives.*
3. *Wives and children removed, because slaves don't require families.*
4. *Walk in crowds, not individually.*
5. *Beaten and terrorized at work.*
6. *Inhuman exploitation . . .*
7. *Ban on organization of any kind.*
8. *Ban on any form of protest or sign of dissatisfaction.*
9. *Every slave dependent for his life on his master . . .*

10. The murderous discipline . . .
11. Compulsion to work . . .
12. Worse off than slaves, because they must look after their own food.
13. Confiscation of property from a dead worker's family, because the right of inheritance has been abolished.
14. Locked inside the residential block.
15. Ban on leaving your apartment and walking in the street after work hours.
16. Limitation of personal freedom, of movement.
17. Worse than slaves, because the latter knew they would remain alive, had some hope to be set free. The Jews are morituri—sentenced to death—whose death sentence [has been] postponed indefinitely, or has been passed.
18. The sick and the weak are not needed, so ambulatory clinics, hospitals and the like have been liquidated.

And the children in the ghettos? Ludwik Hirszfeld remembers those he watched in Warsaw:

The streets are so overpopulated, it is difficult to push one's way through. Everyone is ragged, in tatters. Often they no longer even possess a shirt. Everywhere there is noise and uproar. The thin piteous voices of children crying their wares—"Pretzels, cigarettes, sweets!"—are heard above the din.

No one will ever be able to forget those children's voices. . . .

There are always countless children inside the ghetto. People on the "Aryan" side gape curiously at the piteous spectacle presented by these tattered gangs. In fact, these gangs of children are the ghetto breadwinners. If the German looks away for one second, they run nimbly over to "Aryan" side. The bread, potatoes and other things that they buy are hidden under their rags, and then they have to slip back the way they came.

Not all the German sentries are murderers and executioners but unfortunately, many of them do not hesitate to take up their guns and fire at the children. Every day—it's almost unbelievable—children are taken to hospital with gunshot wounds.

The thousands of ragged beggars are reminiscent of a famine in India. Horrifying sights are to be seen every day. Here a half-starved mother is trying to suckle her baby at a breast that has no milk. Beside her may lie another, older child, dead. One sees people dying, lying with arms and legs outstretched, in the middle of the road. Their legs are bloated, often frost-bitten, and their faces, distorted with pain. I hear that every day the beggar children's frostbitten fingers and toes, hands and feet are amputated.

I once asked a little girl: "What would you like to be?" "A dog," she answered, "because the sentries like dogs."

Yes, they treated dogs better than children. Here is what W. Szpilman saw in the ghetto one day, as he was walking along the inside wall:

I came across a smuggling operation being carried out by children. The actual operation seemed to be over. There was only one thing to do. The little Jewish boy on the other side of the wall had to slip back into the ghetto through the hole, bringing with him the last piece of booty. Half of the little boy was already visible, when he began to cry out. At the same time loud abuse in German could be heard from the "Aryan" side. I hurried to help the child, meaning to pull him quickly through the hole. Unhappily, the boy's hips stuck fast in the gap of the wall. Using both hands, I tried with all my might to pull him through. He continued to scream dreadfully. I could hear the police on the other side beating him savagely. When I finally succeeded in pulling the boy through the hole, he was already dying. His backbone was crushed.

It was only "natural," then, for the children to include death in the games they played. Dr. Aaron Peretz recalls what he saw in the Kovno ghetto:

The children in the ghetto would play and laugh, and in their games the entire tragedy was reflected. They would play grave digging: they would dig a pit and put a child inside and call him Hitler. And they would play at being gatekeepers of the ghetto. Some of the children played the parts of Germans; some, of Jews; and the Germans were angry and would beat the other children who were Jews. And they used to play funerals. . . .

The two-line rhymes of this ghetto song, expressing the Jews' courageous will to survive, were sung to a lilting Hasidic melody.

→≫

Vos darfn mir veynen, vos darfn mir klogn,
Mir veln noch frankn a kadish noch zogn.

Lomir zayn freylech un zogn zich vitsn,
Mir veln noch hitlern shive noch zitsn.

Lomir zich treystn, di tsores fargesn,
Es veln di verim noch hitlern fresn.

Di sonim, vos firn undz dort kayn treblinke,
Zey veln noch vern in der erd ayngezinken.

Mir veln tsuzamen noch orem bay orem,
Imirtseshem tantsn oyf daytshishe kvorim.

Why should we weep, why should we mourn,
We'll live to say the prayer of the dead for Frank.

Let us be gay and tell jokes,
We'll yet live to see Hitler dead.

Let us comfort one another and forget our troubles,
The worms will yet gnaw at Hitler.

The enemies who lead us there to Treblinka
Will yet be sinking into the earth.

Together we will yet, arm in arm,
With the help of God, dance on the graves of the Germans.

9

Gangs of Slaves

The Jews under German control were treated like a natural re-source to be exploited until nothing was left. An official decree began this treatment.

> *All Jews from fourteen to sixty years of age are subject to forced labor. . . . Jews called up for forced labor must report promptly and must bring food for two days and their bedding. Skilled Jewish workers must report with their tools. . . .*

Forced labor began at once, to clear away the rubble of war. At first, when the Nazis needed labor, they would seize people off the ghetto streets. In Warsaw, the Judenrat halted the terrifying press gangs by organizing forced-labor squads and putting them at the disposal of any Nazi agency which wanted them. The labor columns were paid little or nothing to do the emergency day-to-day jobs. Gradually, when large-scale projects began and a more stable kind of labor was required, the Nazis organized special concentration camps for specific use as slave-labor installations. At first, the inmates were used on outdoor projects: to dig canals and anti-tank ditches, to build roads and railways, to reclaim land or to control floods. Then, industrial production was started up, and factories erected near camps, or camps near factories. Jews were used in aircraft plants, steel works, munitions factories, food depots—everywhere the war effort required them.

88

The "useful" Jews were put up for sale by the SS at daily labor rates. The others—the weak, the sick, and the old—were classified as "unproductive" Jews. Their fate was a quicker death. The younger, healthier Jews went more slowly, worked into the grave, starved into the grave. Pay? On some military projects the army allowed about 40 cents a day. The other official agencies usually paid nothing for the forced labor they requisitioned. Food? So little that newcomers lost 50 pounds in weight in the first few months. Hours? Daybreak to nightfall, every single day of the week, all the year round.

Not only the Jews, of course, but civilians all over the conquered territories of Europe were conscripted for labor. They were corralled and herded into boxcars. Often without food, water, or sanitary facilities, they were shipped to Germany. They worked in factories, fields, and mines, and were beaten and starved and often left to die for lack of food, clothing, and shelter. By late 1944 there were 7½ million such civilians, plus another 2 million prisoners of war, grinding out their lives for Hitler's Germany.

The system of forced labor provided the majority of German firms—Krupp, I. G. Farben, Hermann Goering, Siemens, Roechling, etc.—with gangs of slaves. No law protected the worker. The Red Cross was not allowed to intervene.

The industrialists, suffering from a manpower shortage, besieged the SS with applications for slave labor, arguing that only thus could they carry out their "patriotic duty" to the war effort. The businessmen and the SS got along beautifully. The firms profited by the miserable wages they paid directly to the camps that farmed out the workers. (The prisoners never saw one cent of their earnings.) And the SS, collectively and through personal graft, profited by the deals made with the companies.

Living conditions in the camps were wretched, and if disease did not finish them off first, the inmates were marked "unfit for labor" and sent off to a worse fate. The idea was to kill through labor. Of the 35,000 Jews who worked making synthetic rubber for the I. G. Farben *Bunawerk* (Buna plant) at Auschwitz, at least 25,000 died. Their life expectancy was three or four months. In the coal mines it was one month. But it did not bother the corporation executives. Every day there was a fresh delivery of slaves.

The labor camps soon spread over the conquered territories like a giant spiderweb. Most were built close to large towns, within easy reach of railways. Everywhere in the labor camps, Himmler had the SS post signs for the enlightenment of the prisoners. They read:

THERE IS A ROAD TO FREEDOM. ITS MILESTONES ARE:
OBEDIENCE, HARD WORK, HONESTY, SOBRIETY, CLEANLINESS,
DEVOTION, ORDER, DISCIPLINE AND PATRIOTISM.

The prisoners soon knew better. What road to freedom was marked by hunger, cold, filth, and torture?

Reuben Rosenberg, eleven years old when the war began, lived in Lublin. The Nazis seized him for forced labor. They sent him to one camp after another. He tells of his experiences, beginning at Deblin:

I worked at the aviation depot for the Werman firm, later owned by Schultz. The work was difficult, canalization, concrete and other tasks. Sometimes youngsters deliberately wounded their feet on the rails to be freed of the labor for a few days. The work was unbearable. Two boys were killed for stealing potatoes. They were dragged to the cellar of the gendarmerie, where dogs bit them to death. . . .

Then he was sent to Czestochowa:

There were two work places here, the iron foundry, Rakov, and Felzer, an ammunition factory. The food was bad, the labor hard, and we were almost naked. They divided up those from Deblin. There were 700 of us. The three barracks were surrounded by barbed wire. Two people slept on one straw sack; there were 250 men, infested with vermin, sleeping in each barrack. . . . We worked in the iron foundry in two shifts, three shifts in transportation. . . . At Rakov the work—loading iron, tar, coal and coke—was very hard. There were some terrible accidents at the workshops. Men fell asleep from hunger or fatigue at their machines, and their hands or feet would be torn away. . . .

For work we had to rise at 4 A.M., walk 2 kilometers to the station and detour 10 kilometers to Weimar. We worked from nine to four, with frequent rollcalls. There was one loaf of bread and some soup for five people. Twice a week there was sausage. Our work was to clean up the debris after a bombing; there were air attacks every day. We dragged German corpses from the cellars. . . .

Later he moved to Flossenbürg:

At this camp there was a factory that made bazookas. There was one SS man for every four prisoners. Every day 15 men died, aside from those who died from "natural causes." We ran to work. Work intended for 20 people was done by 10. We worked from 6 A.M. to 7 P.M. We collapsed. Many people committed suicide. In two weeks 500 died. Filth, no water, two days without heat, no bath, and no underwear. There was twenty-five lashes for stealing potato peelings. They called us the race gang, communists, cadets, soapbags, criminals, and bolsheviks. . . .

Because things were bad at the front, they hurried us and always beat us at the factory. . . . To load bazookas we had to use picric acid and trotil. We worked without gas masks, and after a few weeks the lungs and feet would cave in. The young were chosen for this task. SS men would kill them while they worked, so there was always a shortage of workers. . . .

One of the workers at Monowitz (the slave-labor camp attached to Auschwitz), which was built for the I. G. Farben Bunawerk, was Kai Feinberg. After the war, he told what slave labor did to his own family:

The conditions were intolerable. . . . On our first day of work, Christmas Eve, 24 December 1942, we had to work through without food until 3 o'clock in the morning of 25 December. Our work consisted of unloading wagons of iron bars and sacks of cement and heavy ovens. . . .

On 5 January 1943 my father was so weakened that he collapsed before my eyes while having to haul along such a 50-kilo sack of cement at a running pace. I wanted to help him but was hit and beaten back by an SS man with a stick. . . .

One of my father's brothers injured himself in the arm while at work and was gassed. My father's second brother died from weakness while at work in Buna one or two weeks after the death of my father.

I myself withstood the work until 15 January 1943; then I got pneumonia and worked again from 15 February until the end of February. Then I was declared unfit for work because I could no longer walk, and was due to be gassed. As it happened no lorry going to the gas chambers came to the Bunawerk that day and I was therefore taken back to the Auschwitz concentration camp.

A young German Jew, Hans Baermann of Cologne, was fourteen when the Nazis forced him out of school. With his parents he was shipped east in December 1941, to the Riga ghetto in Latvia. Two days after their arrival, Hans was among 200 young Jews chosen for forced labor at the nearby Salaspils camp. This is his account of what happened then:

Frozen and starved, we reached a snow-covered clearing that held but a single, large, roofless barracks of wood. Some 4,000 Jews from southern Germany already lived in it, and they attacked us like wolves for food and drink. Our hair was shorn and we were then assigned, three men to a bunk 18 inches high, 6 feet long and less than 5 feet wide. It was bitter cold and the slats were covered with ice. On the third day after our arrival we saw our first bread and a horse-drawn sleigh loaded with potato peelings from the SS kitchen at Riga.

An SS sergeant named Nickel introduced himself as the

92

Commandant, and immediately assigned us to work, to be performed without overcoats and without fires. The construction program embraced 45 barracks in which Latvians and Russians were later quartered. This program was fulfilled, all but 5 barracks. Watchtowers also had to be constructed and the entire area enclosed with barbed wire.

I spent seven months starving in this death camp. In the end I weighed only 80 pounds and was infected with lice. Reduced virtually to a skeleton, I was photographed for the Stürmer [Streicher's anti-Semitic magazine]. Of 15,000 men who passed through this camp, in time, virtually all wasted away. Only 192 survived. I was among them. . . .

The ghettos themselves were integrated as productive units into the German war machine. Inside the Warsaw ghetto, for example, factories operated by German industrialists put tens of thousands of Jews to work making clothing, textiles, brushes, shoes, mattresses, furniture, and barrack doors, windows, and roof sections. Most of the production was intended for the military, but the Germans bribed SS and army officials to divert some of it into private hands. The starved workers got a few zlotys and a sip of soup for twelve hours' work a day.

It was a tragically ironic situation. The German firms had a vested interest in hanging onto profitable ghetto laborers, and so, opposed killing them. And the Jewish workers clung to their jobs, helping the enemy with their own hands, for fear of being sent to the even worse labor camps, and later, the death camps. "The history of man," said Ringelblum, the Warsaw-ghetto archivist, "knows no similar tragedy. A nation that hates the Germans with all its soul can ransom itself from death only at the price of its contribution to the enemy's victory, a victory which means its complete extermination in Europe and perhaps in the whole world."

By the middle of 1944 the Jewish labor force was almost totally destroyed. Valuable as its work was for military needs, that purpose took second place in Hitler's mind to the goal of annihilation.

The exploitation of Jewish workers was merely a preliminary to their execution. Perhaps half a million Jews were killed off at forced labor or died of starvation and disease in the ghettos.

This is a song of the forced laborers whose endless hours of work on starvation rations brought huge numbers to early death.

→»

Zuntog un Montog—ligt men in di griber,
Dinstog un Mitvoch—hot men fiber.
Donershtog un Fraytog—hakt men shteyner,
Shabes hot men tsubrochene beyner.

Shlofn shlofn men in di palatkes,
Nishto kayn hoyzn, nishto kayn gatkes,
Nishto kayn shich, nishto kayn shtivl,
Nishto kayn groshn tsu shraybn a brivl.

Sunday and Monday—we lie in the ditches,
Tuesday and Wednesday—we have the fever.
Thursday and Friday—we break stones,
On the Sabbath, we have aching bones.

We sleep in tents,
We have no pants nor underwear,
We have no shoes, we have no boots,
We haven't a penny to send a letter.

One Little Spark

When news of the forced-labor decree reached the Warsaw ghetto in January 1940, Chaim Kaplan wrote in his diary, "The Jews do not believe that it will come to pass."

Kaplan was principal of a pioneering elementary Hebrew school in Warsaw and the author of books for children on Jewish history. Like Emmanuel Ringelblum, he kept a secret diary. (The small notebooks were smuggled out of the ghetto; Kaplan and his wife are believed to have died in the Treblinka extermination camp.)

Two weeks later, again he was writing:

From the outset the People of Hope did not believe that the decree of forced labor for the Jews would be put into effect. As is the way with Jews, they didn't understand the decree in its simple sense. Because of the magnitude of the destruction contained therein, they didn't believe that even so fierce an enemy as the Fuehrer would put it into actual practice. They tried to find in it some hint for an enormous financial contribution instead. . . .

In another two weeks, he was explaining why the Jews felt this way:

There is no room in our inner feelings for despair and depression. We greet every edict with a deprecating smile, although we are conscious that the creators and enactors of these cruel decrees are psychopaths. . . . A poison of hatred permeates the blood of the Nazis, and therefore all their stupid decrees, the fruit of this hatred, are doomed to failure. Such an awareness saves us from despair. Anything founded upon insanity must not last long.

By the end of May, Hitler's armies had subdued Western Europe. Yet, wrote Kaplan:

Our Jews don't believe in the murderer's victories in France. The newspapers announce victories which cannot be denied, whose truth is apparent—yet the Jews don't admit them. They stick to their conviction: The Germans will end in destruction. They got this far in the years 1914–1918, but nevertheless they were defeated in the end. Knowledgeable people are in mourning, but the masses are happy. They have entered Antwerp? Don't believe them! They conquered Rotterdam? Tell it to Grandma. The people's desire doesn't allow them even to consider the possibility that the murderers will win. The entire world will rise up against them. . . . This is the power of desire. It is the father of all thought.

Later, when mass deportations to mysterious "resettlement" places were sweeping out the ghettos, the same disbelief in reality gripped many. Oscar Pinkas, who lived through it, recalls the mood:

We watched and listened but did not know what it all meant. The normal process of thinking and reacting, the horror of the truth, and the deliberate confusion planted by the Germans, all these combined to produce a frightful weariness, a wish to get it over with—whatever that entailed: deportation, resettlement, concentration camp. . . . When we heard the rushing trains, we cried instinctively, "Heavens, we are all perishing."

96

*But then, once assumed, that knowledge became impossible
to accept. We then went back to our daily routines. . . .*

The "deliberate confusion" was a product of Nazi cunning.
The terror and violence, the contradictory commands, the lies,
the isolation from the outside world, the hunger, the playing off
of one section of Jewry against another—it was psychological
warfare designed to scatter reason and paralyze the will.

How does the mind of the victim work under such conditions
of stress? In May 1942 the Nazis began to visit Jews in their
Warsaw-ghetto apartments at night, and murder them. By shooting, clubbing, throwing them out of the windows. The people
could find no pattern in the isolated murders. None of the victims
knew each other or had anything in common, socially or economically. Then why *these* victims? Kaplan speculates in his diary:

> *In order to comfort ourselves, we feel compelled to find some
> sort of system to explain these nighttime murders. Everyone,
> afraid for his own skin, thinks to himself: If there is a system,
> every murder must have a cause; if there is a cause, nothing
> will happen to me since I am absolutely guiltless.*
>
> *But . . . the system is a lack of system. The guiding
> principle is the annihilation of a specific number of Jews every
> night. They go to the files, indiscriminately draw out a card, and
> whoever is picked, is picked; he is destined to die. . . .*
>
> *People do not want to die without cause.*

Bernard Goldstein said it in somewhat different words: "The
will to live was so strong that it created the illusions necessary to
sustain it."

Some of the Jews of Germany and Austria, who had found no
salvation through conversion, found it in death. With each new
Nazi decree, many killed themselves. But "not so with the beaten
down, shamed, broken Jews of Poland," said Kaplan.

*They love life, and they do not wish to disappear from the
earth before their time. This fact, that we have hardly any*

suicides, is worthy of emphasis. Say what you wish, this will
of ours to live in the midst of terrible calamity is the outward
manifestation of a certain hidden power whose quality has
not yet been examined. It is a wondrous, superlative power with
which only the most established communities among our people
have been blessed.

We are left naked, but as long as this secret power is still
within us, we do not give up hope. And the strength of this
power lies in the indigenous nature of Polish Jewry, which is
rooted in our eternal tradition that commands us to live.
Polish Jewry says, together with our poet laureate Bialik:

> One spark is hidden in the stronghold of my heart
> One little spark, but it is all mine;
> I borrowed it from no one, nor did I steal it
> For it is of me, and within me.

Even during the deportation of over 300,000 Warsaw-ghetto
Jews to the Treblinka death camp, there were relatively few
suicides, Emmanuel Ringelblum noted.

> The large masses of the people, as well as the overwhelming
> majority of the intelligentsia, did not permit themselves to
> break down, and resisted passively as long as it was possible. As
> for the question why did the Jews not defend themselves? The
> answer is: They offered a strong and effective psychic resistance.
> No other people in the world could have endured psychically
> as long as the Jews.

One expression of that endurance was the cultural life that
went on in the ghetto despite all the surrounding horror. Plays
and concerts were allowed by the Germans so long as the drama-
tists and composers were not Aryan and the censor was not
offended. But the Jews in the Warsaw ghetto got around the
restrictions, said the Yiddish actor Jonas Turkow, and satire
mocking the enemy was often performed. Five ghetto theaters

produced plays, in Yiddish or Polish. There were both professional and amateur choruses and orchestras. About 1,800 performances were given in the year 1940–41.

In the Lodz ghetto, too, there was the same spontaneous creation of theatricals, concerts, lectures, classes, and reading circles. Writers wrote, actors acted, musicians played, incredible as it seems to us who never knew that life in death. What was created vanished in the destruction, except for a few things. Among them are these verses by the poet S. Shayevich:

> *The Lord has showered even us with gentle hand:*
> *A double gift—*
> *The death-decree and spring.*
> *The garden blooms, and the sun shines.*
> *And the slaughterer slaughters. . . .*
> *But we crave no recompense or mercy.*
> *For when you slay a man*
> *You slay his God as well.*

Although the ghetto population was constantly changing, through death or deportation, schooling continued. Courses for adults were given in watchmaking, leatherwork, engraving, and drawing. Schools for Jewish children were closed under the pretext of epidemics, but secret or camouflaged schools were set up. The communal kitchens became one excuse for bringing children together in groups. Beneath their jackets they smuggled in the scarce texts and notebooks. N. Korn, the teacher of an underground school in Lublin, recalled the danger in his memoirs:

> *With beating hearts we conducted the lessons, simultaneously on the alert for the barking voices of the SS, who frequently raided Jewish homes. In such a case all incriminating traces immediately disappeared. Gone were books and notebooks. The pupils began to play and the teacher became a customer: in a tailor's house he began to try on clothes and in a shoemaker's house—shoes.*

On the site of a bombed-out house in the Warsaw ghetto, Jewish workers built swings and benches while the students of a graphic-arts workshop painted a fresco of playful animals on a ruined wall. The teachers went on teaching; they wanted the children to believe in a future. In a Jewish paper issued in the Cracow ghetto, a little girl named Martha published this poem:

> I must be saving these days
> (*I have no money to save*),
> I must save health and strength,
> Enough to last me for a long while.
> I must save my nerves,
> And my thoughts, and my mind,
> And the fire of my spirit;
> I must be saving of tears that flow—
> I shall need them for a long, long while.
> I must save endurance these stormy days.
>
> There is so much I need in my life:
> Warmth of feeling and a kind heart—
> These things I lack; of these I must be saving!
> All these, the gifts of God,
> I wish to keep.
> How sad I should be
> If I lost them quickly.

"Even more than bread," said the ghetto poet Leon Staf, "we now need poetry in a time when it seems that it is not needed at all."

As the Nazis began to rob Poland of its cultural treasures, shipping them off to Germany, the Jews worried about the fate of their own libraries. To save a major Jewish collection which had been closed and sealed off by the Nazis, Warsaw Bundists tunneled secretly under the walls and into the building. It took a week to carry out the more important volumes, hiding them under potatoes and coal. Then they set up small mobile libraries for both children and adults, operating secretly out of ghetto homes.

One of the first moves of the Germans had been to close all synagogues, houses of prayer, and ritual baths. They ordered that the Jews be made to work on the Sabbath and even on the High Holidays. But throughout Poland, the High Holidays were celebrated no matter what the Nazis decreed. For Hanukkah of 1940, the blinds in the Warsaw ghetto were drawn in rooms which faced the street, and in nearly every ghetto courtyard the feeling of national kinship was renewed.

At Sukkoth that year, the holiday was celebrated everywhere in the Warsaw ghetto, with the prayer groups saying the wine blessing. A large group of Hasidim (followers of the religious movement founded by Israel Baal Shem Tov) even danced outdoors, on Mila Street, singing the holiday songs in chorus, followed by a large crowd. "When they sang," wrote Kaplan, "they reached such a state of ecstasy that they couldn't stop until some heretic approached them, shouting, 'Jews! Safeguarding your life is a positive Biblical commandment; it is a time of danger for us. Stop this!' Only then did they become quiet. Some of them replied in their ecstasy, 'We are not afraid of the murderer! The devil with him!' "

By 1941 public worship and celebration was forbidden. Nevertheless, Purim of this Jewish year, 5701, was marked in the Warsaw ghetto. At the Zionist soup kitchen on 13 Zamenhof Street, said Chaim Kaplan, they read the Scroll, sang the holiday songs, and even had a bite to eat between numbers—bread and butter, a taste of the traditional poppy-seed tart, and a glass of sweetened coffee. "We came sad and left sad," he wrote, "but we had some pleasant moments in between. . . ."

One of the most moving achievements of the ghetto's underground was the creation and preservation of the Ringelblum Archives. Without them, we would know infinitely less about life in the Jewish communities of occupied Poland. Ringelblum had worked his way through the University of Warsaw, earning his doctorate in the history of Warsaw's Jews. He taught in a Warsaw high school and organized classes for adults throughout Poland. When the war broke out, he was thirty-nine, and in Geneva as a delegate to the World Zionist Congress. (He was a member of the Left-Poale Zionist group.) He could have remained abroad in safety, but he chose to go back to Poland. There he worked in the JDC's Warsaw office.

In the ghetto he gathered around him a secret organization to plan and carry out sociological studies of every aspect of ghetto life under the occupation. There were dozens of trained researchers in the group, teenagers among them. "Our aim was to present the whole truth, no matter how harsh it might be," he said. Papers were presented at secret Saturday meetings (hence the group's name, Oneg Shabbat—the pleasures of the Sabbath) and were discussed and reworked. By many clandestine means the group also gathered documents of both the Germans and the Judenrat, copies of the underground press, leaflets, diaries, poems, photos, all to build a collective portrait of Polish Jewry in World War II. "Death was the constant companion of its workers," said Hirsh Wasser, the secretary of Oneg Shabbat. "Day and night every member was threatened with the greatest danger, of which death was the most comfortable."

Ringelblum also headed the Warsaw ghetto's underground propaganda department and edited its illegal paper, News. In August 1942, when the mass deportations began, the archives and his own journal were buried in the ghetto. Two parts were discovered, in 1946 and 1950; the third part is still missing.

TEREZIN

The heaviest wheel rolls across our foreheads
To bury itself deep somewhere inside our memories.

We've suffered here more than enough,
Here in this clot of grief and shame,
Wanting a badge of blindness
To be a proof for their own children.

A fourth year of waiting, like standing above a swamp
From which any moment might gush forth a spring.

Meanwhile, the rivers flow another way,
Another way,
Not letting you die, not letting you live.

And the cannons don't scream and the guns don't bark
And you don't see blood here.

Nothing, only silent hunger.
Children steal the bread here and ask and ask and ask
And all would wish to sleep, keep silent and
        just to go to sleep again. . . .

The heaviest wheel rolls across our foreheads
To bury itself deep somewhere inside our memories.

(Mif, a child in the Terezin ghetto, 1944)

11

The Final Solution

It is early in February 1942 that rumors of a Nazi decision to exterminate the Jews reach the Warsaw ghetto. Chaim Kaplan notes in his diary a report that the Fuehrer "has decided to rid Europe of a whole people by simply having them shot to death." The same day he mentions that the Judenrat is planning a rollcall of ghetto Jews. People say that deportations begin with such a rollcall.

(Much earlier, in March 1940, it had been whispered to Kaplan that hundreds of young Jewish professionals who had been taken out of the ghetto had been deported to a camp called Auschwitz. But he knew little about that place or what happened to the prisoners there.)

At the end of February 1942 he hears that thousands of Jews have been killed somewhere "by poison gas." But he is sorrowing here and now over the deaths by starvation, in one week, of both his wife's sister and her husband. This is a commonplace in the ghetto, where at every turn one sees living skeletons.

On April 7, Kaplan trembles at the mention of Lublin. There an entire community of 44,000 Jews, he hears, is being wiped off the face of the earth. Panic-stricken Jews are being hunted down by the Nazis and taken "to some unknown place to be massacred." He asks himself, "Why should Warsaw fare better than Lublin?"

On April 12, Ringelblum records rumors that a German extermination brigade has arrived in Warsaw.

The rumors were true. Extermination of the Jews by gas had already begun in Poland. The whirlwind of death had not yet reached Warsaw, only because the gassing installation at Treblinka was not yet complete.

It was no secret in high Nazi circles that Hitler wanted to get rid of all the Jews. He had always said that this was his intention. It was there on the pages of *Mein Kampf*. And it had been repeated time and again in speeches and the press. Again the question: Then why didn't the Jews and others believe what he said?

For one thing, because no sane person took the threats to mean organized mass murder. The Nazis talked of forced emigration, yes, and even put forth a wild plan to convert the island of Madagascar into a concentration camp for all of Europe's Jews. Not until early 1939 did Hitler say publicly that if a war came, it would end in the annihilation of the Jews. But no evidence has come to light that the Nazis had prepared a plan for extermination. Only toward the end of 1940 did secret discussions of such a Final Solution begin.

Still, the groundwork for mass murder had been laid. The Jews had been humiliated and terrorized for years. Couldn't the next, and final, step be foreseen? Some few did predict it, but most people couldn't believe it would happen. Partly because we often screen out of our consciousness what we don't want to hear or can't bear to believe. But perhaps more because there is often a big gap between the declaration of an intention and the act of carrying it out. Who knew—then—whether Hitler really meant to replace the centuries-old policy of expulsion with annihilation? Or whether he would have the opportunity to go that far?

He had started slowly, waiting until his power was total, testing world opinion. And the other nations had done little to oppose or prevent the atrocities the Nazis had committed against the Jews for years. With the war, Hitler saw his chance to carry out the destruction of the Jews. Behind the battle lines he could keep secret the terrible "Final Solution of the Jewish Question."

It had begun in Poland with the mobile killing units and the starving of the ghetto inhabitants. But hunger took its toll too slowly. Some said it would need five years, others, eight years, to finish off the Jews that way. Hitler decided to use faster means.

On July 31, 1941, Goering sent Heydrich orders to make all necessary preparations "for a complete solution of the Jewish question in the German sphere of influence in Europe." Heydrich knew what the cryptic letter meant. He now had full authority to proceed with the killings. He had been preparing for them with the concentration of the Jews in the ghettos. He summoned Eichmann (his expert in Jewish affairs), told him "The Fuehrer has ordered the physical extermination of the Jews," and instructed him to organize the deportations to the death camps.

Eichmann arrived at Maidanek, the death camp near Lublin. "A German police captain there showed me how they managed to build airtight chambers disguised as ordinary Polish farmers' huts, seal them hermetically, then inject the exhaust gas from a Russian U-boat motor." Eichmann passed on Heydrich's order to start "liquidating a quarter million Polish Jews."

Then he went to Lodz, to see how Jews were being gassed. He watched a thousand of them packed into buses with closed windows. Carbon monoxide from the exhausts was piped back into the buses. The buses were driven to pits, the doors opened, and the corpses shoveled out. A Pole with a pair of pliers leaped into the pits, pried open the mouths, and tore out the gold teeth.

Asked to watch the execution through a peephole in a driver's seat, Eichmann declined because, he said, he "simply couldn't look at any suffering." He did observe, however, that the procedure was too slow. Within a few months German technical ingenuity speeded up the process. It could make anything more efficient, even the machinery of death.

After experiments at the Auschwitz concentration camp, whose construction had begun in January 1940, the first permanent death camp was completed at Chelmno. Everything looked ready now. Hans Frank met with his staff to remind them that if the Jews survived the war, victory would be in vain. "Gentlemen," he said, "I must ask you to arm yourselves against all feelings of sympathy. We have to annihilate the Jews wherever we find them and wherever it is at all possible."

The next step was to enlist the active help of all the agencies of the German government. To carry out the Final Solution swiftly and efficiently, the whole State apparatus was needed. The chiefs of these agencies were by now specially picked Nazis. But many of the career men in the civil service, the backbone of the operations, were trained pre-Hitler; many were not even in the Party. Heydrich anticipated great difficulty in getting their cooperation for the extermination.

He was wrong.

He learned how wrong when he called a conference of top ministry officials and SS generals at Wannsee, a Berlin suburb, on January 20, 1942. The aim was to coordinate the material and technical means required for the extermination of the 11 million Jews in occupied countries throughout Europe. The meeting lasted no more than ninety minutes, and was followed by drinks and lunch. Not only did no one object to the plans for the Final Solution, but with "boundless enthusiasm" useful proposals were made for improving upon the extermination process, which was already under way. The bureaucrats competed with each other for the honor of being foremost in this murderous matter.

Eichmann, who was the lowest-ranking official present, said he came away feeling "free of all guilt." If no one, no one at all, among these august personages, was against the Final Solution, then who was he to be troubled?

From the most respectable anti-Semite to the concentration-camp killer, the chain was solid. The Jew-baiter of any kind, as the Final Solution attests, is implicated in the criminal madness of a Hitler. Step by step the "mere" anti-Semite can be drawn into mass murder.

Within a few months of the Wannsee Conference, all the killing centers were ready. In addition to Chelmno, there was Treblinka, for Jews from the Warsaw and Bialystok districts. Sobibor, Belzec, and Maidanek, all in the Lublin district, would take deportees not only from there but from Cracow, Radom, Galicia, Czechoslovakia, and Holland. Auschwitz, located in

Upper Silesia, took Jews from many places, including all the conquered countries.

Trainloads of Jews from all over Europe began to stream into the six killing centers. The movement would not end until the German armies were crushed.

The deportations began in the winter of 1941–42. Even before the killing centers were ready, the Germans started to move the Jews closer to them. The Germans, of course, did not announce their true purpose. They said they intended simply to "resettle" Jews in the East. The "settlers" starved and froze in the temporary quarters. The German Jews were among the first to be "shipped East to work," for the Nazis were eager to rid the Third Reich of the last Jew. Some went to Lodz, others to Riga and Minsk, where they filled up the emptied Russian ghettos.

Jeanette Wolf of Berlin described her transport to Riga in January:

> We rode five days in the cold train without warm food and tortured by thirst. A few people at a time were permitted to leave each car to get water; and a few minutes were allowed for cleaning ourselves in the snow. Men and women had to perform their toilet on the rail embankment in each other's presence. In the terrible cold, hundreds of people froze parts of their bodies and developed gangrenous fingers and toes, and many died after reaching the camp. . . .
>
> At the Shirotava station in Riga, German and Latvian SS welcomed us with sticks and rifle butts. . . . The SS drove us to the ghetto. The houses looked as if vandals had visited them. Floors and stairs were littered with broken furniture and china, torn clothing and shoes, plaster and damaged household articles. Toilets and pipes had been smashed. It was obvious that the previous residents had left in great haste just before we came, but we did not at once understand why. We soon heard rumors that they had been killed. . . .
>
> During the first two weeks we received no food. We looked in the garbage for frozen potato peelings, vegetable refuse, and cleaned, cooked and ate the stuff. We mixed potato peelings

with flour and baked them without fat. *The stoves were broken and smoked heavily. If an army bread truck driving through the ghetto stopped long enough, we stole bread. When food came, it was a starvation ration. . . . Friends who had come with us died of hunger and exposure. Most people had lost their will to live.*

The deportees—all but a few, such as Jeanette Wolf—were annihilated, by shooting squads or by gas.

On July 22, mass deportation from the Warsaw ghetto began. Every day a train packed with at least 5,000 Jews would run the 60 miles from Warsaw to Treblinka. Within two months, 300,000 Jews were sent to their deaths. The Judenrat was given the task of delivering 6,000 Jews a day to the *Umschlagplatz*, a large yard behind a hospital, surrounded by a high brick wall. The Council announced exempt categories: Jews with work certificates; Jews fit for work, and their families; members of the Judenrat, its police and all its many other agencies, together with their families. The list was so long, it made many believe the worst had not yet come. It paralyzed the will to resist or to hide. This was "only" the "resettlement" of the weak and unproductive, people said; it was not the end.

The day after the deportations began, delegates of all Jewish groups met secretly to consider a course of action for the ghetto. Bernard Goldstein, a leader of the underground Bund, tells what his people thought:

All of us felt that active resistance and obstruction of the deportations was the only possible course. The ghetto had no right to sacrifice 60,000 human beings so that the survivors might continue their slave existence a little longer. Whether we could obtain weapons or not, we owed it to ourselves to resist, with bare hands if necessary. We could do at least some damage to the Germans by setting fire to the factories and warehouses inside the ghetto. Would it not be better to die in the flames than to wait our inevitable turn to follow the unfortunate 60,000?

But except for two left-wing Zionist groups, no one else at the meeting supported the Bund's position. They gave way to panic, clinging to the illusions of the majority in the ghetto. In its illegal bulletin, *Storm*, the Bund called on the 60,000 not to report voluntarily for death but to go into hiding, to resist, to fight to the end.

Day after day Chaim Kaplan watched the expulsions from the ghetto.

> *The ghetto has turned into an inferno. Men have become beasts. Everyone is but a step away from deportation; people are being hunted down in the streets like animals in the forest. It is the Jewish police who are cruelest toward the condemned.*

The police ringed a house or a whole block at a time, and went from door to door demanding documents. Whoever had neither the right document nor money enough for bribes was told to gather up a bundle and board the truck at the gate. People were seized on the streets, too, and taken to the *Umschlagplatz* as they were, with no good-byes. It was horrible, says Bernard Goldstein.

> *Children hung onto their fathers, wives to their husbands. They grabbed at pieces of furniture, doorjambs, anything to keep from being dragged away by the police. They clawed at their captors, fighting against death with hopeless desperation. All day, somewhere, one could hear the sounds of the gruesome chase. The cries and weeping of the unfortunates were mixed with the violent abuse and the wild shouts of the police.*

Where were they being taken? How were they being killed? The Bundists were sure this was the fate of the deported. But how to prove it to the ghetto? Zalman Friedrych, one of the young men in the underground resistance movement and as handsomely blond as Hitler's dream Aryan, was assigned to find out. He stole out of the ghetto and made his way to Sokolov, where he learned that a new branch railroad led to Treblinka. In Sokolov he found another comrade, Azriel Wallach, who had just escaped from a work detail at Treblinka. Wallach told him that all the Jews brought to Treblinka were unloaded from the trains, made to undress, and were then led into gas chambers and killed.

Friedrych returned to Warsaw. The Bund published the terrible facts at once in *Storm*, again warning the Jews not to be deceived: "Do not let them destroy you! Do not give yourselves voluntarily into the hands of your executioners!"

After the first week of deportations, the Germans began entering factories and grabbing workers on the job, sometimes taking out the whole shop. The pretense of selection was dropped. Everyone was in danger, and with the warning in *Storm*, few Jews reported voluntarily for deportation now. The Nazis played on their extreme hunger. Jews were offered a big loaf of bread and a tin of marmalade if they would come in themselves. Feigele Wladka, a member of the Bundist youth and active in the resistance, watched them report.

> They are loaded with sacks, baskets, suitcases; they drag with them the last remnants of their poor belongings, and they are all marching in the same direction towards the Umschlagplatz. . . . Some of them are walking slowly, with drooping heads; others move nervously ahead, with unsteady frightened eyes, seemingly in a hurry, as if they were afraid of being forced to go back. . . . Scarcely anyone in the ghetto is surprised at this quiet, resigned marching. From the hiding places and the shops people look at them with deep sorrow, sometimes mixed with a feeling of admiration. . . . "They have found the strength to take a decision." . . . Crushed under the burden of ghetto life, shriveled or swollen from starvation, haunted by the constant fear of being seized, these Jews could no longer go on with their fight. . . .

One of the Bund fighting group, Marek Edelman, was among the Jews waiting in the *Umschlagplatz*. He saw many retreat into the empty hospital building next door, and finding the toilets locked, relieve themselves where they could. The guards ran after them, revolvers ready.

The air is dreadfully sticky, the stench unbearable. I am leaning against the wall in a state of numbness. . . . On the dirty grey wall the design of a heart pierced by the cupid's arrow has been carved awkwardly with a pocketknife. The inscription says, "Blima and Chilek, August 1942" . . . Night is falling. . . . Somewhere near a child is crying. The whining gets on our nerves. The mother rises from the floor and walks toward the door. She passes a window. At the same moment a shot cracks from behind the window. The woman slowly slips down onto the filthy, spittle-covered floor. She is dead. . . .

At night some of the boldest take their chance. They sneak through the halls. At the height of the fifth floor there is a gangplank leading to the roof of the neighboring house on Niska Street. . . . Below, there is a guard watching the court-yard. The first of the fugitives puts his foot on the plank. Now he is walking. The guard fires. The man, pierced by bullets, falls down. The rest of them scuttle down into the halls. On their way they run into the guards. Violent beating starts now, hitting with rifle butts, the crushing of bones. The wounded, lacerated people, blood-spattered, choking and spitting, return to the Umschlagplatz. . . .

Somebody is reaching for poison. He swallows it, washing it down with a little water carefully prepared in a cruet. It was well hidden. It was not discovered during the examination. The man takes the poison in front of all the people. Nobody interferes. He is passing away. He is delivered. . . .

On a hot Wednesday morning early in August, the Nazis came for the children in Janusz Korczak's orphanage in the Warsaw ghetto. Trained as a neurologist and pediatrician, Dr. Korczak was also widely respected as an educator and an author of children's books. He had founded this home for children without parents and given his life to their care. It was in the middle of breakfast that the police ran in, yelling, "All Jews out! Quickly! Quickly!" The 200 children began moving quietly to the stairs, one of them picking up the green flag of their home. Dr. Korczak, who was ill and weak, suffering from a damaged heart, could have stayed behind, with his physician's exemption. But he stood between the Germans and the children.

Down below, on the street, Hillel Seidman happens to be in the crowd gathered to watch. He sees the long line formed in front of the orphanage on Siska Street.

> A long procession, children, small, tiny, rather precocious, emaciated, weak, shriveled and shrunk. They carry shabby packages; some have schoolbooks, notebooks under their arms. No one is crying.
>
> Slowly they go down the steps, line up in rows, in perfect order and discipline, as usual. Their eyes are turned towards the doctor. They are strangely calm; they feel almost well. The doctor is going with them, so what do they have to be afraid of? They are not alone; they are not abandoned.
>
> Dr. Korczak busies himself with the children with a sober earnestness. He buttons the coat of one child, ties up a package of another, or straightens the cap of a third. Then he wipes off a tear which is rolling down the thin little face of a child. . . .
>
> The procession starts out . . . marching quietly and orderly to the place of their untimely doom. The children are calm, but inwardly they must feel it; they must sense it intuitively. Otherwise how could you explain the deadly seriousness on their pale little faces? But they are marching quietly in orderly rows, calm and earnest, and at the head of them is Janusz Korczak.

That same summer, the Germans were demanding 50,000 Jews from the so-called free zone of southern France, whose capital was Vichy. Pierre Laval, a pro-Nazi and the real power in the Nazi-oriented Vichy government, zealously complied. He even proposed that the Germans take all the Jewish children under sixteen. Some of the Jews rounded up were kept in a camp at Drancy, 3 miles outside Paris, waiting for trains bound for

Auschwitz. During the month, 4,000 children who had been left behind by the evacuation of their parents were deported day by day. Georges Wellers describes how it was done:

> On the day of the deportation the children were usually woken at five o'clock in the morning and dressed in the half-light. It was often cold at five o'clock in the morning but nearly all the children went down to the yard very lightly clad. Suddenly aroused from sleep, ill with sleepiness, the littlest ones would begin to cry and, one by one, the others followed their example. They did not want to go down to the yard, struggled and would not let themselves be dressed. Sometimes it happened that a whole roomful of a hundred children, seized with panic and unconquerable terror, no longer responded to the comforting words of the adults who tried vainly to get them to go downstairs. Then the gendarmes were called, who carried the children down, screaming with terror.
>
> In the yard they waited to be called: they often answered wrongly when their names were called out. The older ones held on to the little ones' hands and would not let go of them. There was a certain number of children in each transport added at the end: those whose names were unknown. These were entered on the list by a question mark. It was of no great importance: it was doubtful whether even half of the unfortunate children would withstand the journey. There was no doubt at all that the survivors would be exterminated shortly after their arrival.

In Warsaw, by the end of the summer of 1942, scarcely 65,000 Jews were still alive. The last raids of that period were made on September 21, Yom Kippur. In the lull that followed, leaders of the Zionist and Bundist underground met on the edge of ruined Warsaw with Jan Karski, an agent of the Polish Government-in-Exile, and gave him a message:

> Tell the Polish and Allied governments we are being systematically murdered. Our entire people will be destroyed.

. . . Place this responsibility on the shoulders of the Allies. Let not a single leader of the United Nations be able to say that they did not know that we were being murdered in Poland and could not be helped except from the outside. The democracies cannot calmly put up with the assertion that the Jewish people of Europe cannot be saved.

Five weeks later, with 2 million Jews already murdered, Karski reported what he had learned to leaders of the British and United States governments and to Jewish leaders of Europe and America. Armed with the facts, Shmuel Zygelbojm, the Bund's delegate to the Polish National Council in London, tried—and failed—to break through the world's silence. He killed himself.

This is one version of a ballad, sung in many ghettos, which tells the story of the transports to the death camp at Treblinka.

-»>

In a kleyn shtetl gants fri fartog
Mentshn tserudert, a geveyn un a klog.
M'loyft vi meshuge halb naket un bloyz,
M'hert a geshrey: "yidn fun shtub aroys!"
Zhandarmen, politsey, ukrainer fil,
Tsu dermordn di yidn, dos is zeyer tsil!
M'shist un men shlogt, a moyre, a shrek,
Men traybt di yidn tsum ban avek.
Bashraybn kon es nit kayn feder,
Vi es dreyen zich di reder,
Men firt di yidn oyf kidesh-hashem,
Kayn treblinke, kayn treblinke.

Undzere brider fun yener zayt yam,
Zey konerr nisht filn undzer bitern tam
Zey konen nit filn undzer bitere noyt
Az oyf undz vart yede minut der toyt.
Di milchome vet nemen amol an ek.
Di velt vet derfarn undzer umderherte shrek.
Ongefilt mit veytik iz dos yidishe harts:
Ver vet konen heyln undzer shmarts?
Taychn trern veln rinen,
Ven men vet amol gefinen
Dem grestn keyver fun der velt
In treblinke, in treblinke.

In a little town early one morning
Frightened people, weeping and wailing,
Running about like mad, half naked and undressed,
A cry is heard: "Jews, get out of the house!"
Gendarmes, police, many Ukrainians,
To kill the Jews, that is their aim!
They shoot, they beat, it's terrible, horrible,
They drive the Jews to the trains.
No pen can ever describe
How the wheels go round and round.
As the Jews are being martyred,
Going, going to Treblinka.

Our brothers across the ocean
Cannot feel our bitter pain.
They cannot feel our bitter anguish
As death lurks over us every moment.
The war will end some day.
The world will realize the unheard-of horror.
Our Jewish heart is filled with pain:
Who will be able to heal our hurt?
Rivers of tears will flow,
When they will find some day
The biggest grave in the world
In Treblinka, in Treblinka.

12

The Blue Tattoo

From Warsaw, Vienna, and Berlin, from Rotterdam, Paris, and Brussels, from Rome, Prague, Athens, Budapest, and Belgrade, the Jews were deported to the killing centers of Poland until almost the last days of the war. At the Auschwitz complex alone, 1¾ million Jews died in less than two years. At Maidanek, 1½ million.

It is hard to envisage the organization it took to accomplish that end so swiftly. But the Germans managed it. At Auschwitz, 7,000 of them were devoted to the task. All told, more than 47,000 people staffed the extermination industry. It took time to train them. It took careful planning to design the killing process and collect the tools and materials for it. It took inventiveness to perfect the proper gas for the mass production of corpses and the capacious furnaces needed to consume them. Think of the book-keeping alone—the millions of Jews processed through each camp, each assigned a number, each number entered in the record, then tattooed on the left arm. A business not without some inconvenience caused by prisoners who did not always do what was expected of them—proceed neatly from the entrance gate to the gas chamber. Some died of hunger, some of disease, some of exhaustion, some of beatings or torture or bullets. And these deviations, too, had to be kept track of.

But the German system was up to it. It was a good civil service, every man and woman in the right place, always ready to carry out orders. There seemed no lack of bureaucrats ready to contribute to the Final Solution. Not that the Germans lacked assistants! No, they did not have to do it all alone. They found help wherever they needed it. Among the people of every nation they occupied—yes, in the ghettos and camps, too. Among the Jews themselves were some who served the "master race" as police, spies, informers, and hangmen.

The people who ran the camps were a mixture of SS with long service to the movement and bureaucrats specialized in administrative work. The guards, who came from SS regiments, were notorious for sadism and corruption.

The inmates were destined to be killed quickly. The only reasons some survived for any length of time were that the gas chambers and the crematoriums were temporarily too crowded, or that a number of inmates were needed as labor for camp construction and maintenance or for war production. Living quarters were primitive and filthy, clothing was rags, and food was a starvation diet. Sickness and epidemics were therefore common and deadly.

The shock of arrival in such a hellhole as Auschwitz was conveyed by Viktor Frankl. A Viennese physician, he was among 1,500 Jews traveling by train for several days and nights to an unknown station. They were told it would surely be some munitions factory where they would do forced labor. Frankl heard the engine's whistle, sounding like a cry for help, and then, he said:

> The train shunted, obviously nearing a main station. Suddenly a cry broke from the ranks of the anxious passengers. "There is a sign, Auschwitz!" Everyone's heart missed a beat at that moment. Auschwitz—the very name stood for all that was horrible: gas chambers, crematoriums, massacres. Slowly, almost hesitatingly, the train moved on as if it wanted to spare its passengers the dreadful realization as long as possible: Auschwitz.
>
> With the progressive dawn, the outlines of an immense camp became visible; long stretches of several rows of barbed wire fences; watchtowers; searchlights; and long columns of

*ragged human figures, grey in the greyness of dawn, trekking
along the straight desolate roads, to what destination we did
not know. There were isolated shouts and whistles of command.
We did not know their meaning. My imagination led me to see
gallows with people dangling on them. I was horrified, but this
was just as well, because step by step we had to become
accustomed to a terrible and immense horror. . . .*

Then the train moved into the station. Voices shouted commands in rough, shrill tones, the doors were flung open, and squads of prisoners with shaved heads and in striped uniforms stormed inside. They took charge of the new arrivals, grabbing their baggage and searching them for smuggled items—gold, silver, jewels. Everything they tried to keep or hide was stripped away and taken to warehouses to be sorted, packed, and sent off to Germany. From one such camp alone, a train of ten cars packed with clothing, shoes, and sacks of women's hair left for Germany every day. It is strange that most Germans claimed not to have known about the camps when they were wearing secondhand clothing with labels from cities all over Europe. Where did they think it came from? The gold teeth and fillings of the dead were melted down and converted into ingots stored in the vaults of the central bank of Germany. The women's hair was combed, cut, spun into thread, and made into industrial felt from which slippers were produced for the sailors in German submarines. Nothing was wasted, everything was turned into profit in this last stage of the looting process.

Over the main gate at Auschwitz was a big sign. It read: "*Arbeit macht frei*"—Labor liberates. Leaving the train, Frankl and the others were told to fall into two lines, men on one side, women on the other, in order to file past a senior SS officer.

*Instinctively, I straightened on approaching the officer. . . .
Then I was face to face with him. He was a tall man who looked
slim and fit in his spotless uniform. What a contrast to us,
who were untidy and grimy after our long journey! He had
assumed an attitude of careless ease, supporting his right elbow*

with his left hand. His right hand was lifted, and with the forefinger of that hand he pointed very leisurely to the right or to the left. None of us had the slightest idea of the sinister meaning behind that little movement of a man's finger, pointing now to the right and now to the left, but far more frequently to the left.

It was my turn. Somebody whispered to me that to be sent to the right would mean work, the way to the left being for the sick and those incapable of work, who would be sent to a special camp. I just waited for things to take their course, the first of many such times to come. . . . The SS man looked me over, appeared to hesitate, then put both his hands on my shoulders. I tried very hard to look smart, and he turned my shoulders very slowly until I faced right, and I moved over to that side.

Passing the first selection, Frankl was sent to a shed where the new arrivals were disinfected. Some naively asked the old prisoners, there as helpers, if they could keep a wedding ring or a medal or a good-luck piece. Frankl tried to take one of the helpers into his confidence.

Approaching him furtively, I pointed to the roll of paper in the inner pocket of my coat and said, "Look, this is the manuscript of a scientific book. I know what you will say, that I should be grateful to escape with my life, that that should be all I can expect of fate. But I cannot help myself. I must keep this manuscript at all costs; it contains my life's work. Do you understand that?"

Yes, he was beginning to understand. A grin spread slowly over his face, first piteous, then more amused, mocking, insulting, until he bellowed one word at me in answer to my question, a word that was ever present in the vocabulary of the camp inmates. "Shit!" At that moment I saw the plain truth and did what marked the culminating point of the first phase of my psychological reaction: I struck out my whole former life.

120

Primo Levi, a Jewish chemist, was deported from Italy to Auschwitz late in 1943. He too passed the first selection and was put in the work camp, Monowitz, where 40,000 prisoners were making a kind of rubber called Buna. On arrival he was stripped naked, his hair was shorn off, and he was then showered and disinfected. Rags and a broken-down pair of boots with wooden soles were thrown at him. Barefoot and naked, with the clothing in his hand, he was made to run 100 yards, over the blue and icy snow of dawn, to a hut where he was allowed to dress. And then he experienced a sensation something like Frankl's.

> When we finish, everyone remains in his own corner and we do not dare lift our eyes to look at one another. There is nowhere to look in a mirror, but our appearance stands in front of us, reflected in a hundred livid faces, in a hundred miserable and sordid puppets. We are transformed into the phantoms glimpsed yesterday morning.
>
> Then for the first time we become aware that our language lacks words to express this offense, the demolition of a man. In a moment, with almost prophetic intuition, the reality was revealed to us: we had reached the bottom. It is not possible to sink lower than this, nor could it conceivably be so. Nothing belongs to us anymore; they have taken away our clothes, our shoes, even our hair; if we speak, they will not listen to us, and if they listen, they will not understand. They will even take away our name: and if we want to keep it, we will have to find in ourselves the strength to do so, to manage somehow so that behind the name something of us, of us as we were, still remains.

Levi's number—174517—was tattooed on his left arm in a swift and slightly painful operation. The prisoners stood in an alphabetized line and moved past a man with the short needle jutting out of the pointed tool. Only by showing his number could 174517 get bread and soup. It took many days for the habits of freedom to wear off. He would still look for the time on his wristwatch, only to find his "name" there instead, tattooed in bluish numerals beneath the skin.

When the new arrivals asked questions of the old-timers, they were always given the same replies: You are not at home. This is not a sanitorium. There is no why here. The only way out is up the chimney.

Primo Levi met a boy of about sixteen the first day. He was a Polish Jew working as an ironsmith. They exchanged names but could not go much further in the only tongue they shared, a miserable German. The boy, Schlome, asked the man, Primo:

> "Where is your mother?"
> "In Italy." Schlome is amazed: a Jew in Italy? "Yes," I
> explain as best I can, "hidden, no one knows, run away, does
> not speak, no one sees her." He has understood; he now gets
> up, approaches me, and timidly embraces me. The adventure is
> over, and I feel filled with a serene sadness that is almost joy. I
> have never seen Schlome since, but I have not forgotten his
> serious and gentle face of a child, which welcomed me on the
> threshold of the house of the dead.

In the work camps, people fell into one of two categories, the saved or the drowned, as Levi called them. The struggle to survive was without letup. Everyone was "desperately and ferociously alone." The men who crumbled were called "mussulmen." In a few weeks they would be ashes in a field and crossed-out numbers in a register. They died alone, leaving no trace in the memory.

Those with energy and acuteness—the organizers, the operators, the people who knew how to fight for material advantages and reputation—had a chance to live longer. It was easy to sink, to go under. Only the exceptional survived more than three months. The others were done in before they could adapt themselves. They made up the anonymous mass of the camps.

The exceptional won jobs as kapos (foremen), cooks, nurses, night guards, hut sweepers, superintendents of latrines and showers. Most of them, in Levi's view, became the type developed in a system of slavery when a few slaves are offered a position of privilege for which they must betray their natural solidarity with their comrades. Levi observed what happens to such a man:

> He will be withdrawn from the common law and will become untouchable; the more power that he is given, the more he will be consequently hateful and hated. When he is given the command of a group of unfortunates, with the right of life or death over them, he will be cruel and tyrannical, because he will understand that if he is not sufficiently so, someone else, judged more suitable, will take over his post. Moreover, his capacity for hatred, unfulfilled in the direction of the oppressors, will double back, beyond all reason, on the oppressed; and he will only be satisfied when he has unloaded onto his underlings the injury received from above.

How such a kapo could behave was described by Nathan Sienicki, one of the Jews deported from France to Auschwitz:

> Our job was to carry planks and panels of wood for the construction of new huts. Our boss was a Polish kapo called Rene, whose number was 25. He was a common criminal and wore the letter "M" on his chest, which distinguished him as a murderer. . . . His cruelty was unbelievable. He would beat us without stopping and force us to run on the job. Every morning we started out with 120 people in his group, but more than half would be dead before the day was over. An average of 70 people a day . . .

Most of the prisoners, said Levi, could rely only upon their own strength to survive. To survive without the loss of dignity and the death of conscience was given to very few. Levi learned how quickly one's own moral world could be given up when hunger swamped the spirit.

> A fortnight after my arrival I already had the prescribed hunger, that chronic hunger unknown to free men, which makes one dream at night, and settles in all the limbs of one's body. I

have already learnt not to let myself be robbed, and in fact if
I find a spoon lying around, a piece of string, a button which
I can acquire without danger of punishment, I pocket them and
consider them mine by full right. On the back of my feet I
already have those numb sores that will not heal. I push
wagons, I work with a shovel, I turn rotten in the rain, I
shiver in the wind; already my own body is no longer mine: my
belly is swollen, my limbs emaciated, my face is thick in the
morning, hollow in the evening; some of us have yellow skin,
others grey. When we do not meet for a few days, we hardly
recognize each other.

How did it happen that Primo Levi was one of the handful to
live to tell his story? He said it was because he chanced to meet
Lorenzo. Lorenzo was an Italian civilian worker, not a prisoner,
who brought him a piece of bread and the remainder of his own
ration every day for six months. He gave him a vest of his own,
full of patches. He wrote a postcard for him, mailed it to Italy,
and brought him a reply.

For all this he neither asked nor accepted any reward,
because he was good and simple and did not think that one did
good for reward. . . . However little sense there may be in
trying to specify why I, rather than thousands of others, managed to survive the test, I believe that it was really due to
Lorenzo that I am alive today; and not so much for his material
aid as for his having constantly reminded me by his presence, by
his natural and plain manner of being good, that there still
existed a just world outside our own, something and someone
still pure and whole, not corrupt, not savage, extraneous to
hatred and terror; something difficult to define, a remote
possibility of good, but for which it was worth surviving. . . .
Thanks to Lorenzo, I managed not to forget that I myself was
a man.

Nor was he the only one not to forget. Levi told of the Greek
Jews:

> Those admirable and terrible Jews of Salonika, tenacious,
> thieving, wise, ferocious and united, so determined to live, such
> pitiless opponents in the struggle for life, those Greeks who
> have conquered in the kitchens and in the yards, and whom
> even the Germans respect and the Poles fear. They are in their
> third year of camp, and nobody knows better than they what
> the camp means. They now stand closely in a circle, shoulder
> to shoulder, and sing one of their interminable chants. . . .
> Their amazing consciousness of the survival of at least a po-
> tential human dignity made of the Greeks the most coherent
> national nucleus in the Lager [camp], and in this respect, the
> most civilized.

Wachsmann was another man Levi remembered from his barracks in Auschwitz. He had been a *melamed*, or teacher, in the
cheder, or elementary Hebrew school, of his Galician village, and
famed as a healer, too. "Nor am I far from believing it," said Levi,
"when I think that this thin, fragile and soft figure has managed
to work for two years without falling ill and without dying, but on
the contrary is lit up by an amazing vitality in actions and words
and spends long evenings discussing Talmudic questions incom-
prehensibly in Yiddish and Hebrew with Mendi, who is a mod-
ernist rabbi."

Sometimes, in the long winter nights, a *badchen*, or storyteller,
would come secretly into the barracks, look around cautiously,
then sit down on Wachsmann's bunk. At once a small crowd
would gather, silent and attentive.

> He chants an interminable Yiddish rhapsody, always the
> same one, in rhymed quatrains, of a resigned and penetrating
> melancholy (but perhaps I only remember it so because of the
> time and the place that I heard it?); from the few words that
> I understand, it must be a song that he composed himself, in
> which he has enclosed all the life of the Lager in minute detail.
> Some are generous and give the storyteller a pinch of tobacco
> or a needleful of thread; others listen intently but give
> nothing.

Many survivors tell of the same dream, a dream they dreamed many times in the death camps. The elements are always the same. The dreamer is at home with his family, telling them of what has happened in the camp. It is an intense pleasure to be there, among loved ones, and to have so much to tell them. But as the dreamer recounts his experiences, he notices his listeners are not following him. They act indifferent, they interrupt to talk among themselves of other things; it is as if the dreamer is not there. Finally the listeners leave without saying a word to the dreamer.

Awake, the dreamer feels a desolation that is unbearable. It is anguish in its pure state. The pain of each day, suffered again in the night.

13

Zyklon B

And what of death itself in the camps? The death they were designed for, death by gas? In Auschwitz the Jews were killed by a product called Zyklon B. It was hydrogen cyanide, efficient in large rooms. It was made into bluish pellets, which were packed into small canisters. Poured through openings in the ceilings of the killing chambers, the Zyklon turned into gas and did its job.

Zyklon was manufactured by the Dessauer Works and was sold not only for killings but to fumigate ships and buildings and disinfect clothing. The SS bought it for the death camps. SS First Lieutenant Kurt Gerstein handled the payments. Gerstein, thirty-four when the war began, had been trained as a mining engineer. He was also a national official of the YMCA in Germany, in charge of a special program in biblical studies. He joined the Nazi movement when he was young but soon became disillusioned because of its war against the Christian Church. For spreading anti-Nazi propaganda, he was sent to a concentration camp in 1936. Released, he was admitted to the SS, which he joined, he said, in order to expose it to the world. In the summer of 1942 the SS sent him to the Polish death camp called Belzec, to deliver some experimental Zyklon B. There he witnessed the mass extermination of Polish Jews by carbon monoxide.

He tried to tell the Pope's representative in Berlin what he had seen, believing that if the truth were known, the German people would rise up. But he was turned away. Then he wrote a report of his experience and asked the office of the Archbishop of Berlin to forward it to the Pope. On the train returning from Belzec, he had met a Swedish diplomat stationed in Berlin, and stayed up all night to tell him the terrible story. The diplomat sent a report to Sweden, but the Swedish government did not publish the report or forward it to the Allies until the war was over. Even the Dutch resistance movement, which learned Gerstein's story, refused to disclose it, because "nobody would believe it."

What did Gerstein see at Belzec? The following is taken from his own handwritten account:

> . . . In the hot August weather the whole place smelt like the plague and there were millions of flies everywhere. Right by the small two-track station there was a large shed, the so-called cloakroom, with a large counter where valuables were handed over. Then there was a room containing about 100 chairs—the barber's room. Then an outdoor path under birch trees with a doubled barbed-wire fence on the left and right, with the sign: "To the inhalation and bathrooms." In front of us a sort of bathhouse with geraniums, then a few steps, and then three rooms each on the right and left . . . with wooden doors like garages. In the rear wall, scarcely visible in the darkness, large sliding doors. On the roof, as a "witty little joke," the Star of David . . .

Early the next morning he saw the train come in: 45 cars carrying 6,700 people, of whom 1,450 were already dead on arrival. Children looked out the barred windows, their faces pale, their eyes filled with the fear of death. When the train stopped, Ukrainian guards tore open the doors and whipped the people out onto the platform. All had to strip naked and give up their clothes, shoes, valuables, spectacles, artificial limbs, and their hair.

> Then the procession started to move. With a lovely young girl at the front. They all walked along the path, all naked, men, women, and children. . . . Mothers with their babies

at the breast came up, hesitated, and entered the death chambers. A sturdy SS man stood in the corner and told the wretched people in a clerical tone of voice: "Nothing at all is going to happen to you! You must take a deep breath in the chambers. That expands the lungs. This inhalation is necessary because of illness and infection." When asked what was going to happen to them, he answered, "Well, of course, the men must work, building houses and roads, but the women don't have to work. Only if they want to, they can help with the housework or in the kitchen."

This gave some of these poor people a glimmer of hope that lasted long enough for them to take the few steps into the chambers without resisting. The majority realized—the smell told them—what their fate was to be. So they climbed the steps and then they saw everything. . . . They hesitated, but they went into the gas chambers, pushed on by those behind them, or driven by the leather whips of the SS. Most of them without saying a word. A Jewess of about forty, with eyes blazing, called down upon the heads of the murderers the blood being spilt here. Hauptmann Wirth personally gave her five or six lashes in the face with his riding whip. Then she too disappeared into the chamber. Many people were praying. . . .

The chambers filled. . . . People were standing on each other's feet. . . . The SS forced as many in together as was physically possible. The doors closed. Meanwhile the others were waiting outside in the open air, naked. . . . Twenty-five minutes went by. . . . Many were now dead. One could see that, through the little glass window through which the electric light lit up the chamber for a moment. After 28 minutes only a few were still alive. At last, after 32 minutes everyone was dead.

Men of the work squad opened the wooden doors from the other side. . . . The dead were standing upright like basalt pillars, pressed together in the chambers. There would not have been room to fall down or even to bend over. One could see the families even in death. They were still holding hands, stiffened to death, so that it was difficult to tear them apart in order to clear the chamber for the next load. The corpses were thrown *out—wet with sweat and urine, soiled with excrement, menstrual blood on their legs. Children's bodies flew through the air. There was no time to lose. The whips of the Ukrainians whistled down on the backs of the work squad. Two dozen dentists opened the mouths with hooks and looked for gold. Gold on the right, without gold on the left. Other dentists used pliers and hammers to break gold teeth and crowns out of the jaws. . . . The naked corpses were carried in wooden barrows just a few meters away to pits.*

At Belzec, death by monoxide gas took much too long. Rudolf Höss, the SS commandant of Auschwitz, preferred Zyklon B, because it worked faster—in 3 to 15 minutes, depending upon climatic conditions. The most efficient way of disinfecting the world of Jews was the goal of his Party. As Himmler said, "Anti-Semitism is the same as delousing. Getting rid of lice is not a question of ideology; it is a matter of cleanliness. In just this same way anti-Semitism for us has not been a question of ideology but a matter of cleanliness." Once he told his co-workers that the elimination of the Jews "is a page of glory in our history."

The disposal of the bodies was another problem for German ingenuity to solve. At first the bodies were buried in mass graves in the woods. But the decaying corpses left odors that spread for miles, and when the rate of killing increased, the space needed for graves was enormous. Worse, mass graves were evidence of mass killings. So cremation, first in small ovens and then in giant crematoriums, was tried. By 1944, transports came so fast that over 10,000 Hungarian Jews were being gassed per day, and 20,000 Lodz Jews. The ovens couldn't process that many bodies. At Auschwitz they turned to burning the corpses in open pits. This proved to be the cheapest and most efficient method. As Raul Hilberg says, "it took millennia in the development of Western culture" to reach this unlimited capacity for human destruction. The record at Auschwitz was 34,000 people killed and destroyed in 24 hours, through continuous day and night shifts.

In the name of "medical science" the Nazis made special use of the doomed Jews. The victims of these experiments numbered in the hundreds of thousands. Only a handful survived to tell the story at the Nuremberg Trials of the Nazis after the war.

The origin of this practice went back many years. It began on January 2, 1934, when Nazi laws were adopted for the sterilization of the "unfit." Who was to decide who was unfit? "Without the smallest pity," Hitler said that year, he could eliminate millions among the "inferior races that breed like vermin." On the day World War II began, he had launched a program to eliminate "unfit" Aryans. He signed an order allowing doctors to give "mercy deaths" to the "incurably sick." Carbon-monoxide chambers were built to carry out this "euthanasia program." Between December 1939 and August 1941, about 50,000 to 60,000 Germans—children and adults—were secretly killed by lethal injections or in gassing installations designed to look like shower rooms. It was a foretaste of Auschwitz. The victims were taken from the medical institutions and put to death. Their relatives were never consulted or told what had happened. They were simply sent the ashes, never the body, and warned not to demand explanations or to "spread false rumors." It was impossible to squelch suspicion. In December 1940 the Vatican condemned the "mercy killings" as "contrary to both natural and divine law." Two German bishops and a cardinal also spoke up, protesting the gassing of fellow Germans. (They are not known to have protested when non-German Christians or Jews were the victims.) Hitler stopped the gassing in Germany almost at the moment he began it, on a vastly greater scale, in Poland.

There were two types of medical experiments. One was for the usual goals of medical research: to test a drug, a serum, a treatment, a hypothesis. But the Nazis did not rely on volunteer subjects; they forced the camp prisoners to undergo the tests. The German air force, for example, wanted to carry out high-altitude tests on humans, but because the tests were so dangerous, nobody would volunteer. They tried monkeys; that proved unsatisfactory. So air force doctors asked Himmler to put human beings at their disposal. "Gladly," he replied. Jews at the Dachau camp were chosen and locked into the special chamber the air force had provided; then the pressure was altered to simulate atmospheric conditions at extra high altitudes. Eighty died in the "sky ride machine," as the victims called it, and another 129 were killed after "survival" of these experiments.

Freezing experiments were carried out next. Prisoners were forced to stand naked out-of-doors from 9 to 14 hours in below-freezing temperatures. Then they were "warmed up" in a variety of ways, including the use of the most obscene sadism, to see at what point they showed vital life signs. The victims either died in the tests or were killed immediately afterward. (One of the most prominent Nazi scientists who gave conceptual guidance to the tests was Dr. Hubertus Strughold. He came to the United States after the war to pioneer in the development of American space medicine.)

It might be a German army doctor doing research on jaundice or a German chemical company testing a drug against typhus. They all came to the SS for permission to draw upon its huge supply of doomed Jews. Of course each request was for "habitual criminals" as experimental subjects. That was a blind for the conscience. For the choice would inevitably fall upon the "race-defiling Jewish habitual criminals."

Many experiments had nothing to do with attempts to heal the sick. They were experiments in killing; human guinea pigs were used to find out how to widen the destruction process, how to cut down on or get rid of "undesirable, inferior" populations, such as Jews and Gypsies. X rays were used on the sexual organs of young Jewish men to test new methods for mass sterilization. Castration of men was tried at both Auschwitz and Ravensbruck. Chemical irritants were inserted in the uteri of Jewish women to render them sterile, and 300 who did not die from this were then gassed.

All such experiments led to nothing except the deaths of the victims. The tests proved that the racial theory of inferior beings was a poison that had no limit to its destructiveness.

What kind of physician would take part in such work? Professor Johann Kremer was an SS doctor at Auschwitz. He had been a professor of anatomy at the University of Munich before the war. His diary entries for 1942 reveal something of his mentality. On September 2, he witnessed execution by gas for the first time; 918 Jews from France were killed.

> After what I have seen today, Dante's Inferno seems almost a comedy.

On September 5, he was present when 800 sick women were removed from the camp hospital and exterminated.

> Horror of horrors. Thils was right when he told me that here we were at the world's anus.

The next day, Sunday, he noted:

> We had an excellent lunch today—tomato soup, half a chicken and roast potatoes, cake and delicious vanilla ice cream.

On September 9, he was even happier.

> Received the highly welcome information that I was divorced from my wife on the first of this month. I see colors again: a black curtain has been lifted from my life!

Then, with no change of tone:

> Later in my capacity as doctor, was present at the punishment by whipping of 8 prisoners and an execution by small-bore rifles. Was given soap flakes and two bars of soap.

On September 20:

> This Sunday afternoon from three to six o'clock listened to a concert given by the camp orchestra in beautiful sunshine. Conducted by conductor of the Warsaw State Opera. Eighty musicians. For dinner there was roast pork. For supper baked tench.

BOOK THREE

Spirit of
Resistance

14

To Die with Dignity

Three times a week little Sima smuggled Jews out of the Minsk ghetto, evading the SS guards, and led them to the forests of Staroje-Sielo, 50 kilometers away.

Who was Sima? We know about her underground work from the memoirs of Jacob Greenstein, a partisan (an anti-Nazi fighting behind the lines) in the Minsk region.

> Sima was a twelve-year-old girl with blonde hair, blue eyes, and dimples that showed when she talked. Her parents perished in the first German pogrom. In the beginning Sima lived outside the ghetto and carried out important assignments for the underground party committee. Later when we began to lead Jews out of the ghetto, Smolar brought the little girl to the ghetto and she became our contact with the forest.
>
> No assignment was too difficult for Sima. Before going out on a mission, she listened carefully to the given instruction; then she would repeat what she was told, trying hard not to miss a single word. Her small pistol was always in the special pocket sewn into her coat. Before starting out, she would always point to it and say, "Don't worry, the Fritzes will not take me alive."
>
> On cold winter nights Sima would sneak out of the ghetto through an opening beneath the barbed wire fence. She returned to the ghetto through the cemetery. There were times

*when she did not succeed in getting into the ghetto at night.
When this happened, she would spend the night, hungry and
cold, in some bombed-out building, and remain there throughout the next day. At dusk, when the Jews returned from work,
she would stealthily join their column, and together with them
enter the ghetto. After the liquidation of the Minsk ghetto,
Sima participated in the combat operations of the partisan
detachment.*

Sima had an indomitable will to live. She resisted the Nazis,
and she survived. Later, when the Germans, now losing the war,
were driven out in summer, 1944, Sima marched through Minsk in
the front ranks of the partisans. Hers was one of the many forms
of resistance to Hitler's persecution. Wherever there was oppression, resistance of some kind emerged. The watchword of the
Jewish resistance was: "Live and die with dignity!" And despite
the greatest terror, hunger, and privation, Jews upheld that
watchword. They did not want simply to vanish silently from the
earth.

Acts of resistance were countered by the Nazis with a violence
almost beyond belief. In 1941, a group of Dutch Jews dared to
attack German police in Amsterdam. Hannah Arendt reports
their punishment:

*Four hundred thirty Jews were arrested in reprisal and they
were literally tortured to death, first in Buchenwald and then in
Mauthausen. For months they died a thousand deaths, and
every single one of them would have envied his brethren in
Auschwitz and even in Riga and Minsk. There exist many
things considerably worse than death, and the SS saw to it that
none of them was ever very far from their victims' minds and
imagination.*

Under such conditions, those who conducted an organized and
armed resistance were a minority. That even such a minority
existed was a miracle. The right question to ask, Elie Wiesel has

said, is not: Why didn't *all* the Jews fight? but How did *so many* of them?

Another question to examine is: What was the degree of resistance among non-Jews? Hitler's armies swept over most of Europe with incredible speed. Everyone attributed it to the superior power of the German military forces. The vanquished nations, all of them, had trained and equipped armies. The Jews had nothing. The Nazis killed myriads of people in the parts of Russia they occupied, a territory whose population greatly outnumbered the German troops. How much resistance did Hitler encounter there? Millions of Russian captives were transported to German prisons and labor camps and treated so brutally that 5 million of them died. How many riots or acts of resistance took place among them? Yet no one accuses them of going like sheep to slaughter. No, the vast majority in the prisoner-of-war camps behaved much as did the civilians in the occupied countries. They were inert, passive; they did what they were ordered to do, hoping simply to survive. A minority chose to collaborate with the Nazis. Another minority chose to actively resist.

The purpose here is not to criticize or demean others, only to indicate how hard it is for anyone to resist a ruthless totalitarian power which commands modern weapons and employs elaborate means to crush opposition.

Even so, throughout occupied Europe, when the terrible truth about the Final Solution became clear to some Jews, they urged the others to resist physically. Realists accepted the fact that Hitler meant to annihilate every Jew in Europe, but the majority of Jews could not believe this would happen. Partly because the Germans shrouded their evil work in utter secrecy. Partly because the Germans used many forms of deception to confuse and mislead their victims. And perhaps most importantly, because the very idea of mechanical and systematic mass murder struck most people—everywhere in the world—as utterly inconceivable. It seemed infinitely different from the earlier examples of what came to be known as genocide. It went far beyond the reach of the human imagination. As Dr. Louis de Jong, a Dutch historian of the Holocaust, once said, "Our mind, once having grasped the facts, immediately spewed them out as something utterly alien and unnaturally loathsome." A group of Jehovah's Witnesses, who were put in the death camp at Birkenau, by the side of the gas chambers and crematoriums, said later, "One day we would believe our own eyes; the next day we would simply refuse to do so." Another Hollander, Emile Franken, was one of a group in Birkenau which saw the crematorium chimneys smoking day in and day out. But the inmates, "the people themselves," he said, "pretended that the place was a brickyard or a soap factory. This mass delusion lasted for four weeks." He was the only one among them who could accept the unbearable truth.

The gas chambers spelled death not only for oneself but for husband, wife, children, grandparents, relatives, friends. How many among the millions who died in them could face that awesome truth? Professor de Jong concludes:

> We should be committing an immense historical error, were we to dismiss the many defense mechanisms employed by the victims—not constantly, mind you, but by way of intermittent distress signals—as mere symptoms of blindness or foolishness; rather did these defense mechanisms spring from deep and inherent qualities shared by all mankind: a love of life, a love of family, a fear of death, and an understandable inability to grasp the reality of the greatest crime in the history of mankind, a crime so monstrous . . . that even its perpetrators (the sadists and other perverts among them excepted) were unable to dwell on their activities for too long.

As some Jews became convinced that their people were doomed, the natural question to ask was: How then shall we die? One answer was to frustrate the enemy by not making it easy for him: Do not commit suicide; stay alive as long as you can. The simple act of living on became a form of passive resistance. Many expressed that resistance by carrying on their traditional religious life—praying, singing, studying the Talmud, observing the Holy Days—and their cultural activities in the ghettos. Others hid from the enemy as long as they could. Some bore children as if to say, No matter what you do, the generations will go on.

Other Jews, who began to understand that Nazi terror was a totally different order of life, chose more active ways of responding to it. They felt it was hopeless to rely on legal methods in such a morally criminal system. So people learned how to use bribery, smuggling, forgery, theft, spying, sabotage, violence. They saw these as weapons of defense against a power committed to their destruction. They bribed the enemy; they smuggled food and people; they stole bread and guns; they forged papers—birth and baptismal certificates, residence cards, ration cards, work cards, registration forms, passports. They planted spies in the enemy's ranks; they sabotaged war production; they blew up trains and bridges and buildings; they shot and stabbed and poisoned Hitlerites.

The essential fact is that one can resist in a great many ways, by acting and yes, sometimes, by refusing to act. Armed fighting, for those physically able to undertake it, will usually do the most damage to the enemy. And, of course, there were armed battles. That aspect of Jewish resistance—apart from the Warsaw Ghetto Uprising—is almost ignored in the earlier accounts of the Holocaust. One reason for the neglect is the fact that historians based themselves largely on the captured Nazi documents, which gave only a one-sided version of what happened. As the years pass, documentation of resistance by the Jews increases in many languages, especially Yiddish. This includes not only memoirs written during the Holocaust and after liberation but depositions of witnesses, records of trials, and thousands of oral interviews with survivors all over the world.

Some historians, such as Raul Hilberg, argue that the "Jews of all regions and all classes failed to resist in significant measure throughout the destruction process." It all depends upon the definition of resistance. Hilberg limits it to armed fighting. He excludes bribery, ransom, and rescue as only "alleviation," and flight and hiding he calls simply "evasion." But the resistors themselves and some of the research organizations devoted to the study of the Holocaust (Yad Vashem in Israel and YIVO Institute for Jewish Research in New York) commonly include as honorable examples of resistance what Professor Hilberg would leave out.

To account for his view, Hilberg and others claim that the Jewish tradition of 2,000 years in the Diaspora was one of non-resistance to and compliance with oppression. That view is countered by many who interpret Jewish history differently. A Polish Jewish writer, M. Edin, has this to say:

> Some naive researchers and publicists discovered the Jews for the first time in the ghetto barricades. These writers say that the Jews had not fought since Maccabean times . . . that only in the presence of death in the ghetto did the Jew take to arms. This is not true. We shall not discuss here the fighting tradition of the Jewish masses of the nineteenth century, beginning with exploits of Berek Yoselevich's division [in the Polish uprising of 1832]. But only a superficial acquaintance with the participation of the Jewish workers and the Jewish intelligentsia in the labor movement of Poland and Russia from its inception down to the Nazi attack is enough to refute this view. For the Jews manifested heroism not only in cases of individuals like Shulman, Hirsh Leckert, Naftali Botwin and Engel, but even more importantly, on the part of the Jewish working masses as a whole. From this working class tradition and from the intellectual and moral training and ideology of the working class movement did men and women like Joseph Levartovsky, Andjei Schmidt and a legion of Jewish resistance heroes, known and unknown, draw strength in this most tragic period. . . .

Here the writer is stressing one of the two traditions in Jewish history—the tradition of physical resistance to persecution. That pattern of resistance, as he implies, came out of a historical experience developed over a long period of time. Each nation has traditions and values shaped by its own past. America and France have had a revolutionary tradition since the late eighteenth century. The Poles, too, beginning with the insurrection of 1794 and the many that broke out during the next hundred years. And the

142

Yugoslavs, since their struggles against the Turks. The Czechs took a somewhat different course, after the terrible defeat of the Hussite rebellion in the fifteenth century. Under Hapsburg domination they developed methods of passive resistance which they later used against the Nazis.

Another critic of Hilberg is the historian Reuben Ainsztein. His 900-page study of Jewish resistance in Nazi-occupied Eastern Europe thoroughly documents all aspects of Jewish action in defense of life and dignity. He asserts that in charging Hitler's victims with cowardice, Hilberg has laid Jewish behavior to a history of passivity in the Diaspora. Ainsztein refutes this by a fresh examination of the Jews in history, showing them to have been neither born victims nor born martyrs. He presents a detailed survey of the Diaspora Jew as soldier, seaman, corsair, merchant-adventurer, and explorer. The tradition of the Jewish fighter in antiquity never died, he says. "The role of the fighter . . . in ensuring Jewish survival is . . . at least as important as that of the religious martyr."

Jewish methods of resistance to oppression have not been uniform. Dispersed throughout many varying cultures, the Jews were inevitably affected by their interactions with their host societies. The intellectuals, the assimilated part of the middle class, and the working class absorbed the traditions and values of those nations. What about the Jews who maintained their religious orthodoxy? Philip Friedman, a Jewish historian born in Galicia, who was active in the anti-Nazi underground in Poland, explains how their traditions influenced the question of resistance:

> . . . The large mass of Orthodox Jews, particularly in
> Eastern and Southeastern Europe, had quite a different attitude
> to those problems. Whereas most other nations have legacies
> of heroism in which heroism means physical and military
> prowess, in the case of Orthodox Jewry the concept of heroism
> is interwoven with the idea of spiritual courage, of sacrifice for
> the sake of religion, known in Hebrew as Kiddush Hashem
> (Sanctification of God's Name). This was the main form of
> resistance carried on by the Orthodox Jews. It was a resistance

stemming from religious inspiration and it contained a deeply rooted ancestral heritage epitomized by the saying, "not by force but by the strength of the spirit."

This attitude had been maintained during many centuries of religious persecution. Its essence is epitomized in the idea that the evil of the world should not be fought and cannot be defeated by physical force, because the struggle between good and evil will be decided elsewhere, by Divine Providence; it will by no means be decided by physical warfare. In accordance with this view, the true weapon is the weapon of conscience, prayer, religious meditation and devotion, and not armed resistance.

The Orthodox Jew did not believe that it was possible or even desirable to resist the Nazis in any other way. They believed that the recital of a chapter of the Psalms would do more to affect the course of events than the killing of a German —not necessarily immediately but in the infinite course of mutual relations between the Creator and His creatures.

"Not by force but by the strength of the spirit . . . " An example of what that means comes from an eyewitness account of what happened in the Polish town of Dabrowa when the Germans found Rabbi Isaac and his Hasidic disciples hiding in an underground shelter. The Nazis drove them to the local Jewish cemetery. Waiting for the Germans in their hideout, the Hasidim were dressed in their praying shawls and had a bottle of vodka which they managed to bring to the cemetery. There, facing their executioners, as the account goes, "they drank lechayim (to life) to each other, held hands and began to dance, and were shot down as they danced. The Germans were so enraged by the scene, which they had failed to prevent, that they slit the Jews' bellies and trampled on them until the bowels came out."

Keeping these traditions in mind, what can be learned from the history of resistance movements? There are basic conditions necessary for their success. One is a favorable place to fight—such as mountains, forests, marshes. These existed in Europe but were denied the Jews because they were locked behind ghetto walls. All their moves could be observed and controlled. To start an underground conspiracy under such conditions and to link it with others was neither easy nor safe. Smuggling weapons into the ghetto required great courage and ingenuity. And getting fighters out of a ghetto—studded with spies and surrounded by guards—and into the forests and mountains was even harder.

That very decision—whether to stay in the ghetto with the mass of Jews or to escape and fight outside—was an agonizing one to make. Many passionate debates took place over the moral issue. Usually they ended with the resistance forces staying inside. They helped the inmates of the ghetto struggle against oppression and then led the fight against the deportations to the death camps. They left only when there was no longer any chance to be useful in the ghetto.

The ghetto Councils, faced with the choice—to resist or not to resist—did not act on a rigid pattern. There were variations, but the end remained the same. In Vilna, the Judenrat did whatever the Germans asked. Its head, Jacob Gens, seems even to have used Jewish police to assist at mass executions. And Gens himself forced the resistance leader Itzik Wittenberg to give himself up to the Nazis. (The Germans killed Wittenberg and two months later, shot Gens.) In Kovno, while the Council seemed to be carrying out Nazi orders, its leader, Dr. Elkhanen Elkes, worked secretly with the resistance; and the Jewish police chief, Moshe Levin, doubled as a resistance leader, smuggling out many young Jews to join the partisans. In Lodz and Warsaw, the Councils opposed resistance. In Lvov, two Council heads heroically refused to collaborate with the Nazis.

The resistance movements in the ghettos challenged the position of those Councils which believed that by working for the Germans, the Jews would save themselves. The partisans of the Vilna ghetto, as early as January 1942, seven months before the deportation of Jews to Treblinka began in Warsaw, published a call which warned that "The fate of the Jews under Hitlerite occupation is total annihilation, regardless of the economic interests of the Germans. Brothers! Away with the illusion that we will

be saved by virtue of economic necessity! . . . The destruction
. . . is a systematic process which sooner or later will include
everyone. . . ."

The historian Isaiah Trunk concludes that "the majority of the
Councils were against the idea of organized resistance." He cites
town after town where the Councils tried by every means to
oppose the resistance movements. There was one Council head,
Moshe Merin of Bedzin-Sosnowiec, who betrayed many young
people to the Nazi executioners and was himself sentenced to
death by the underground movement. Trunk also lists a smaller
number of Councils which supported the resistance. Among the
leaders were such men as Eliyahu Myshkin of Minsk and Abraham
Gefner of Warsaw. In Iwaniska, Chaim Rabinowicz, a rabbi who
was a member of the Council, helped some 300 young people
escape to the woods, where they had a chance to take revenge on
the enemy.

There were Council members who remain controversial figures
today. One such is Adam Czerniakow, head of the Warsaw
ghetto. He committed suicide when the Nazis ordered him to
supply 10,000 Jews a day instead of 6,000. Some hold he was a
martyr, because he killed himself rather than carry out the order.
But the poet Yitkhok Katzenelson, active in the Warsaw resistance, asked, How do you distinguish between handing over 10
rather than 6 Jews? "How many more than 6 are 10? To 6 you
agree, but at 10 you object?"

Trunk reports that, of the some 700 people he has listed who
were members of 404 Councils, 182 were killed before the deportations began, 21 resigned, 13 were dismissed or arrested, 9 committed suicide, 26 died "natural" deaths, 383 were shipped to
death camps, and 86 escaped.

Under such enormous pressure, manipulated by the diabolical
methods of the Nazis, people were understandably deluded. Some
collaborated, some collapsed, some even served as agents of the
Gestapo. What happened under Hitlerism echoed what had happened under czarism a hundred years earlier. In the time of Czar
Nicholas I, the traditional Jewish community councils had been
ordered to supply boys to serve in the army for twenty-five years.

146

The sons of the rich, the gifted few, and the promising Talmudic scholars escaped service, while the children of the poor and the helpless were seized by the Jewish councils and handed over to the army. There was often the same injustice and inhumanity in the Nazi ghettos. A tiny minority of Jewish officials and racketeers lived (for a time) in relative ease, while the poor carried the heaviest burdens of taxation, forced labor, starvation, and deportation. In his Warsaw-ghetto diary, Emmanuel Ringelblum cried out passionately, "The entire activity of the Jewish Council is one shocking injustice against the poor."

The most useful way to examine the record of the Judenrat might be from the perspective of Jewish history, rather than as a matter of making moral judgments on individuals. The best members of the Jewish Councils meant to save lives. If they collaborated, it was to keep as many Jews as possible alive until the defeat of Germany. But the lesson for the world now is that collaboration only made the Councils accomplices to mass murders. Ber Mark, a historian of the Warsaw Ghetto Uprising, sees the actions of the collaborationist Councils as one of two lines of development in Jewish history:

> One—self-defense, resistance and struggle; the other—accommodation and desertion. One—joining the liberation movements of mankind; the other—fear of the Authority and isolating oneself in a spiritual ghetto. One—an honorable struggle for national rebirth, for national rights, for a free Jewish people among free peoples; the other—pleasing the reactionary ruler, submission to the oppressor, and deserting one's own people. In the conditions of the ghetto this meant: the line of resistance versus the line of the Judenrat.

Whatever its internal problems, and no matter where it operated, the resistance movement needed the friendly help of the non-Jewish populations. Only from them could come essential information, food, shelter for the sick and wounded, and hiding places for partisans and weapons. But in very few Nazi-occupied countries could the Jewish underground find friends among the general populations. The Jews felt themselves terribly alone in their struggle. Even sympathetic non-Jews wavered in their support, fearing the cruel punishment of the Nazis. But more often the local people were indifferent or actively hostile to the Jews. They did not look upon the Jewish cause as their own.

Nor could the Jewish underground count upon the Allied governments fighting Germany or the governments-in-exile from their Nazi-occupied countries for the supply of arms. No country treated the Jewish resistance on equal terms with its own national underground. Whatever weapons the Jews received came too few and too late. They were forced to buy arms through illegal channels, paying black-market prices, or to make their own in small and secret shops. Their weaponry was pathetic against the power of German guns.

As for leadership, the most promising was eliminated early by the Nazis. Hitler's policy of quick arrest, imprisonment, and execution of political and labor leaders, intellectuals, and professionals, including seasoned soldiers of earlier wars, decapitated the potential resistance. It was therefore the Jewish youth organizations of all kinds that became the source of resistance leadership. Denied the experience and example of their elders, they had to learn everything for themselves.

Nevertheless, Jews took part in the resistance in all countries. In two ways: as members of the national resistance movements or as part of the specifically Jewish resistance. In the first case, as Henri Michel, historian of the European resistance movements, points out, they were often the leading spirits in the resistance. In his own country, France, he wrote that the Jews "made the greatest contribution of anybody in proportion to their numbers among the population as a whole." At least a million Jews fought in national armies of the Allies or in the resistance forces, a fact not to be forgotten.

Jewish underground groups were of many political beliefs, each growing and learning on its own, usually with few or no links to other groups. Because the Nazi extermination machine went into high gear so early in the war, the Jewish groups had little time in which to develop. The Nazi mobile killing squads began their work in 1939, and annihilation by gas started in the fall of 1941. Within two years the ghettos of Europe were emptied by death.

Worst of all for members of the Jewish underground was the hopelessness of their fight. They faced total destruction, and they all knew it. They had no homeland they could call their own, no place they could dream of returning to. Members of the non-Jewish resistance fought to win back their political freedom and to live at peace once again in their own homes. That was a simple goal, an end to all this terror, which they could hold in sight. But for the Jews there was no such hope to cherish and struggle for. Their only goal was to die with dignity and honor.

15

I Want to Live

Passive resistance was one of the many forms in which the Jews carried on the struggle against the Nazis. Do not think that because arms were not used, it meant no risk. Out of principle or religious belief, some people would not take up a gun. Yet they suffered and died rather than give in to Nazism. There were the prayer groups who congregated in the ghettos and camps, disobeying German orders not to. Jews lost their lives while rescuing Torah Scrolls from burning synagogues. The Hasidim prayed and sang in ghetto streets, even as the Germans clubbed them down. There were many who acted as Janusz Korczak did when he chose death with his orphanage children rather than accept exemption for himself. In Lodz, an underground group monitored Allied radio broadcasts and spread the news until they were betrayed. Writers and actors dared torture and death to satirize the Nazis in ghetto theaters. Teachers took the same chances when they conducted secret schools for children.

It was in Berlin that one of the most incredibly courageous Jewish resistance groups operated. Incredible because, first, it was formed in the very heart of Hitler's Germany. And second, because most of the 32 members of the group were only eleven to fourteen years of age when Hitler came to power. By the time they became active, the four leaders were nineteen years old. These were two married couples, Herbert and Marianne Baum, and Sala and Martin Kochmann.

The Baum group, as it came to be known, started in 1937 with social gatherings at the home of the Baums at Stralanerstrasse 3. The young people met to hear music and talk. Soon the group began discussing politics and the plight of the Jews. Most of the boys and girls were Zionists; two were Communists.

A year later came *Kristallnacht*. The Nazis put about a thousand young Jews to work in the Siemens electric motor plant in Berlin, segregating them in special departments under slave-labor conditions. Herbert and Martin, classmates at school and now old friends, were among them. With their wives, they decided to set up a secret unit to organize a Jewish resistance group. Herbert was allowed to be the one Jew at Siemens who could speak for the others to the factory overseer in charge of Jews. With his small group, Baum succeeded in recruiting many other young Jewish workers.

During 1939 and 1940, the underground group tried to do cultural work among the city's Jews and to lift the morale of those who had sunk into despair. Baum protested to the factory against the low wages and brutal working conditions of the Jews. But in vain, of course.

The group at Siemens began to draw in Jewish youths from other factories. Early in 1941 a man who had escaped from Buchenwald brought them news of the actions of a Jewish resistance group in the concentration camp, led by Rudi Arndt, a young man well known to Berlin's Jews. He had been murdered by the SS a few months earlier. Arndt's example inspired the Baum group to try bolder resistance actions. When the German-Soviet war began in June 1941, the group gained confidence. They felt the Hitler regime was doomed now and they must do all they could to help speed its end.

They began distributing pamphlets and leaflets against the war and Hitlerism, getting them into homes, offices, and factories. Two young women, non-Jewish office workers, joined the group and helped by typing stencils at home.

At night the young people took terrible chances by posting up their broadsides and painting slogans on the walls. Besides sharing in such work, the members had the responsibility of educating

151

people politically wherever they were, and of raising the morale of the Jews around them.

As the deportation of German Jews continued, Baum procured forged Aryan documents in the hope of saving his group, should they fall victim to mass roundups. It cost a great deal to do this and to buy food for group members who were starving on the pitiful rations allotted Jews. The group had to find funds somewhere. They planned and carried out two daring robberies that produced valuable goods which they were able to exchange for cash.

In May 1942, Goebbels opened an exhibition in Berlin called "The Soviet Paradise." Its aim was to persuade the Germans that the war against Russia was necessary; and it was timed to divert attention from German defeats in the East. The Baum group decided to destroy the exhibition. One night seven of them, led by Herbert and Marianne, entered the hall and started a fire with explosives. They left safely as the flames shot up, destroying part of the exhibit before firemen could arrive.

The Gestapo arrested the seven within a few days, then used the fire as an excuse to round up 500 innocent Jews. The Nazis shot half of them and sent the other half to the Sachsenhausen camp.

Herbert Baum was tortured by the Gestapo and beaten to a bloody pulp. Then they dragged his half-dead body through the Siemens plant and demanded that he identify his accomplices. He refused to betray anyone. The Gestapo then said he had committed suicide, but other prisoners testified later that he had been tortured to death.

By the end of the year, the whole Baum group had been captured. Most were condemned to death by a "people's court" and decapitated. Three of the women were given prison terms and sent to concentration camps, where they all died.

Gestapo records found after the war show that some of the young men and women proudly admitted they had shared in the resistance movement. None expressed regret or asked for mercy. One of them, Lotte Rothholz, said under interrogation: "One must use every opportunity to fight against the present regime. I, personally, am not schooled in politics. . . . But one thing was clear to me: as a Jew I must not lag behind. . . . My ties were and remain with Baum."

Such heroic actions were rare inside Germany but more common outside. In the Lithuanian town of Marcinkonis, the Germans lined up freight cars early one November morning in 1942 and ordered the Jews to board them for deportation. The whole community of 370 Jews refused. Four of the local Jews, in a collective report, described what happened:

> Ahron Kobrovsky, President of the Judenrat, cried out, "Jews, whoever wants to live, let him run where he can! The play is with the devil!" The Jews began to run toward the ghetto fence. . . . The commandant began shooting his automatic pistol in all directions. His subordinates did likewise. Cries of women and children were heard and the groans and rattling sounds of the wounded and dying. Everybody ran from the ghetto. The fence was broken down. The panic and pandemonium in the ghetto was indescribable. There were not a few cases of Jewish men beating the armed murderers with their bare fists and trampling them underfoot. The shooting on every side became intensified. Many dead and wounded fell. Groans and wails filled the air. The Germans did not succeed in catching alive one single Jew, man, woman or child, to throw into the freight cars. One hundred five Jews remained lying dead in the ghetto and outside the enclosure. . . .

Jews sometimes set their ghettos afire when the Nazis came to deport them, and in the confusion that followed, took flight. Escape to the forest was often attempted, or hiding in the homes of Christians. Enormous ingenuity, labor, and daring went into the creation of hiding places. There were tunnels dug to the "Aryan side," breaks made under and over and through ghetto walls, burrows built beneath cellars and around sewers. Whole families shared in this form of resistance to Hitler's sentence of death.

Sabotage was resistance, too. In the Minsk ghetto, members of the underground who worked in German factories sabotaged production. Jewish tailors stitched uniforms so that they would come apart, and shoemakers put nails in soles so as to cripple the wearers. Leather goods and textiles were shipped out with secretly produced chemicals, introduced at the last minute, which ruined them for use. The smuggling and other illicit methods used to gather food are another example of passive resistance. Masses of Jews did their best to thwart regulations aimed at destroying the ghetto by hunger.

In the Minsk ghetto the first Judenrat worked closely with the resistance movement. When the Germans ordered the Council to collect fur coats for the army's winter campaign, the Judenrat delivered only half to the Germans. The other half was sent to the partisans, the resistance fighters in the forest. Trapped finally by the Nazis, the whole first Judenrat, except for one member, was publicly executed.

In Kovno, the Jews joining the resistance took this oath:

> I promise to fight with all my powers against the Nazi occupation; to endanger their encampments; disrupt their transport; burn and blow up bridges; destroy railroads; organize and help carry through acts of sabotage at every opportunity and under all circumstances, without sparing myself—and when necessary, to offer up my life.

It was in that Lithuanian ghetto that Leib Segalov burned down three huge ammunition and winter-clothing storehouses. And Yankel Kopelman set fire to a train carrying German reinforcements to the front. Two other resistance members, Mayer Luria and Feivel Forad, were killed while destroying an artillery train.

No one knows how many survived in bunkers—the underground hiding places in the fields and woods. Sometimes it was one person alone; sometimes a small group. They depended upon nearby peasants for food and warnings, or had to forage for themselves, secretly and by night. Moses Feigenbaum, a Polish Jew, was one of four fugitives who dug a pair of bunkers in an orchard close

154

to his own town. His mother, wife, child, and sisters had all been killed by the Nazis. Two Polish women and a young farmhand gave the group help. Feigenbaum told their story:

> With no possibility of washing regularly, we became filthy and vermin-ridden. Delousing was to be, in fact, an important part of our daily routine. Yet when we had completed our bunkers and lay all day without a lick of work to do, we found we'd have to think of a way to keep busy. To begin with, we decided to make our bunkers more comfortable, to turn them into tiny underground cabins instead of the living graves they were. There was plenty of wood only 6 kilometers away, and we made several nightly forays. . . .
>
> After we had tidied the bunkers and covered the wooden floor and walls with straw mats, it was our turn to clean up: nor did we skimp on soap or water. Finally we changed our underwear. Clean and comfortable at last. . . . We grew hungry and began to wish for some home cooking. We managed to get hold of a primus stove. . . . There were lots of things for our table in the fine orchards where we were living. . . .
>
> When sleep will not come, you remember the times you hoped for such a hiding place; now that you have it, you are apathetic and only long for death. . . . In the evening we sit around a pot of warm food, talk and play dominoes. By day we read—if there is something to read. When there is nothing else to do, we sleep. Generally, we sleep a great deal. Though our dreams are bad, it is better than being awake. . . . The tedium of our underground existence becomes unendurable at last. So overpowering is my desire to see another face that I decide to tempt fate by visiting my town. . . .

Feigenbaum crawled through deep snowdrifts to reach his town. In the Jewish quarter he found only ruined buildings and empty houses. Every trace of the Jewish cemetery had been destroyed. He learned that the Germans were rapidly retreating before the Russian Army, which would soon be near.

*I cannot leave without passing our house. As I draw near,
I seem to hear my father's voice, bidding me welcome. I want
to fall down and kiss the cold stones. But I only stand there,
like a Jew at the Wailing Wall. . . .*

Young Abraham Lipser went into hiding, too, but by a different means. He was nineteen when the Germans began to herd Polish Jews into ghettos. With the other six members of his family, who lived in the village of Janow, he was sent to a transit camp. The filthy barracks housed 45,000 Jews. Within seven weeks, 30 percent of them died. One day thousands were picked out and ordered to board trains bound for an unknown station. The Lipser family felt lucky to be together, seated not in one of the cattle cars but in an old passenger coach. Abraham described their departure:

*There were tears on my mother's face; my father's lips moved
silently, in prayer. I looked through the battered window; the
camp was behind us. Suddenly the news spread along the
grapevine that we were headed for Auschwitz. I shuddered. SS
guards patrolled the corridor outside. No escape that way. I
looked at my mother, crouching in a corner of our compartment, her face buried in her hands. It seemed as though we had
stopped breathing. Then I began to think: I am young. . . . I
want to live. . . . I must try my luck and jump off this death
train. . . .*

*I fell back in my seat, laughing like a lunatic. My father shook
his head and motioned me to keep quiet; my mother continued
to weep quietly. Slowly, it grew dark. Suddenly, I rushed to the
window, pulled it open, and threw myself clear. A hail of
bullets from the guns of the guards on top of the train swept to
the right and left of me. I lay motionless. What if the train
should stop? But the train moved on, and now I was alone, with
agonized thoughts of my parents, whom I had left behind. My
knee was bleeding profusely; no matter, I had escaped.*

I crawled through a thicket and found myself on the highway outside Janow. Going back would have been sheer folly. But a lifelong friend of my father's—a Gentile—had a farm and homestead nearby and I headed there. The old man stared at me, utterly bewildered. "Is it really you?" he whispered. Murmuring a prayer in Polish, he took me by the hand, and drew me over the threshold. Our situation was precarious. If I were found, my father's friend and all his family would be exterminated. "But," he added, after a moment's reflection, "I'll take that risk." He proposed to dig a hole in the stable, cover it with boards and pile straw and manure on top. "I'll bring you three square meals a day," he said. "You need fattening up badly." I squeezed his hand without a word; but I knew he understood.

Lipser stayed in that dark hole for two years. In 1944, unable to bear the isolation any longer, he left, made his way to Warsaw, obtained a forged passport, and moved through Austria and Italy to Cyprus and, finally, Palestine. He and one brother were the only ones in the family to survive.

May Day, the traditional labor holiday, became the occasion for demonstrating defiance of the Nazi edict against celebrating it. The Polish town of Menzerzyce had a large number of Jewish workers, mostly brushmakers. It had been a center of the Bund before the war. The Germans were constantly carrying out manhunts on the streets to obtain forced labor. Jews lived in daily fear of capture. Despite that, on May Day the workers marched through the town in small, silent groups. They said nothing, sang nothing. But the whole town saw, and took courage from, their extraordinary demonstration.

Golda Cuker was one of the young underground Bundists in Menzerzyce. Married to a brushmaker, she had two little girls. The Germans had taken several hundred men from the town and put them in a labor camp nearby. Because Golda looked like a Pole, her job in the Bund was to make the rounds of the villages to scrounge food for the starving inmates of the labor camp. She also tried to find secret hideouts for Jewish children on the farms of the peasants. One day, while on such a mission, she disappeared. Her younger sister, doing the same work, suffered the same fate.

It is hard to draw the line between passive and active resistance. The Jew in a ghetto garment factory who chose on his own to sabotage German army uniforms was resisting the Nazis. Not with the gun, with the needle. Acts of sabotage carefully prepared and carried out under direction from an underground center were a more effective form of resistance, perhaps, but each act required the same moral courage.

Another distinction to be made between forms of active resistance is between the armed and the unarmed. The young Jews of occupied France offer a superb example of unarmed resistance. After the big roundup of nearly 13,000 Jews on July 16, 1942, there remained thousands of boys and girls between eleven and eighteen who had escaped the police net. Overnight they became outlaws—their families, homes, funds gone. Many joined the French resistance—the men, women, and children who worked to combat the French Nazi-collaborators and the occupying Nazi forces. Within the Jewish Scout Organization, which had been much like any scout movement before the war, was formed a group of youngsters who carried on unarmed resistance work. Called "The Sixth," they organized a network of small shops which forged "Aryan" documents. (One of the boys, Maurice Lobenberg, proved so resourceful, he produced several hundred identity cards a day.) They founded a string of safe hiding places for Jewish children and adults, supplying the fugitives with identity papers. They brought their charges food and clothing and visited them regularly. Much of this work was done for foreign Jews living in France, Jews especially exposed to danger because they could not speak French and had no local connections. "The Sixth" made contacts with the religious orders, Protestant and Catholic clergy, and friendly municipal authorities and police. They worked with professional smugglers to get fugitives safely across the mountains into refuges abroad. They rescued over 3,000 adults and 1,000 children. At a price: of the 88 boys and girls in "The Sixth," 4 were shot to death by the Nazis, and 26 were deported to death camps.

In occupied Belgium, young Jews set fire to a train carrying raw materials to Germany. They raided bureaus which printed meal tickets, acquiring over a quarter million a month that way. In one coup they stole all 275,000 meal tickets carried on a train heading from Brussels to Ghent. Half the tickets they gave to the resistance and to Jews; the rest they sold to get funds for their work.

JEWISH PARTISAN SONG (ZOG NIT KEINMOL)
Words by Hirsh Glick

Translated from the Yiddish by Aaron Kramer

Never say that there is only death for you
Though leaden skies may be concealing days of blue—
Because the hour we have hungered for is near;
Beneath our tread the earth shall tremble: We are here!

From land of palm-tree to the far-off land of snow
We shall be coming with our torment and our woe,
And everywhere our blood has sunk into the earth
Shall our bravery, our vigor blossom forth!

We'll have the morning sun to set our day aglow,
And all our yesterdays shall vanish with the foe,
And if the time is long before the sun appears,
Then let this song go like a signal through the years.

This song was written with our blood and not with lead;
It's not song that birds sing overhead,
It was a people, among toppling barricades,
That sang this song of ours with pistols and grenades.

So never say that there is only death for you.
Leaden skies may be concealing days of blue—
Yet the hour we have hungered for is near;
Beneath our tread the earth shall tremble: We are here!

ZOG NIT KEINMOL

Words by
HIRSH GLIK

March

Zog nit kein - mol az du geist dem letz - tn
pal - men land biz vai - tn land fun

veg.   Ven him - len blai - e - ne far shte - in bloi - e
shnei,   Mir ku - men on mit un - zer pain mit un - zer

teg.   Ku - men vet noch un - zer ois - ge - benk - te sho, S'vet a
vei.   Vu ge - fa - ln s'iz a shpritz fun un - zer blut, Shpro - tzn

poik ton un - zer trot mir zai - nen do.   Ku - men vet noch un - zer ois - ge - benk te
vet dort un - zer gvu - re un - zer mut.   Vu ge - fa - ln s'iz a shpritz fun un - zer

sho,   S'vet a poik ton un - zer trot mir zai - nen do.   Fun gri - nem
blut,   Shpro - tzn vet dort un - zer gvu - re un - zer mut.

Fine

5 times

16

Ghetto Uprising

Few people realize how widespread armed resistance to the Nazis
was in the several hundred ghettos of occupied Europe. The
Jewish underground organizations made the preparations in many
places, but in others the rebellions were spontaneous. Tuczno, a
small town in the Ukraine, was one such place. The Jews of all
the neighboring towns were wiped out by the Germans with the
help of the anti-Semitic Ukrainians. But Tuczno's Jews were
spared for a time because many worked in the two factories
producing badly needed leather and cloth. Late in the summer of
1942, the Germans ordered a ghetto wall to be built around the
town's 3,000 Jews. A month later, armed Germans and Ukrainians
surrounded the wall as a Gestapo officer ordered all the Jews to
assemble at the gate for deportation. What the Jews did then is
told by Mendel Mann, who learned the story when he later
reached the town with the Russian Army:

> Tuvia Tchubak . . . son of a blacksmith, and another Jew
> named Taflik began to exhort the people not to obey the
> German command but to gather in the synagogue instead.
> When the synagogue was filled, one Jew leaped to the platform
> and called out: "Resist! Do not go voluntarily like sheep!"
> Another jumped on a bench and cried out: "Jews! You should
> know that the pits have already been dug at the Katowice

forest!" The young people were in a fighting mood. One of them shouted: "Let's set the ghetto on fire! Burn it down! Burn everything!"

From somewhere barrels of kerosene were rolled out. Jews fetched ladles, pots, jugs, and other kitchen utensils and filled them with kerosene. Even children came running with pots. The few Orthodox Jews did not participate. They gathered in the large synagogue and read the Psalms.

When night fell, the Jews put the torch to the kerosene-soaked houses. Flames shot up in the air. Soon the whole ghetto was on fire. The Germans and Ukrainians, taken unaware, were stunned and confused, and the Jews turned the confusion into their advantage.

"Smash the fence!" someone cried out. The youths attacked the Germans and Ukrainians with hatchets. From some houses shots rang out and grenades were thrown. Jews stormed the wall and began to run in the direction of the forest, leaving behind them a burning ghetto. The flames were visible for miles around. . . . About 2,000 of the Jews reached the forest, though they fled under continuous German fire and were frequently attacked on the way by Ukrainians who lay in wait in their scattered huts.

By the fall of 1942, only 65,000 Jews were still alive in the Warsaw ghetto that had once held nearly half a million people. The ghetto was a tiny fragment of its old self, clumps of tenements surrounded by high fences of wood or barbed wire. Inside, a small number of left-wing Zionists and pioneer Zionist youths were planning resistance through the Jewish Fighting Organization (JFO) led by twenty-four-year-old Mordecai Anielewicz. Their few arms and explosives were either smuggled in or manufactured in crude workshops within the ghetto. In January 1943, Himmler visited Warsaw and ordered mass deportations to the death camps to resume. On January 18, the ghetto was surrounded, and 8,000 Jews were told to muster for deportation. Although taken by surprise, the ghetto fighters launched guerrilla attacks upon the Nazi forces. The Germans were astounded by the sudden and unexpected armed counterattack. A thousand Jews were killed within a few days, and 6,500 were taken off to death camps. But German losses were heavy, too. The JFO had proved the Nazi "supermen" were not invincible. And now the mass of Jews surviving in the ghetto gave active support to the Jewish boys and girls who had determined to meet the enemy with guns, even though it meant certain death.

The Nazis had to give up their plans for the peaceful, orderly obliteration of what had been the largest Jewish community in Europe. Over the next few months the smaller ghettos nearby were destroyed, as well as Cracow, one of the oldest Jewish communities in Poland. Meanwhile the JFO had grown to nearly 700 fighters, organized into 22 groups. The ghetto people had built bunkers for hiding and defense and had linked them with underground passages so that people could move from house to house and street to street. The fighters collected food, smuggled in or made more arms, and rid the ghetto of informers. Although an appeal for aid was rejected by the Poles outside, preparations for battle went on.

On April 19, German army, police, and SS units invaded in force—tanks, artillery, machine guns—under orders to crush the resistance and destroy the Warsaw ghetto. With revolvers, grenades, rifles, and bricks, the Jews fought back. They battled the Nazis on the streets and in the courtyards, from sewers and rooftops, showing a will to resist that electrified the world. The revolt lasted for weeks, enraging the Nazi leadership, who had thought their vastly superior numbers and firepower would eliminate the ghetto swiftly. In his diary for May 1, Goebbels noted "the exceedingly serious fighting in Warsaw between . . . our own Wehrmacht [armed forces] . . . and the rebellious Jews. . . . It shows what is to be expected of the Jews when they are in possession of arms. . . ."

After four weeks of continuous fighting, the ghetto had still not surrendered, although most of the revolt's leaders had been killed. On May 16, the German commander General Stroop claimed in his official report that the ghetto "no longer exists." The scattered remnants of Warsaw's Jews, hiding in the ruins, clashed here and there with Germans. Some of the fighters survived to take part in the Polish uprising more than a year later, in August 1944. To the Warsaw ghetto goes the honor of carrying out the first major civilian revolt against the Nazis in all of occupied Europe.

A month after the Warsaw Ghetto Uprising, the Jews of Bialystok defended themselves when Nazi troops began to liquidate their ghetto. Bialystok, a Polish city surrounded by immense forests, was a large textile center. When the Germans captured it in 1941, they massacred Jews by the thousands, day after day. Once they crammed several hundred into a synagogue and burned them alive. The murder stopped for a time when the Nazis decided to make use of the city's productive capacity. They pushed the Jews behind ghetto walls and forced them to labor. A resistance movement sprang up, with diverse political wings. One of them was the *Hehalutz*, a pioneer Zionist youth group led by Mordecai Tenenbaum. An extraordinary document exists, recording a debate in the Hehalutz executive committee over what resistance policy to follow. These excerpts show the tormenting decisions the young fighters faced:

MORDECAI: . . . *The few people sitting here are the last Halutzim in Poland. We are entirely surrounded by the dead. . . . We have to decide what to do tomorrow. . . . We can do two things: decide that with the first Jews to be deported now from Bialystok, we start our counterattack, that from tomorrow on nobody is allowed to hide during the action. Everybody will be mobilized. We can see to it that not one German leaves the ghetto alive, that not one factory is left standing. . . . Or we could decide to escape to the woods. . . . Each one of us will have to decide about his own life or death. But together we have to find a collective answer to the common question. . . .*

ISAAC: *What we're really debating is two different kinds of death. Attack means certain death. The other way means death two or three days later. . . .*

HERSHL: . . . *Only one thing remains for us: to organize collec-*

tive resistance in the ghetto, at any cost . . . to write a proud chapter of Jewish Bialystok and our movement into history. . . . Our duty is clear: with the first Jew to be deported, we must begin our counteraction. If anyone succeeds in taking arms from the murderer and going into the woods—fine. . . . I have lost everything, all those near to me; still, there persists the desire to live. But there is no choice. If I thought that not only individuals could save themselves but 50 or 60 percent of the ghetto Jews, I would say that our decision should be to remain alive at any cost. But we are condemned to death.

SARAH: . . . It is better to remain living than to kill five Germans. In a counteraction we will all die, without any possible doubt. On the other hand, in the woods 40 or 50 percent of our people can be saved. That will be our honor and that will be our history. We are still needed; we shall yet be of use. . . .

ENOCH: No illusions! We have nothing to expect but liquidation to the last Jew. We have a choice of two kinds of death. The woods won't save us, and certainly rebellion in the ghetto won't. There remains for us only to die honorably. . . . The woods offer greater opportunities for revenge, but we must not go there to live on the mercy of peasants, to buy our food and lives for money. Going to the woods should mean to become active partisans, but that requires arms. . . . If we do have enough time left, we should acquire arms and go to the woods. But if the Nazi action intervenes, we must answer as soon as they touch the first Jew. . . .

ETHEL: Concretely—if an action is started in the next few days, then our only choice can be a counteraction; but if we are granted more time, we should work along the lines of taking to the woods. I hope I can be equal to the duties that will be imposed on us. It may be that in the course of events I shall be strengthened. In any case, I am resolved to do everything that needs to be done. . . . We are going to perform a desperate act, whether we want to or not. Our fate is sealed, and there remains for us only the choice between one kind of death and another. I am calm.

Tenenbaum's own conviction prevailed: that the duty of the resistance was to fight inside the ghetto. In July 1943, the resistance groups finally achieved unity in the Anti-Fascist Fighting Bloc. Only a month later, the Nazis sent in troops to destroy the 40,000 Jews in the Bialystok ghetto. All the resistance had to fight with were twenty-five rifles, a hundred small arms, a few tommy guns, one machine gun, some hand grenades, and axes, scythes, knives, and bayonets. The Nazis drove the Jews into six narrow streets of the ghetto. The resistance forces tried to breach the ghetto wall so that everyone still alive could make for the forest to join up with the partisans. They failed. Miserably armed and with no room to maneuver, they had no chance against tanks and armored cars. "Even if we are too weak to defend our lives," said the resistance proclamation posted on the ghetto walls, "we are strong enough to defend our Jewish honor and human dignity, and thus prove to the world that we are captive but not defeated."

In four days of August 1943, the Jews of Bialystok were annihilated. And so it went—in Warsaw, Minsk, Slonim, Nieswiez, Czestochowa, Glebokie, Lachwa, Mazowiecki, Kleck, Breslau—Jews in the ghettos took up arms to resist their slaughter. Many Jews, like those of Tuczno, escaped to the forests or mountains and formed or joined partisan units. After Germany attacked Soviet Russia, guerrilla fighting increased. With Russia in the war, the Communists became much more active in the resistance movement throughout Europe. In Eastern Europe, when the Russian Army took the counteroffensive, the partisans often linked up with Russian-led guerrilla units.

The Jews who had survived the rebellion against the Nazis in Marcinkonis escaped to the forest. Their region, on the border between Lithuania and Byelorussia (in the western region of Soviet Russia), was a battleground for German army units and Russian partisans. The commander of the Russian partisans, a Jew named Davidov, befriended the Marcinkonis Jews, equipping them with weapons dropped by parachute. He forbade non-Jewish partisans to molest them. The Marcinkonis partisans, under their chief, Yitzhok Kobrovsky, plunged into guerrilla warfare. They derailed a military train and blew up a locomotive in their first action. Then they wrecked a dozen ammunition cars and ruined stretches of railway tracks. Their success led many other Jews hiding in the forests to join the partisans.

The Minsk ghetto supplied more Jews for the partisan movement than any other ghetto in Eastern Europe. Over 10,000 escaped into the forest with the help of the ghetto underground; they formed 7 partisan detachments. Some of them were mixed with non-Jewish Byelorussians, and the others were either all Jewish or mainly Jewish. One unit, headed by the underground leader Zorin, established a Family Camp of 600 men, women, and children. Its function was to supply the partisan units with boots and clothing and to operate a central laundry, bakery, and hospital for them. A combat section made up of the Family Camp's younger members protected the group and took part in the operations of other partisan units, too. Unlike the general population of Poland, the Byelorussians were friendly to Jews and made it possible for thousands to survive. The Jewish and Byelorussian undergrounds worked in close collaboration.

Another family unit of forest fighters was led by the three Bielski brothers of Byelorussia. It began in December 1941 when their parents were killed by the Germans. With 15 other Jews— friends and relatives from nearby villages—they formed a guerrilla unit armed with six rifles bought from a peasant. Their first action was to shoot a German guard and take his rifle and ammunition. That winter Jews streamed into their camp, and within a year the Bielski division of 500 fighters was ambushing German troops, dynamiting their trains, and wrecking their communications. The group gave protection to many old men and women and to children, although they hampered movement and drained food supplies. But noncombatants helped by cooking, building barracks, staffing the infirmary, and teaching the children. One of the major actions of the Bielskis was to wreck the granaries and burn the farms the Germans had taken over to support their armies. As the Wehrmacht retreated in the summer of 1944, the Bielski unit took part in the heavy fighting. Over 1,000 Jews in the family unit survived, thanks to the protection of the partisans.

Especially useful to the forest fighters were Jewish physicians and medical workers. One of the many who earned combat leadership was Dr. Ezekiel Atlas, a young Polish Jew educated as a physician in Western Europe. When the ghetto of Dereczyn was destroyed by the Nazis in July 1942, a handful of Jews escaped to the forest. Dr. Atlas molded a Jewish partisan unit out of them. To avenge the loss of their families, they attacked the German garrison in Dereczyn one night. After several hours of fighting, they captured 44 Germans, most of them police, and shot them in the same square where the Nazis had slaughtered Jews only three weeks earlier. This action, one of the first victories by a partisan unit, won wide recognition for the fighting talents of Jews. Atlas, whose parents and sister had been killed by the Nazis, would say to his partisans, "Our private lives finished on the day our fellow Jews were massacred. Every day of life that is given us belongs not to ourselves but to our slaughtered families. We must avenge them." A little man, Atlas looked funny wearing boots far too big for his small feet. He carried a submachine gun and a pistol, and the pockets of his ragged army pants bulged with hand grenades. He was enormously popular with his men. His unit destroyed bridges, blew up trains, and salvaged equipment and weapons abandoned by the German troops. In one attack on a German garrison, they killed 127 soldiers and captured 25 wagon-loads of weapons. Dr. Atlas' military career lasted less than six months. Only thirty-two, he was killed in December 1942 when Germans attacked his unit.

Just as heroic were the young men and women who acted as couriers between the partisans in the forests and the underground inside the ghettos. Zelda Tregar carried messages from partisan units into the Vilna ghetto, slipping through the barbed wire and past the sentries at least eighteen times. And from the ghetto she carried dozens of guns back to the guerrilla bases. She smuggled herself into several concentration camps and guided some of the prisoners to freedom. Four times she was captured by the Nazis, and four times she escaped from their hands.

Vitka Kempner had the same indomitable spirit. Like Zelda, she was one of the Vilna-ghetto fighters who fled to the forest to continue resistance. Once she hauled a suitcase packed with explosives into Vilna, a distance of 20 miles, and blew up an electric generator. Another time she slipped into the concentration camp at Kailis and led 60 prisoners to partisan camps. By herself she succeeded in capturing 2 Gestapo agents.

The core of partisan action was physical force. Any available weapon and any imaginable means were used to kill the Nazi enemy and thwart his murderous plans. The risks were enormous, and the casualties high. To die of a bullet was the easiest death to be faced. Many died gruesome and lingering deaths devised by experts in torture. And they died at the hands not only of Germans but of anti-Semitic and greedy Poles, Lithuanians, Hungarians, Rumanians, Letts, Estonians, Ukrainians . . . even other, native guerrilla bands. While fighting to destroy the Nazis, many of these peoples were just as hostile to the Jews, and freely plundered and butchered them.

This was the tragic case in Eastern Europe. It was not the same in Western Europe. The French historian of the Holocaust, Leon Poliakov, explains why:

> Great as was the tragedy of the Western Jews, it was not marked by the same brutality as in the East. The causes were various: on the one hand, the Jews in the West were more assimilated to their non-Jewish environment, they were few in number and were more widely distributed among the general population; on the other hand, the enemy pursued a different policy in the West than in the East. In the West he acted with greater cunning and circumspection, to avoid shocking the native population, which was not as contaminated with the germ of anti-Semitism as the peoples of Eastern Europe. The chief factor, however, was the attitude of the native population and the sympathy the Jews in the countries of the West received from their fellow citizens. The difference is most clearly revealed in the numerical comparison of the number of Jews who perished. In Poland more than 90 percent of the Jews were liquidated, in France . . . the losses were less than 30 percent.

In Nazi-occupied Paris there was a Jewish partisan unit which lived an altogether different life than the forest partisans of Eastern Europe. One of its leaders was Abraham Lissner, a veteran of the International Brigades who fought against Franco in Spain in the 1930s. In his diary he recorded what was required of a partisan in Paris:

1. Sever relations with everyone who is not connected with the underground organization.
2. Abandon one's legal residence and begin living alone on an illegal basis.

These strict measures had to be adopted so that the partisan, if arrested, would not drag others along with him. A partisan must spend his entire day outdoors even when he has no special reason for being on the street. To avoid arousing suspicion of his concierge and neighbors, he has to leave his room every morning at the same time, as though he were going to work, and return in the evening like all the other residents. Full-time partisans receive a monthly wage from the organization, since they have no other means of earning a living. A single partisan gets 1600 francs [$36.54] a month; a married one with one child gets 1900. On this salary the partisan must pay the rent for his room and eat every meal in a different restaurant.

Jewish women shared the danger equally with the men.

Like the men, they carry out sabotage acts, using time bombs and grenades. One day three of these women lost their lives in the course of carrying out their duty. As they came out of the Métro station Porte d'Orleans, they were caught in a police roundup, which is a daily occurrence in Paris. One of the women, Helen Kro, who was carrying the grenades, was the first to be caught. The police took her home, hoping to find there a weapons cache. While they were searching, Helen threw herself out of the window rather than fall into the hands of the Gestapo. She was killed instantly. The other two, who were also caught by the Vichy police, were later deported and were never heard from again.

Partisan plans could go terribly wrong, as Lissner's Paris diary showed:

April 1942: Our leadership decided that on May 1 the Jewish partisans should carry out an anti-German act of a military character by placing a time bomb close to a barracks occupied by German soldiers. Salek Bot, a young violinist, and Hersz Zimmerman, an engineer, undertook the difficult task of preparing the explosive.

April 27: Today the Jewish partisans suffered a severe loss. As our two comrades were putting together the bomb, in a small hotel room in the fifth arrondissement, something went wrong. The bomb exploded, killing Salek on the spot and critically wounding Hersz. But that was not all. After the explosion the police occupied the hotel room and succeeded in arresting 17 of our comrades who, not knowing about the accident, had come to see Salek and walked into a police trap.

But there were many successes, too.

November 10, 1942: Today Marcel Rayman and Nathan Lemberger placed a time bomb at the window of a hotel on Montmor, which is inhabited by high-ranking German officers, causing great damage.

November 15: A group of Jewish partisans, led by Mayer List, today placed two time bombs at the window of a German military barracks on rue de Vaugirard, killing several Hitlerites while they were eating breakfast. In this action two Jewish women participated. They carried the bombs.

November 26: Today the Jewish partisans have to their credit two anti-German acts. They bombed a hotel on rue St. Florine, and they placed two time bombs on a street not far from Place de la Concorde, where German soldiers usually pass in groups.

The bombs exploded just as the soldiers arrived, causing severe losses in their ranks. Both acts went through without a mishap.

Sometimes the Jewish partisans worked with others in joint actions. Germans holding key positions in occupied nations were the targets of assassination. Karl Ritter was the aide to Fritz Sauckel, the head of Hitler's compulsory-labor service. Ritter had deported hundreds of thousands of Frenchmen to Germany for slave labor. The partisan chiefs condemned him to death and assigned three men to carry out the sentence: a Spaniard; a German anti-Fascist; and Marcel Rayman, a young French Jew. The three waited for Ritter near his garage one September morning in 1943. As his car came out, the Spaniard fired at him. Ritter tried to leap out of his car, but Rayman shot him dead. Caught later and tortured for three months by the Gestapo, Rayman said to the Nazis: "I'm a Jew, and as a Jew I could not live without fighting against you." He was executed in February 1944.

Marching songs such as this were popular
among the young people's groups in the ghettos.
They were written to inspire purposeful
defiance of the Nazi war machine.

→»

Nor, bruder, an anderer ritm
Vet bald tsu dayn oyer dergeyn,
Un di, vos far shrek
Geven ersht farshtekt,
Shpanen mit undz nit aleyn.
Tsu eyns, tsvey, dray,
Tsu eyns, tsvey, dray,
Di geslech, dem toyer farlozt!
S'hot der trot aza klang
Gor anander gezang,
Ven du geyst un du veyst shoyn farvos.

But, brother, another rhythm
Will soon reach your ear,
And those who were hidden
In fear only yesterday,
Now march right along with us, not alone.
And one, two, three,
And one, two, three,
Leave the lanes and the gates behind!
For your step now resounds
With a new kind of sound,
When you march and know the reason why.

Revolt in the Death Camps

Even in the death camps there were bloody uprisings against the fate Hitler had decreed. That there could be any resistance within the camps seems almost impossible. The divisions among the prisoners were many: a score of different languages; a whole range of political beliefs; varying religious faiths; differences in class origin, in education, and in occupation or profession. These differences the SS were always ready to intensify in order to keep the inmates disunited.

And what time was there to think or plot, when the tiny spark of energy or spirit that might still live within a prisoner went into finding the extra morsel of food to stay alive or to stave off the next blow from a brutal kapo? To plan resistance, conspirators need to be able to meet and talk. But these prisoners were never alone. They slept, ate, washed, toileted, and worked, always under watchful eyes and listening ears. Cut off from the world outside, pitted against one another, it was natural to sink into hopelessness.

How could resistance be organized under such conditions? Yet it was. Small, inadequate, but it did appear. Shaye Gertner, who was fourteen when he was deported from Lodz to a camp, told how even in Dachau a group of prisoners practiced sabotage. He was one of the slave laborers in a munitions plant dug into the earth below Dachau. They made a weapon called "Fau 1."

We not only produced bombs but manufactured the entire apparatus, including five bombs and a bombing vessel. . . . Former Soviet officers working with us taught us the art of sabotage. They taught us to drop a few straws into receptacles filled with gasoline. When the mechanism would be heated, the straws would ignite and cause havoc. We also mixed sand with the powder. The sabotage was not carried out carefully, and one day all the apparatus was destroyed in the same manner. A military commission investigating the explosion found sand and straw. A rollcall of those employed in the tunnel followed, separating the Jews, the Poles and the Russians. Every tenth man was condemned to death—160 deaths all told. Thereafter, the supervisor was most rigorous. At the least suspicion 30 to 50 workers would be hanged. Later we resumed the sabotage so that the two or three parts of the apparatus would be defective.

In Treblinka, a young Jew from Warsaw, who worked in one of the companies handling disposal of the victims, saw his wife and child being taken to the gas chamber. He pulled out a concealed knife and stabbed the SS guard to death. The same desire for revenge burned in most hearts, but only in some did it develop into a plan for revolt. In Treblinka, the revolutionary was a fifty-year-old doctor from Warsaw named Julian Chorazyski. He gathered a small group of plotters, among them Stanislaw Kohn. They figured out a way to get dynamite and arms, but before they could move ahead, the doctor was caught and took poison. His place was taken by Galewski, an engineer from Lodz, and a Jewish army officer from Czechoslovakia, Captain Zielo.

When the last transport of Jews from Warsaw brought in news of the ghetto revolt, the conspirators decided this was the time for their uprising. But months dragged on before they were ready. And day after day they watched thousands of Jews, stripped naked, lining up before the building which contained the twelve gas chambers. Finally the conspirators fixed the time to act: Monday, August 2, 1943, at 5 P.M. The plan was to ambush and kill the chief murderers, disarm the guards, cut the telephone wires, and then destroy the killing center by fire. They would do this by filling a disinfectant sprinkler with gasoline stolen from camp trucks, spraying the gas over all the buildings they could, and then, at a given signal, hurling hand grenades at the "disinfected" sites to set them on fire. After this, they would free the Poles from a camp a mile away, join up with them, and escape to the woods to organize a partisan band. Only the 60 people who planned the revolt knew its details. As Stanislaw Kohn told:

At two in the afternoon the distribution of weapons began. Young Salzberg and the other boys searched their employers' huts for weapons and took them to the garage. . . . The door of the armory was opened with our key and Jacek, the Hungarian boy, slipped inside, climbed onto the windowsill at the end of the room, cut out a small square in the glass with a diamond and handed out the bombs and other weapons to Jacob Miller . . . who put them on his refuse cart. The arms were carried to the garage. . . .

Spirits grew agitated and no one could keep the secret. The leaders therefore decided to start the revolt an hour before the agreed time. Punctually at four the messages were sent to all groups with orders to assemble immediately in the garage to get their weapons. Rudek from Plotzk was responsible for the distribution.

Anyone coming to fetch weapons had to give the password, "Death," to which the reply was "Life!" "Death—Life!" "Death—Life!" Cries of enthusiasm arose as the long-hoped-for guns, revolvers and hand grenades were distributed. At the same time the chief murderers of the camp were attacked. Telephonic communication was cut and the watchtowers were set on fire with gasoline. Captain Zielo attacked two SS guards with an ax and made his way to us to take over the command.

Near the garage stood a German armored car, but Rudek had swiftly immobilized the engine. Now the car served as a lair from which to fire on the Germans. Our gunfire felled the

Sturmführer *Kurt Majdkur and other German dogs. The armory was taken by assault and the weapons distributed. We already had 200 armed men. The others attacked the Germans with axes and spades.*

We set fire to the gas chambers, burned the fake railway stations with all the notices . . . burned the barracks. . . .

The flames and the reports of the firing roused the Germans, who began to arrive from all sides. SS and police arrived from Kosow, soldiers from the nearby airfield and finally a special section of the Warsaw SS. Orders had been given to make for the neighboring forest. Most of our fighters fell but there were many German casualties. Very few of us survived.

Of the 700 prisoners drawn into the action, about 150 to 200 managed to escape. And of these, only a dozen lived through the war. More than 20 Germans were killed in the revolt. But the number who survived or the number who died is not a measure of the revolt's success. The Treblinka resistance had known they could get no support from the outside. Their goal had been to destroy the killing center. As Samuel Rajzman, one of the few survivors, said later, "We realized our aim fully and in martyrdom. Treblinka was wiped out. A fortress of horrible Nazism was erased from the face of the earth."

Scarcely two months later, another revolt occurred in the death camp of Sobibor. Here is the terse report of it made by the Order Police in the district of Lublin on the next day, October 15:

On October 14, 1943, at about 5 P.M., revolt of the Jews in SS-camp Sobibor, 25 miles north of Chelm. They overpowered the guards, seized the armory, and after firefight with camp garrison, fled in unknown direction. Nine SS murdered, 1 SS man missing, 2 foreign guards shot to death.

Approximately 300 Jews escaped; the remainder were shot to death or are now in camp. Military police and armed forces were notified immediately. The area south and southwest of Sobibor is now being searched by police and armed forces.

The uprising was all the more extraordinary because it came out of an underground movement that originated only three weeks before the attack. Its leader was Alexander Pechersky, a Jew and a Russian Army officer captured by the Germans. He directed about 70 other Jewish prisoners of war. Those who escaped split up. The Polish Jews went west, toward Chelmno, where they knew the language and the people. The Soviet Jews headed east. The Dutch, French, and German Jews knew not where to turn in this strange land. Half the escapees were killed quickly—by land mines, SS, police, troops, pursuing planes, and anti-Semitic Poles. The group that followed Pechersky, some 60 men and women, reached safety in a Russian partisan camp. Research indicates that 10 SS men and 38 Ukrainian guards were killed.

Two days after the uprising, Himmler ordered Sobibor to be totally destroyed. The revolt had succeeded in eliminating a death factory which had taken the lives of 600,000 Jews.

One year later, and another revolt in a death camp. This time at the largest—Auschwitz. It happened not long after the Nazi killers recorded the highest number of victims to be destroyed in one day: on July 24, 1944, they gassed and burned 46,000 Jews at Auschwitz.

The Russian armies were taking Poland from the Nazis. Soon they would reach the death camps. The Germans wavered over whether to blow up the crematoriums or to keep their fires burning. They decided to speed up the death machine.

For months the underground in Auschwitz had been trying to reach the outside world with convincing proof of Hitler's stepped-up exterminations. Their hope was to break through the universal indifference toward the condemned Jews. The reports which had already been sent abroad had not convinced any of the Allied governments to act. The underground decided that only the personal testimony of prisoners would achieve their aim.

But how get a prisoner out of Auschwitz? Its combined labor and death camps were encircled by electrified barbed wire, deep ditches, high watchtowers. Guards and informers were everywhere. For 40 kilometers around, the territory had been declared "prohibited" and cleared of all civilians. Still, prisoners did escape. At least 230 attempts have been recorded; about 80 succeeded. Of these, five were not personal flights but escapes of Jewish prisoners organized by the underground to tell the world what was happening inside the death factory. The five were Siegfried Lederer, Walter Rosenberg, Alfred Wetzler, Arnost Rosin, and Czezlaw Mordowicz. The first man escaped on April 5, 1944; the next two on April 7; and the last two on May 27. Their detailed eyewitness testimonies, given to both private and governmental agencies, were accompanied by concrete proposals that the Allied governments should bomb from the air the gas chambers, the crematoriums, the industrial plants, and the railway lines used for the daily transports. They urged that public threats of retaliation be given repeatedly over the radio, and they asked that the Vatican issue a strong condemnation of the Nazi crimes. The hope was to prevent the final stage of the extermination process being prepared by the Nazis for the spring of 1944.

But what was done? Only verbal protests were made. Nothing practical was attempted in answer to the appeals. The reply of the United States government, for instance, was that the planes for bombing raids on the camps could not be spared in the midst of war. "Such an effort, even if practicable, might provoke even more vindictive [acts] by the Germans," said John J. McCloy, the U.S. Assistant Secretary of War.

The only thing left for the prisoners to do was to try to destroy Auschwitz by themselves.

One day Rosa Robota, a twenty-three-year-old Jewish prisoner (from the Polish town of Ciechanow) who worked in the clothing-supply section of Auschwitz, was approached by a stranger. Rosa was a member of *Hashomer Hatzair*, the Socialist-Zionist youth movement which prepared people for kibbutz life in Palestine. The stranger was Noah Zabladowicz, a member of the Jewish underground in the camp. He told her the organization was planning a general uprising during which they wanted to blow up the gas chambers and crematoriums. They needed explosives to do it. Since she had friends from her hometown who worked in the explosives section of the Krupp munitions plant at Auschwitz, would she try to get those young women to help?

Rosa was eager to carry out the task. Her own family, together with almost all the other Jews of Ciechanow, had been sent to the gas chamber. She hated the Nazis. She soon had 20 young women smuggling dynamite and explosive charges out of the plant. They hid the tiny dynamite wheels in their bras or in secret pockets of their clothing. The material was made into bombs by a Russian prisoner who used empty sardine tins for casings. The bombs were then hidden in various parts of the huge camp. One cache was hidden by the Sonderkommando who lived next to the crematoriums where they worked. The Sonderkommando was the group of Jewish prisoners assigned by the SS to spend the last few months of their lives operating the crematoriums. Each group was then itself gassed and replaced by another crew. Rosa brought the bombs to the Sonderkommando, who hid them in the handcarts in which the corpses of prisoners who had died in the barracks were taken to the crematoriums.

Before the uprising could take place, the Sonderkommando learned that their turn to be gassed was imminent. They had no choice but to act now or go to their deaths passively. They blew up Crematorium Number 3, killing 4 SS men and wounding others. Then they broke through the barbed wire and fled. About 600 prisoners got loose in the uproar, but the Nazis hunted them down and killed them.

With the help of informers, the SS traced the trail of the explosives to the young women in the munitions plant. Three who worked there—Esther, Ella, and Regina (their full names are unknown)—together with Rosa Robota, were seized for grilling. Fearing Rosa would not be able to withstand the terrible torture, the underground found a way to get her friend Noah in to see her. The Jewish kapo let him into her cell, and then left them alone briefly. Noah reported later:

> When I became accustomed to the dark, I noticed a figure wrapped in torn clothing, lying on the cold cement floor. She

turned her head toward me and I hardly recognized her. After several minutes of silence she began to speak. She told me of the sadistic methods the Germans employed during interrogations. It is impossible for a human being to endure them. She told me that she took all the blame upon herself and that she would be the last to go. She had betrayed no one.

I tried to console her but she would not listen. I know what I have done, and what I am to expect, she said. She asked that the comrades continue with their work. It is easier to die when one knows that the work is being carried on.

I heard the door squeak. Jacob ordered me to come out. We took leave of each other. It was the last time that I saw her.

Rosa gave Noah a last message for the underground. It ended with the Hebrew greeting of the Hashomer Hatzair: "Khazak v' hamatz"—Be strong and brave.

Soon after, all the Jewish prisoners in the camp were marched to the execution site. They stood at the foot of the gallows and watched as Rosa and her three comrades died. Auschwitz had not broken them. While they lived, they fought back.

The Only Hope Left

Russian troops advanced into Poland, freeing prisoners in the Maidanek death camp in July 1944. Even as the Germans, knowing they had lost the war, retreated, they saw to it that half a million Hungarian Jews were gassed in day-and-night operations in Auschwitz. Not until the end of November did that death machine halt. The SS blew up the crematoriums, destroyed the camp records, and burned the vast storehouses of looted property. To prevent the liberation of survivors in the other camps of Poland and the Baltic region, the SS pushed them west, back toward Germany, throughout the bitter winter months. They dumped the prisoners inside Germany, where Hitler was making his last stand. Given no food, ravaged by typhus, the human wrecks died by the tens of thousands. Just as freedom came in sight . . .

In the last days of the war, the Nazi leaders holed up in Hitler's concrete bunker beneath the debris of bombed Berlin. A week before Germany surrendered, Hitler committed suicide. In his final testament he continued to vilify the Jews, "the universal poisoner of all nations." They had caused the war, not he. He charged the new leaders of Germany to "uphold the racial laws."

A few weeks before the war's end, seventeen-year-old Elie Wiesel was one of the 20,000 prisoners still alive in Buchenwald. The SS decided to evacuate them all before the American troops could reach them. As they began taking their last victims to the assembly point, shots rang out and grenades exploded all over the camp. The resistance had chosen this moment to revolt. The SS fled; the underground was in charge. Wiesel describes the moment:

> At about six o'clock in the evening, the first American tank stood at the gates of Buchenwald.
>
> Our first act as free men was to throw ourselves onto the provisions. We thought only of that. Not of revenge, not of our families. Nothing but bread.
>
> And even when we were no longer hungry, there was still no one who thought of revenge. On the following day, some of the young men went to Weimar to get some potatoes and clothes—and to sleep with girls. But of revenge, not a sign.
>
> Three days after the liberation of Buchenwald I became very ill with food poisoning. I was transferred to the hospital and spent two weeks between life and death.
>
> One day I was able to get up, after gathering all my strength. I wanted to see myself in the mirror hanging on the opposite wall. I had not seen myself since the ghetto.
>
> From the depths of the mirror, a corpse gazed back at me.
>
> The look in his eyes, as they stared into mine, has never left me.

Twenty months after he had been taken prisoner in Italy and deported to Auschwitz, Primo Levi came home.

> Of 650, our number when we had left, three of us were returning. . . . My house was still standing, all my family was alive, no one was expecting me. I was swollen, bearded, and in rags, and had difficulty in making myself recognized. I found my friends full of life, the warmth of secure meals, the solidity of daily work, the liberating joy of recounting my story. I found a large clean bed, which in the evening (a moment of terror) yielded softly under my weight. But only after many months did I lose the habit of walking with my glance fixed to the ground, as if searching for something to eat or to pocket hastily to sell

for bread; and a dream full of horror has still not ceased to visit me, at sometimes frequent, sometimes longer, intervals.

It is a dream within a dream, varied in detail, one in substance. I am sitting at a table with my family, or with friends, or at work or in the green countryside; in short, in a peaceful relaxed environment, apparently without tension or affliction; yet I feel a deep and subtle anguish, the definite sensation of an impending threat. And in fact, as the dream proceeds, slowly or brutally, each time in a different way, everything collapses and disintegrates around me, the scenery, the wall, the people, while the anguish becomes more intense and more precise. Now everything has changed to chaos; I am alone in the center of a grey and turbid nothing, and now, I know what this thing means, and I also know that I have always known it; I am in the Lager once more, and nothing is true outside the Lager. All the rest was a brief pause, a deception of the senses, a dream; my family, nature in flower, my home. Now this inner dream, this dream of peace, is over, and in the outer dream, which continues, gelid, a well-known voice resounds: a single word, not imperious, but brief and subdued. It is the dawn command of Auschwitz, a foreign word, feared and expected: Get up, 'Wstawàch!

What of the future? Was there any hope for the Jews of Europe, the remnant, the one out of three, still alive? As Primo Levi was journeying home from Auschwitz to Italy, his train passed through Germany, and he caught a glimpse of the future.

After Munich we realized that we had taken on board an entire contingent: our train consisted no longer of 60, but of 61 cars. A new car was traveling with us towards Italy at the end of our train, crammed with young Jews, boys and girls, coming from all the countries of Eastern Europe. None of them seemed more than twenty years old, but they were extremely self-confident and resolute people; they were young Zionists, on their way to Israel, traveling where they were able to, and finding a path where they could. A ship was waiting for them at

*Bari; they had purchased their car, and it had proved the
simplest thing in the world to attach it to our train: they had not
asked anybody's permission, but had hooked it on, and that
was that. I was amazed, but they laughed at my amazement:
"Hitler's dead, isn't he?" replied their leader, with his intense
hawklike glance. They felt immensely free and strong, lords
of the world and of their destinies.*

Many East European Jews who outlived Hitler felt they could
no longer stay in their homeland. One of them was Tuviah Friedman, who later became known as a hunter of Nazi criminals.
Poland after the war only tolerated the Jews, while pretending
that anti-Semitism no longer existed. Friedman decided to leave
for Palestine, to join with Jews from all over the world in the fight
for a national home. Early one morning in the spring of 1946,
together with a group of others, he climbed down a mountain and
crossed the Polish border into Czechoslovakia.

*I looked behind me, at Poland. My father and his father were
buried there. Jews had lived in Poland for a thousand years,
their condition fluctuating like the fever of a malaria patient.
One hour back, I thought, is the country in which I was born,
to which I had shown allegiance, which I had tried to love;
now, here, with a packful of clothing, happy that I had succeeded in crossing its frontier, I sat catching my breath, gather-
ing up my strength for an unknown future. I had perhaps a
total of ten dollars, and some socks and shirts and underclothing.
Everything else was in my heart.*

A few months later Poland proved how right Tuviah Friedman
had been. A pogrom erupted in Kielce on July 4, 1946. A mob
stormed the Jewish community center and murdered 41 Jews. Like
a string of bombs, pogroms exploded all over the country.

After the great hour of liberation, many of the ex-prisoners
suffered intense attacks of depression. They were no longer
Untermenschen, but did going on with life make any sense? No
one was left to live for. There was no home to return to.

Then they began to think, Maybe somebody else is alive. Wife, husband, parents, children, friends, people in the hometown? Simon Wiesenthal saw the day he had prayed for all those years—the day the last SS man ran away, as American tanks rumbled into the Mauthausen camp. But he didn't believe in miracles. He *knew* all of his people were dead. His wife—buried in the rubble of Warsaw. His mother—dead in the death camp of Belzec. Still, he wrote the Red Cross in Geneva; they replied that his wife was dead. He watched the other survivors begin their hunt.

There was no mail service. The few available telephone lines were restricted to military use. The only way to find out whether someone was alive was to go and look. Across Europe a wild tide of frantic survivors was flowing. People were hitch-hiking, getting short jeep rides, or hanging on to dilapidated railway coaches without windows or doors. They sat in huddled groups on hay carts, and some just walked. They would use any means to get a few miles closer to their destination. To get from Linz to Munich, normally a three-hour railroad trip, might take five days. Many of them didn't really know where to go. To the place where one had been with his family before the war? To the concentration camp where the family had last been heard of? Families had been torn apart too suddenly to make arrangements for the day when it would be all over.

. . . And yet the survivors continued their pilgrimage of despair, sleeping on highways or in railroad stations, waiting for another train, another horse-drawn cart to come along, always driven to hope. "Perhaps someone is still alive. . . ." Someone might tell where to find a wife, a mother, children, a brother—or whether they were dead. Better to know the truth than to know nothing. The desire to find one's people was stronger than hunger, thirst, fatigue. Stronger even than the fear of border patrols . . . of men saying, "Let's see your papers."

And then the miracle: his wife had survived. They found each other six months after the war ended.

The Wiesenthals, husband and wife, were among the lucky

ones. Hitler's Final Solution had not destroyed all of Europe's Jews. Not quite all. One out of ten of Poland's prewar Jewish community of 3.3 million was still alive in 1945. But for most of those who had escaped the gas chambers, this place could no longer be home. Even when governments changed, Jews saw that they could still be victims. Through all of Poland's shifts—from czarist province to independent republic and now to postwar Communist state—there was one constant: anti-Semitism.

Palestine was the only hope left. Governments throughout the world had refused to take Jews in when they were trying to flee Hitler. None offered to take in the remnant now. The illegal entry to Palestine, which had begun when Britain curbed immigration in 1939, continued after the war. By 1947, 113,000 Jewish refugees had slipped through the barriers. The violent struggle for Palestine among Jews, Arabs, and the British went to the United Nations for solution. The United Nations agreed on a partition plan for separate Jewish and Arab states in Palestine. The Jews accepted the proposal; the Arabs refused it. The British departed, and the independent state of Israel was proclaimed on May 14, 1948.

The immediate consequence was the invasion of Israel by seven Arab states. A UN truce ended the war, leaving Israel with more territory than the UN Partition Plan had allotted it. The new state opened its doors to the ingathering of exiles. Thousands of Jewish settlers from all over the world, aided by the Joint Distribution Committee, made their way to Israel. (One out of every seven Israelis in those early years came out of a concentration camp. One out of every three Israelis had lost one or more relatives to Hitler's extermination machine.) By 1975 Israel's Jewish population stood at 2.6 million.

The hope of finding common ground between Arabs and Jews is still alive, although challenges from the Arab world resulted in the two wars of 1967 and 1973. To Jews everywhere, Israel was defending the right of the Jewish people to exist. It was a right Jews had to secure for themselves. They could count on no one else. Thousands of years of bitter experience had taught them that as long as Jews were a minority, they would always be persecuted. The Holocaust had signified their near-destruction. It had happened once; it could happen again.

And the rest of the world? It did little about the Jews during the war, and not much more after it.

What about the perpetrators of the crime? The four leading Allied powers—the United States, the Soviet Union, Britain, and France—debated what to do about them. Finally it was agreed to try the instigators of the war for their "crimes against humanity." The chief charge was that of aggressive war. In preparing for the Nuremberg Trials of 1945 and carrying them out, the prosecutors gave evidence demonstrating that the Germans had committed enormous crimes against humanity. Robert H. Jackson, the U.S. Chief Prosecutor at Nuremberg, said the world had never "witnessed slaughter on such a scale, such cruelties and inhumanities, such wholesale deportations of people into slavery, such annihilations of minorities. . . . If we cannot eliminate the causes and prevent the repetition of these barbaric events, it is not an irresponsible prophecy to say that the twentieth century may yet succeed in bringing the doom of civilization."

The first trial began late in 1945 before an international military tribunal. The 22 men in the dock had held key positions in the Nazi machinery of destruction. Now they claimed ignorance. They "did not know," they said, that the Jews were to be exterminated. Even so, they protested that whatever they did, they did under orders. From whom? From Adolf Hitler, of course.

When this trial ended in October 1946, 12 of the defendants were sentenced to death, 3 to life imprisonment, 4 to lesser terms, and 3 were acquitted. There was no popular movement to launch mass trials of the huge number of Germans who were part of the death machine. Not even among the Jews. The trials of "lesser offenders" that followed were the result of a tangled elimination process, chiefly in the American and British zones of occupied Germany. Less than 200 men all told were brought into court in the American zone. They included generals, judges, industrialists, physicians, concentration-camp administrators, and leaders of the mobile killing squads. After judgment, great reductions of sentence were often given by the U.S. High Commissioner to Germany and his clemency board.

The Germans themselves did little to punish their own war criminals. The small number convicted in German courts got unbelievably easy sentences, and they and the great number who were exonerated went back to their everyday lives, shrugging off the past. Many retired with pensions. Some entered politics, rising to high office. There were many notorious Nazis who disappeared immediately after the war, finding refuge in Spain, Latin America, the Middle East, and the United States. (Adolf Eichmann was one of those discovered in hiding and tried in 1961 for his crimes.)

Later, the West German government offered "amends" to the Jews. Three measures were adopted: restitution, reparations, and indemnification. These provided benefits only to the surviving victims; nothing was done to compensate for the 6 million dead.

Restitution meant the return of identifiable property to the original owner or payment for it if he did not wish to take it back. The total amounted to several hundred million dollars. Reparations were paid as the result of a treaty made in 1952 between West Germany and Israel. Israel received some $700 million in commodity shipments; and survivors in other countries, about another $100 million. Through the indemnification program, West Germany paid for various kinds and degrees of losses suffered as the direct or indirect result of official German action. The full benefits went only to victims who had resided on German soil at some time.

THE DEATH TOLL

Country*	Jewish population, September 1939	Number of Jews dead	Percentage of Jews dead
Poland	3,300,000	2,800,000	85.0
Soviet Union (occupied area)	2,100,000	1,500,000	71.4
Rumania	850,000	425,000	50.0
Hungary	404,000	200,000	49.5
Czechoslovakia	315,000	260,000	82.5
France**	300,000	90,000	30.0
Germany	210,000	170,000	81.0
Lithuania	150,000	135,000	90.0
Holland**	150,000	90,000	60.0
Latvia	95,000	85,000	89.5
Belgium**	90,000	40,000	44.4
Greece	75,000	60,000	80.0
Yugoslavia	75,000	55,000	73.3
Austria	60,000	40,000	66.6
Italy**	57,000	15,000	26.3
Bulgaria	50,000	7,000	14.0
Miscellaneous#	20,000	6,000	30.0
Totals	8,301,000	5,978,000	72.0

* Considered within prewar borders
** Figures include Jewish refugees
\# Denmark, Estonia, Luxembourg, Norway, and the city of Danzig, Poland

(Source: Hannah Vogt, THE BURDEN OF GUILT)

Never to Forget

This, then, is not the Holocaust—what words can be equal to it?—but merely something about it. We who did not live it can know at least this much.

To forget what we know would not be human.

To remember it is to think of what being human means. The Holocaust was a measure of man's dimensions. One can think of the power of evil it demonstrated—and of those people who treated others as less than human, as bacteria. Or of the power of good—and of those people who held out a hand to others.

By nature, man is neither good nor evil. He has both possibilities. And the freedom to realize the one or the other. "The power of choosing between good and evil," said the early Christian philosopher Origen, "is within the reach of all."

There are forces at work in the world which cut off human response. They make it possible for people to commit terrible crimes without knowing or feeling they are doing wrong. Eichmann was one such person. He saw himself as only a tiny cog in the machine destroying inhuman objects, the Jews. He was "doing his duty." He was the product of a totalitarian state. Such systems deform and depersonalize those they rule. Whether of the right or the left, they make functionaries out of us, mere nobodies reduced to so much machinery.

Thus it is that the massacre of a whole people can be organized and carried out by the State, relying upon this "human" machinery. The individual conscience vanishes in the face of "orders from superiors." Only a few people in Germany still made their own judgments of right or wrong, and acted accordingly. They did not let the State decide for them; they took personal responsibility in questions of morality. Even under the worst conditions of terror some people will resist evil.

If there had been more people like that—not only in Germany but everywhere—the Holocaust might not have happened. Before the war started, there were many chances to save the Jews. The world was indifferent. After the war began, there were still ways to save some. The will to do it was not there. The conscience of man, the sympathy of one human being for another, failed. Perhaps, it could be argued, by that time it was too late. But who even tried hard enough?

If few did, then it is hard to believe that the shock of Auschwitz makes impossible another Holocaust. Emil Fackenheim, the philosopher and a survivor of the Holocaust, asks: "Is the grim truth not rather that a second Holocaust has been made more likely, not less likely, by the fact of the first? For there are few signs anywhere of that radical repentance which alone could rid the world of Hitler's shadow."

In Indochina, in Indonesia, in Biafra, in Bangladesh, there have been mass exterminations: all post-Hitler. Who speaks of them now? Hitler himself, contemplating the extermination of the Jews, said, Who remembers that the Turks massacred a million Armenians only a little while ago?

Indifference is the greatest sin.

It can become as powerful as an action. Not to do something against evil is to participate in the evil. Karl Jaspers, the German philosopher, wrote shortly after the Holocaust that every German was to be blamed for "crimes committed in his presence or with his knowledge. If I fail to do whatever I can to prevent them, I too am guilty. If I was present at the murder of others without risking my life to prevent it, I feel guilty."

From Alexander Donat, a survivor of the Warsaw ghetto, there is this last word:

The shame and horror of our century have to do with the conduct of the European powers, the Gentile world. Even if not one Jew had resisted, there would be no justification either to condemn the victims or to divert attention from the crimes of the murderers. The central issue must not be forgotten: it is a moral issue, the issue of what the world has done and permitted to be done. To insist upon making the world uncomfortable with the memory of its guilt is a necessity for that moral reconstruction which may alone prevent a repetition of our Holocaust.

CHRONOLOGY

1933

Jan.	30	Germany's President Hindenburg appoints Adolf Hitler, head of the Nazi party, as Reich Chancellor (Prime Minister).
Feb.	2	Political demonstrations are banned in Germany.
	27–28	Reichstag fire. State of emergency declared. Constitutional rights suspended.
Mar.	5	Last general election to Reichstag: Nazis receive 44% of vote. First "individual acts" against Jewish citizens.
	23	First concentration camps: Dachau opens.
Apr.	1	First official boycott of Jewish shops and businesses throughout Germany.
July	14	Nazi party made Germany's one and only legal party. Political opposition punishable by law. Jews deprived of German citizenship.
Dec.	1	Hitler declares German state and Nazi party are one by law.

1934

Jan.	2	Laws for sterilization of "unfit."
Aug.	2	On death of Hindenburg, Hitler becomes Germany's Head of State and Commander-in-Chief of Armed Forces.

1935

Sept.	15	Reichstag passes anti-Semitic Nuremberg Laws: the "Reich Citizenship Law" defines "Jews" and "mixed-blood" status, and the "Law for the Protection of

German Blood and German Honor" prohibits marriage between Jews and Aryans.

1936

Mar.	7	German troops occupy the Rhineland, violating the Versailles treaty.
Oct.	25	Hitler and Mussolini form Rome-Berlin Axis for war.
Nov.	25	Germany and Japan sign military pact.

1937

July	16	Buchenwald concentration camp opens.
Nov.	5	Hitler discloses war plans at secret meeting.

1938

Mar.	13	German army takes over Austria and applies anti-Jewish laws.
Apr.	22	Decree issued to eliminate Jews from Germany's economy and to take over their assets.
June	15	Arrests begin of all "previously convicted Jews," including those convicted of such minor offenses as traffic violations.
July	6	At international conference at Evian, France, participating nations fail to provide refuge for German Jews.
Sept.	29	In Munich pact, Britain and France agree to allow Hitler's annexation of Czech Sudetenland.
Oct.	5	Passports of German Jews marked with letter "J."
	28	Thousands of Jews in Germany expelled into Poland.
Nov.	7	Herschel Grynszpan shoots member of German embassy staff in Paris, resulting in:
	9	"Night of Broken Glass" (*Kristallnacht*), in which government organizes pogroms against Jews throughout Germany.
	12	At Nazi conference on "Jewish problem," Goering orders "expiation payment" by Jews and their exclusion from economic and cultural life. About 26,000 Jews arrested and sent to concentration camps; 1,000 killed.
	15	Jewish children expelled from German schools.
Dec.		Decree orders "Aryanization" (compulsory expropria-

tion) of Jewish shops, industries, and businesses throughout Germany.

1939

Jan.	1	German Jews compelled to use first name of "Sarah" or "Israel."
	30	In Reichstag speech, Hitler prophesies "the extermination of the Jewish race in Europe" in case of war.
Mar.	15	German troops occupy Czechoslovakia, without opposition from other nations.
Aug.	23	Germany and Soviet Union sign non-aggression pact.
Sept.	1	Germany invades Poland: World War II begins. SS and German army cooperate in widespread pogroms and mass executions in Poland.
	3	Great Britain and France declare war on Germany.
	27	Poland surrenders to Germany. Forced labor announced for Polish Jews.
Oct.	12	Nazis begin deporting Jews from Austria and Moravia to Poland.
Nov.		Hans Frank made Governor General of occupied Poland: establishes first Polish ghetto; begins to set up a Jewish Council (*Judenrat*) in each city.

1940

Jan.		First resistance actions by Jewish youth in Poland.
Apr.	9	German invasion of Denmark and Norway.
May	10–18	German invasion of Holland, Belgium, Luxembourg, France. Holland surrenders. Belgium surrenders. Auschwitz concentration camp (later to become a death camp) opens.
June	10–22	Italy enters war as Hitler's ally. France surrenders.
Sept.	27	Japan joins Germany and Italy to form Axis Powers. Soon Hungary, Rumania, and Slovakia join Axis.
Nov.	15	Warsaw ghetto sealed off.
Dec.		Emmanuel Ringelblum begins work on secret archives of Jewish life in Warsaw ghetto.

1941

Feb.	22	Deportation of Dutch Jews to Mauthausen concentration camp begins; Holland's workers strike in sympathy with Jews.

June	22	Hitler breaks non-aggression pact with Stalin; invades Soviet Union. Nazi massacres begin in Eastern Europe.
July	12	Britain and Soviet Union sign military treaty to cooperate against Hitler.
	31	Goering appoints Heydrich to carry out "Final Solution of the Jewish Question."
Sept.	1	Jewish star introduced: all German Jews (ages six up) must wear it, beginning September 19.
Oct.	14	German Jews deported to Lodz, Poland (beginning of general deportations from Reich).
Dec.	7	Japanese attack Pearl Harbor. U.S. joins Allied Powers (Britain and USSR) in war against Axis Powers.
	8	Chelmno death camp begins functioning. Jewish partisans begin operating in Minsk area.

1942

Jan.	15	Nazis begin transporting Jews from Lodz to Chelmno death camp.
	20	Wannsee conference on Nazi plan to exterminate European Jews.
	21	Unified Partisan Organization set up in Vilna ghetto. Jewish resistance groups grow throughout Eastern Europe.
April		Transports from ghettos to death camps extend over Poland.
June	1	Treblinka death camp opens. Jewish star introduced in Nazi-occupied France and Holland.
July	22	Jews offer armed resistance during liquidation of Nieswiez ghetto. Similar actions follow in other ghettos.
	28	Jewish Fighting Organization (JFO) set up in Warsaw ghetto.
Oct.	4	All Jews in German concentration camps ordered deported to Auschwitz.
Dec.	17	Allied nations pledge punishment for extermination of Jews.

1943

| Jan. | 18 | Warsaw-ghetto Jews launch first civilian armed resistance to Nazis: four days of street fighting. |

Apr.	19	At Bermuda conference, U.S. and British delegates fail to produce plans for saving Nazi victims.
Feb.	2	German Sixth Army surrenders at Stalingrad: turning point of war.
Mar.		Transports to death camps increase from many parts of Nazi-occupied Europe.
	13	New crematoriums open in Auschwitz.
Apr.	19	Warsaw Ghetto Uprising begins.
June	11	Deportation of Jews from Polish ghettos to death camps ordered. Deportations extended to Soviet ghettos.
Aug.		Russian army captures Kharkov. Revolt in Bialystok ghetto. Inmates revolt in Treblinka death camp.
Oct.	1	Expulsion of Danish Jews ordered: Danish underground rescues 7,000; only 475 captured by Germans.
	14	Inmate uprising in Sobibor death camp.
	20	UN War Crimes Commission set up.

1944

June	6	D-Day: Allied invasion of Nazi-occupied Western Europe begins in Normandy, France.
July	20	Attempted assassination of Hitler fails.
	24	Russian troops liberate Maidanek death camp.
Aug.	6	SS begins to drive concentration-camp inmates back into interior of Germany, as advancing Soviet army threatens to free them.
	23	Paris liberated by Allies.
Oct.		Last gassings in Auschwitz.
	26	Himmler orders destruction of Auschwitz crematoriums, as Nazis try to hide evidence of death camps.

1945

Jan.	11	Soviet troops take Warsaw.
	17–26	Soviet troops liberate 80,000 Jews in Budapest; take Auschwitz, find a few thousand survivors.
Feb.	4	Allies in Yalta conference plan spheres of influence for postwar Europe.
Apr.	11–28	U.S. troops liberate Buchenwald and Dachau. British troops liberate Belsen concentration camp. Soviet

troops reach outskirts of Berlin. Nazis evacuate prisoners from Sachsenhausen and Ravensbruck camps. SS commits last massacres.

	30	Hitler commits suicide in Berlin bunker.
May	2	Berlin surrenders.
	7	Germans surrender to Allies unconditionally.
Aug.	6	First atom bomb dropped by U.S. on Hiroshima, Japan.
	15	Japan surrenders: World War II ends.
Nov.	22	Nuremberg Trials of Nazi leaders begin.

BIBLIOGRAPHY

What crystallized the decision to write this book was a pamphlet by Henry Friedlander called *On the Holocaust: A Critique of the Treatment of the Holocaust in History Textbooks.* * (Professor Friedlander, a German Jew, was eleven years old when the Nazis deported him to the Lodz ghetto and from there to Auschwitz.) A study of American high school textbooks, he said, showed that "their treatment of Nazism was brief, bland, superficial, and misleading." Racism, anti-Semitism, and the Holocaust were either ignored or dismissed in a few lines. History textbooks designed for the colleges and universities were "not substantially better." He quotes the anti-Nazi historian Golo Mann: "Darkness hides the vilest crime ever perpetrated by man against man."

Beyond the bounds of the traditional textbook there is a large literature on many aspects of the Holocaust. A bibliography of those studies is available in English, prepared by Jacob Robinson: *The Holocaust and After: Sources and Literature in English*, Israel Universities Press, Jerusalem, 1973. It includes books, articles, films, plays, television productions, and even reviews of books. The 353 pages contain 6,637 entries.

My purpose was to write a short book, a book that could be read by young and old, by people who know little or nothing about the Holocaust. I have tried to provide enough historical background to make its place in time clear. The military aspects of the war it is linked to are only touched upon, nor is there much detail on the inner politics of the Nazi regime or the international politics which are inseparable from the event.

My focus is the human experience: what happened to the Jews of Europe, what it meant to them, and what it means for all the rest of us, Jews and non-Jews alike. This is told in their own words as much as possible. There is no attempt to be comprehensive. A book of this kind can only suggest the nature of what many agree is the most significant and terrible event of the twentieth century.

* Anti-Defamation League of B'nai B'rith, New York, 1973.

For those who want to read more, there are now several large-scale histories of the Holocaust. The newest is by Lucy Dawidowicz: *The War Against the Jews 1933–1945*. The others, also listed in the history section of this bibliography, are by Hilberg, Levin, Manvell, Poliakov, and Reitlinger.

The titles in my bibliography are chiefly those I made use of myself. They are presented under various headings somewhat arbitrarily, in order to help readers find the material of their special concern. Obviously, there is considerable overlapping; the divisions are not rigid. I have omitted references to articles in historical journals, especially the many I drew from in the *Yivo Annual of Jewish Social Science*. Nor do I include important literary materials—novels, stories, poems, plays—or what can be found in the nonprint media—films, filmstrips, slides, tapes, exhibits, recordings. Lists of such material can be obtained from the American Association for Jewish Education, 114 Fifth Avenue, New York, N.Y. 10011.

A final word on the oral history of the Holocaust. A number of institutions here and abroad are conducting oral history programs on the Holocaust. They are taping and transcribing interviews with survivors and, sometimes, with the next generation as well. The largest such collection is at the Yad Vashem Institute in Jerusalem.

Anti-Semitism

*Arendt, Hannah, *The Origins of Totalitarianism*. Cleveland: The World Publishing Company, 1958.

Cohn, Norman, *Warrant for Genocide: The Myth of the Jewish World-Conspiracy and the Protocols of the Elders of Zion*. New York: Harper & Row, Publishers, Inc., 1969.

Davies, Alan T., *Anti-Semitism and the Christian Mind: The Crisis of Conscience After Auschwitz*. New York: Herder & Herder, 1969.

*Flannery, Edward H., *Anguish of the Jews: Twenty-Three Centuries of Anti-Semitism*. New York: The Macmillan Company, 1965.

Littell, Franklin, *The Crucifixion of the Jews*. New York: Harper & Row, Publishers, Inc., 1975.

*Mosse, George L., *Germans and Jews: The Right, the Left, and the Search for a "Third Force" in Pre-Nazi Germany*. New York: Howard Fertig, Inc., 1970.

Poliakov, Leon, *The Aryan Myth*. New York: Basic Books, Inc., Publishers, 1974.

* Available in paperback.

Samuel, Maurice, *The Great Hatred*. New York: Alfred A. Knopf, Inc., 1948.

*Schweitzer, Frederick M., *A History of the Jew Since the First Century A.D.* New York: The Macmillan Company, 1971.

Weinreich, Max, *Hitler's Professors*. New York: YIVO, 1946.

History

Dawidowicz, Lucy S., *The War Against the Jews 1933–1945*. New York: Holt, Rinehart and Winston, Inc., 1975.

Fisher, Julius S., *Transnistria: The Forgotten Cemetery*. New York: A. S. Barnes & Co., Inc., Yoseloff, 1969.

Fishman, Joshua R., ed., *Studies on Polish Jewry, 1919–1939*. New York: YIVO, 1974.

*Hilberg, Raul, *The Destruction of the European Jews*. New York: Quadrangle/The New York Times Book Co., 1961.

*———, ed., *Documents of Destruction*. New York: Quadrangle/The New York Times Book Co., 1971.

*Hitler, Adolf, *Mein Kampf*. Boston: Houghton Mifflin Company, 1943.

*Jarman, T. L., *The Rise and Fall of Nazi Germany*. New York: New York University Press, 1956.

Katz, Robert, *Black Sabbath: A Journey Through a Crime Against Humanity*. New York: The Macmillan Company, 1969.

*Kogon, Eugen, *The Theory and Practice of Hell: The German Concentration Camps and the System Behind Them*. New York: Octagon Books, Division of Farrar, Straus & Giroux, Inc.

*Levin, Nora, *The Holocaust: The Destruction of European Jewry, 1933–1945*. New York: T. Y. Crowell Co., 1968.

Levy, Claud, and Tillard, Paul, *Betrayal at the Vel D'Hiv*. New York: Hill & Wang, 1969.

Manvell, Roger, and Fraenkel, Heinrich, *The Incomparable Crime: Mass Extermination in the Twentieth Century: The Legacy of Guilt*. New York: G. P. Putnam's Sons, 1967.

Pilch, Judah, ed., *The Jewish Catastrophe in Europe*. New York: American Association for Jewish Education, 1968.

Poliakov, Leon, *Harvest of Hate: The Nazi Program for the Destruction of the Jews of Europe*. Westport, Conn.: Greenwood Press, Inc., 1971.

Presser, Jacob, *The Destruction of the Dutch Jews*. New York: E. P. Dutton & Co., Inc., 1969.

*Reitlinger, Gerald, *The Final Solution: The Attempt to Exterminate* the Jews of Europe, 1939–1945. New York: A. S. Barnes & Co., Inc., 1961.

*Schoenberner, Gerhard, The Yellow Star: The Persecution of the Jews in Europe, 1933–1945. New York: Bantam Books, Inc., 1973.

The Nazi Regime

*Allen, William Sheridan, The Nazi Seizure of Power: The Experience of a Single German Town, 1930–1935. New York: Franklin Watts, Inc., 1965.

*Bullock, Alan, Hitler: A Study in Tyranny. New York: Harper & Row, Publishers, Inc., 1964.

Dallin, Alexander, German Rule In Russia, 1941–1945: A Study of Occupation Policies. New York: St. Martin's Press, Inc., 1957.

*Heiden, Konrad, Der Fuehrer: Hitler's Rise to Power. Boston: Houghton Mifflin Company, 1944.

Merkl, Peter H., Political Violence Under the Swastika. Princeton: Princeton University Press, 1975.

*Neumann, Franz, Behemoth: The Structure and Practice of National Socialism. New York: Harper & Row, Publishers, Inc., 1966.

Noakes, Jeremy, and Pridham, Geoffrey, Documents on Nazism, 1919–1945. New York: The Viking Press, Inc., 1974.

Reitlinger, Gerald, The S.S.: Alibi of a Nation, 1922–1945. New York: The Viking Press, Inc., 1957.

*Schoenbaum, David, Hitler's Social Revolution: Class and Status in Nazi Germany, 1933–1939. New York: Doubleday & Co., Inc., 1967.

Stern, J. P., Hitler: The Fuehrer and the People. Berkeley: University of California Press, 1975.

*Trevor-Roper, Hugh R., The Last Days of Hitler. New York: The Macmillan Company, Collier Books, 1966.

Personal Accounts

Cohen, Elie A., The Abyss: A Confession. New York: W. W. Norton & Company, Inc., 1973.

Donat, Alexander, The Holocaust Kingdom: A Memoir. New York: Holt, Rinehart and Winston, Inc., 1969.

*Frank, Anne, The Diary of Anne Frank. New York: Pocket Books, 1971.

Frankl, Viktor E., *From Death-Camp to Existentialism: A Psychiatrist's Path to a New Therapy.* Boston: Beacon Press, Inc., 1959.

*Goldstein, Bernard, *The Stars Bear Witness.* New York: The Viking Press, Inc., 1949.

*Goldstein, Charles, *The Bunker.* New York: Atheneum Publishers, 1970.

Hart, Kitty. *I am Alive.* London: Abelard-Schuman, Ltd., 1961.

Heimler, Eugene, *Concentration Camp.* New York: Pyramid Communications, Inc., 1961.

Kantor, Alfred, *The Book of Alfred Kantor.* New York: McGraw-Hill, Inc., 1971.

*Katsh, Abraham, ed., *The Warsaw Diary of Chaim A. Kaplan.* New York: The Macmillan Company. Collier Books, 1973.

Kruk, Herman, *Diary of the Vilno Ghetto.* New York: YIVO, 1961.

Lengyel, Olga, *Five Chimneys: The Story of Auschwitz.* Chicago: Ziff Davis Publishing Co., 1947.

*Levi, Primo, *Survival in Auschwitz: The Nazi Assault on Humanity.* New York: The Macmillan Company, Collier Books, 1961.

Lind, Jacov, *Counting My Steps: An Autobiography.* New York: The Macmillan Company, 1969.

Meed, Vladka, *On Both Sides of the Wall: Memoirs from the Warsaw Ghetto.* Israel: Ghetto Fighters' House and Hakibbutz Hameuchad Publishing House, 1972.

*Nyiszli, Miklos, *Auschwitz: A Doctor's Eyewitness Account.* New York: Frederick Fell, Inc., 1960.

*Ringelblum, Emmanuel, *Notes from the Warsaw Ghetto: The Journal of Emmanuel Ringelblum.* New York: McGraw-Hill, Inc., 1958.

Shapell, Nathan, *Witness to the Truth.* New York: David McKay Co., Inc., 1974.

Wells, Leon W., *The Janowska Road.* New York: The Macmillan Company, 1963.

*Wiesel, Elie, *Night.* New York: Hill & Wang, 1960.

The Judenrat

Trunk, Isaiah, *Judenrat: The Jewish Councils in Eastern Europe under Nazi Occupation.* New York: The Macmillan Company, 1972.

Tushnet, Leonard, *The Pavement of Hell: 3 Leaders of the Judenrat.* New York: St. Martin's Press, Inc., 1972.

Yivo, *Imposed Jewish Governing Bodies Under Nazi Rule*. New York: YIVO Institute for Jewish Research, 1972.

Resistance

Ainsztein, Reuben, *Jewish Resistance in Nazi-Occupied Eastern Europe, with a Historical Survey of the Jew as a Fighter and Soldier in the Diaspora*. New York: Barnes & Noble, Inc., 1974.

*Bauer, Yehuda, *They Chose Life: Jewish Resistance in the Holocaust*. New York: The American Jewish Committee, 1973.

Donat, Alexander, *Jewish Resistance*. New York: Warsaw Ghetto Resistance Organization, 1964.

*Elkins, Michael, *Forged in Fury*. New York: Ballantine Books, Inc., 1971.

Friedman, Philip, *Their Brothers' Keepers*. New York: Crown Publishers, Inc., 1957.

Horbach, Michael, *Out of the Night*. New York: Frederick Fell, Inc., 1967.

Kimche, John and David, *The Secret Roads: The "Illegal" Migration of a People, 1938–1948*. London: Secker & Warburg, 1954.

Mark, Ber, *Uprising in the Warsaw Ghetto*. New York: Schocken Books, Inc., 1975.

Michel, Henri, *The Shadow War: Resistance in Europe 1939–1945*. New York: Harper & Row, Publishers, Inc., 1973.

*Suhl, Yuri, ed., *They Fought Back: The Story of the Jewish Resistance in Nazi Europe*. New York: Crown Publishers, Inc., 1967.

Refugees and World Response

Bauer, Yehuda, *Flight and Rescue: Brichah*. New York: Random House, Inc., 1970.

Feingold, Henry L., *The Politics of Rescue: the Roosevelt Administration and the Holocaust, 1938–1945*. New Brunswick, N.J.: Rutgers University Press, 1970.

*Flender, Harold, *Rescue in Denmark*. New York: Simon & Schuster, Inc., 1963.

Friedman, Saul S., *No Haven for the Oppressed: United States Policy Toward Jewish Refugees, 1933–1945*. Detroit: Wayne State University Press, 1973.

*Morse, Arthur D., *While Six Million Died: A Chronicle of American Apathy*. New York: Random House, Inc., 1967.

Postwar Trials

*Arendt, Hannah, *Eichmann in Jerusalem: A Report on the Banality of Evil.* New York: The Viking Press, Inc., 1964.

Hausner, Gideon, *Justice in Jerusalem.* New York: Harper & Row, Publishers, Inc., 1966.

Robinson, Jacob, *And the Crooked Shall be Made Straight: The Eichmann Trial, the Jewish Catastrophe, and Hannah Arendt's Narrative.* New York: The Macmillan Company, 1965.

*Wiesenthal, Simon, *The Murderers Among Us.* New York: McGraw-Hill, Inc., 1967.

Anthologies

Friedlander, Albert H., *Out of the Whirlwind: A Reader of Holocaust Literature.* New York: Union of American Hebrew Congregations, 1968.

*Glatstein, Jacob; Knox, Israel; and Margoshes, Samuel, eds., *Anthology of Holocaust Literature.* New York: Jewish Publication Society of America, 1969.

Halperin, Irving, *Messengers From the Dead: Literature of the Holocaust.* Philadelphia: The Westminster Press, 1970.

Korman, Gerd, ed., *Hunter and Hunted: Human History of the Holocaust.* New York: The Viking Press, Inc., 1973.

Search for Meaning

Berkovitz, Eliezer, *Faith After the Holocaust.* New York: KTAV Publishing House, Inc., 1973.

Borowitz, Eugene. *How Can a Jew Speak of Faith Today.* Philadelphia: The Westminster Press, 1969.

Cohen, Arthur A., *Arguments and Doctrines: A Reader of Jewish Thinking in the Aftermath of the Holocaust.* New York: Harper & Row, Publishers, Inc., 1970.

*Fackenheim, Emil L., *God's Presence in History: Jewish Affirmation and Philosophic Reflections.* New York: Harper & Row, Publishers, Inc., 1972.

*Rubenstein, Richard L., *After Auschwitz: Radical Theology and Contemporary Judaism.* Indianapolis: The Bobbs-Merrill Co., Inc., 1966.

*Wiesel, Elie, *One Generation After.* New York: Random House, Inc., 1970.

Bradfisch, Otto, 64
Buch, Walter, 54
Buchenwald camp, 28, 138, 151, 182–183, 196; revolt in, 183, 199
Bund, Jewish Labor, 62, 63, 100, 109, 110, 111, 114, 115, 157

camps. See concentration camps, death camps, labor camps, names of individual camps
Catholic Center, 18, 20
Catholic Church, Jews and, 3–5, 54–55, 60, 127–128, 131
Chamberlain, Houston S., 8, 10
Chamberlain, Neville, 44
Chelmno camp, 106, 107, 198
children: in Auschwitz, 122; in Baum group, 149–153; beaten at school, 35–36; bound for Israel, 184–185; deported from France, 114; deported from orphanage, 112–113; in forced labor, 90–93; in French resistance, 158; in Hitler Youth, 39; in ghettos, 85–87; made informers, 22–24; murdered by killing squads, 66–70; poem by, 103; as saboteurs, 174–175; in secret schools, 99–100; in underground, 137–138
Chorazyski, Julian, 175
Christianity, Jews and, 3–6, 30, 153

Christian Social Workers' party, 8
collaboration, 145–147
Communists, 18, 19, 20, 28, 151, 166
concentration camps, 26, 27–30
conversion to Christianity, 32
Cracow ghetto, 78, 100, 107, 163
Crusades, x, 4
Cuker, Golda, 157–158
Czechoslovakia: subjugation of, 44, 59, 196, 197; Jews in, 44
Czerniakow, Adam, 146
Czernowitz ghetto, 79
Czestochowa, 90

Dabrowa, 144
Dachau camp, 28, 55, 131, 174, 195, 199
Dawidowicz, Lucy, 58–59, 202
death camps, Jewish losses in, 117, 178. See names of individual camps
Deblin, 90
deportations of Jews, 96, 98, 108, 162; from Austria, 117, 197; from Belgium, 117; from Czechoslovakia, 107, 117, 197; from France, 113, 117, 123, 133; from Galicia, 107; from Germany, 108, 117, 152, 198; from Greece, 117, 124–125; from Holland, 107, 117, 197; from Hungary, 117, 130; from Italy, 117, 121; from Lithuania, 153; from Yugoslavia, 117

Jewish Fighting Organization, 162–164, 198

Jewish self-defense. See resistance

Jews: assets taken, 196; assimilation of, 32, 61–62; and Atonement Payment, 56, 196; awareness of Holocaust events, 33; boycott against, 34, 195; businesses Aryanized, 56, 196; converting, 32; curfew for, 37; death toll of, 190; denied jobs, 34–35, 196; denied public relief, 56; of Eastern Europe, 60–65, 169; emigration of, 35, 42–47; expelled from schools, 196; forced labor of, 53, 56–57, 88–94; homes looted, 52, 54; identification of, 37–38; imprisoned, 52; lose German citizenship, 37, 195; mass arrests of, 43, 52, 196; in mixed marriages, 37, 196; murdered, 52, 196; and Nuremberg Laws, 36–38, 195; offered "amends," 189; Orthodox, 143–144; as outsiders, 32; of Poland, 59–65; and quota system, 37; rescue by Christians, 53; segregation of, 37; shops ransacked, 51–52, 54; starvation of, 80, 81, 106; stereotypes of, 4, 7; and suicide, 97–98, 140, 146, 152; synagogues destroyed, 43, 51, 53, 164; wages cut, 57

Jong, Louis de, 139–140

Judaism, 6

Judenrat. See Jewish Councils

Kaplan, Chaim, 95–96, 97–98, 101, 104, 110

Karski, Jan, 114–115

Katzenelson, Yitkhok, 146

Kempner, Vitka, 168

Kielce pogrom, 185

killing squads. See *Einsatzgruppen*

Kobrovsky, Ahron, 153

Kobrovsky, Yitzhok, 166

Kochmann, Martin, 150–153

Kochmann, Sala, 150–153

Kohn, Stanislaw, 175–177

Kopelman, Yankel, 154

Korczak, Janusz, 112–113, 150

Korn, N., 99

Kovno ghetto, 145, 154

Kremer, Johann, 132–133

Kristallnacht (Night of Broken Glass), 51–57, 151, 196

Kro, Helen, 170

Krupp, A. G., 89, 180

labor camps, 88–94

Laval, Pierre, 113

"Law for the Protection of German Blood and German Honor," 36–37

League of Anti-Semitism, 8

League of Nations, 43

Lederer, Siegfried, 179

Lemberger, Nathan, 171

Levi, Primo, 121–125, 183–185

Levin, Moshe, 145

Ley, Robert, 22

Libau, M. I., 52–53

Lichtenberg, Bernard, 55

Peretz, Aaron, 86–87
Pinkas, Oscar, 96–97
poems, 98, 99, 100, 103
pogroms, x, 54, 56, 60–61, 63, 185, 197
Poliakov, Leon, 169
Popovicz, Traian, 79
population, Jewish: of Austria, 43; of Eastern Europe, 60; of Europe, 107; of Germany, 31, 35; of Israel, 187; of Poland, 59, 187; of Soviet Union, 65; of United States, 45; of Warsaw, 77, 114, 162
Protestant churches, Jews and, 5, 54–55

Rabinowicz, Chaim, 146
racism: and anti-feminism, 26; doctrine of, xi–xii, 73, 201; against Jews, 59, 61, 73; against Poles, 59
Rajzman, Samuel, 177
Rath, Ernst vom, 51, 56
Ravensbruck camp, 28, 131, 199
Rayman, Marcel, 171, 172
Red Cross, 89, 186
refugees. See emigration
Reich Association of Jews in Germany, 56
Reichstag fire, 19, 195
Representative Council of Jews in Germany, 38, 56
resistance, Jewish, 137–181, 197, 198; active, 109, 111, 158; armed and unarmed, 158, 161; in Belgium, 159; in Berlin, 150–153; condi-
tions of, 144–145, 147–148; in death camps, 174–181; degree of, 139, 141; in the Diaspora, 142–143; forms of, 140–141, 143–144, 153–159; in France, 148, 158–159, 170–172; in Holland, 138; and Jewish Councils, 145–147; led by youth, 148, 150–153, 161–164; passive, 98, 143, 150, 158; in Russia, 137–138; by women, 165, 168–169, 170, 179–181
Rhineland, remilitarized, 42, 59, 196
Riga ghetto, 92, 108–109, 138
Ringelblum, Emmanuel, 84–85, 93, 95, 98, 101–102, 104, 147, 197
Ritter, Karl, 172
Robinson, Jacob, 201
Robota, Rosa, 179–181
Roechling, 89
Roehm, Ernst, 21
Rome-Berlin Axis, 196
Roosevelt, Franklin D., Jewish refugees and, 43, 45
Rosenberg, Reuben, 90–91
Rosenberg, Walter, 179
Rosin, Arnost, 179
Rothholz, Lotte, 152–153

SA (Storm Troopers), 21, 34
sabotage, 141, 152, 153–154, 158, 159
Sachsenhausen camp, 28, 29, 199
St. Louis (ship), 46–47
Salaspils camp, 92

Warsaw Ghetto Uprising, 141, 147, 162–164, 175, 198, 199
Weidemann, *Landesbischof*, 55
Weimar Republic, 12, 13, 32
Weizmann, Chaim, 42
Wellers, Georges, 114
Wetzler, Alfred, 179
Wiesel, Elie, 138–139, 182–183
Wiesenthal, Simon, 186
Wilhelm II, 11
Wittenberg, Itzik, 145
Wladka, Feigele, 111
Wolf, Jeanette, 108–109
women: as deportees, 108–109; position under Nazis, 25–26; in resistance, 81, 157–158, 165, 168–169, 179–181

World War I, 11–13, 31, 40, 44, 61, 96
World War II, 46, 58, 131, 197, 200

Yad Vashem, 141
Yivo Institute for Jewish Research, 141–142
Yosselevscka, Rivka, 66–70
youth, under Nazism, 22–24

Zabladowicz, Noah, 179–181
Zimmerman, Hersz, 171
Zionists, 62, 101, 102, 110, 114, 151, 162, 164, 179, 184–185
Zygelbojm, Shmuel, 115
Zyklon B gas, 127

Format by Kohar Alexanian
Set in 11 pt. Electra
Composed and bound by American Book–Stratford Press, Inc.
Printed by The Murray Printing Company
HARPER & ROW, PUBLISHERS, INCORPORATED

MAP OF EUROPE SHOWING CAMP AREA

Atlantic Ocean

North Sea

Baltic Sea

Mediterranean Sea

Copenhagen

North Sea

Hamburg

NEUENGAMME

Bremen

PAPENBURG

RAVENSBRUCK

SACHSENHAUSEN

Amsterdam

BERGEN–BELSEN

Berlin

DORANORDHAUSEN

Leipzig

BUCHENWALD

Frankfurt

THERESIENSTADT

FLOSSENBÜR

Nuremberg

NATZVILLER

DACHAU

LANDSBERG

Munich

MAUTHAUSE

Zurich

Bern

X Extermination Camps

● Concentration Camps

• Towns

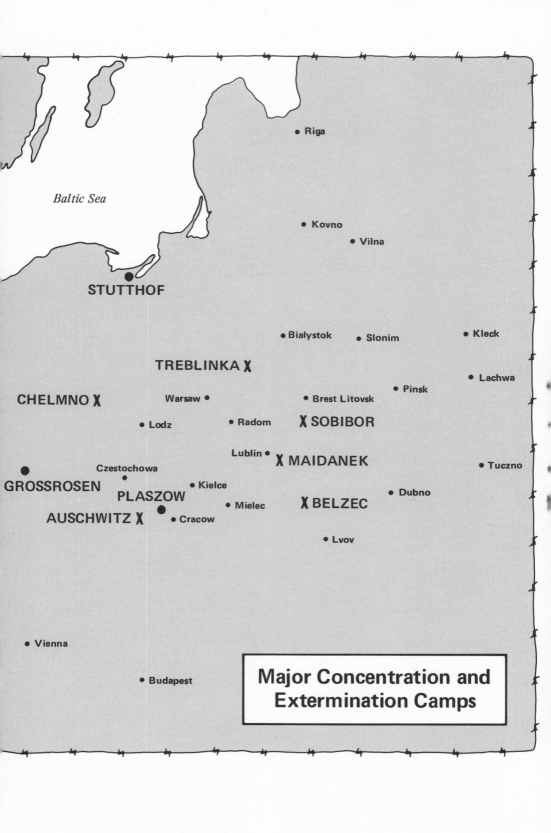

Baltic Sea

• Riga

• Kovno

• Vilna

STUTTHOF

• Bialystok   • Slonim   • Kleck

TREBLINKA X   • Lachwa

CHELMNO X   Warsaw •   • Brest Litovsk   • Pinsk

• Lodz   • Radom   **X SOBIBOR**

Lublin • **X MAIDANEK**

Czestochowa   • Tuczno

GROSSROSEN
          • Kielce
PLASZOW
                  • Mielec   **X BELZEC**   • Dubno
AUSCHWITZ X   • Cracow

                                    • Lvov

• Vienna

• Budapest

**Major Concentration and
Extermination Camps**

Historians speak of Hitler's destruction of 6 million Jews during World War II as the Holocaust. Yet the human meaning of such brutal statistics has been hard to grasp. Now Milton Meltzer turns statistics back into people, as the men, women, and children who lived the Nazi terror tell it in their own words.

While the narrative exposes the roots of German anti-Semitism, Hitler's rise to power, and the workings of the Nazi death-machine, the author connects us to individual Jews' experiences recorded in private letters and diaries, memoirs, poems, and songs. These moving personal accounts reveal everyday life in the Nazi ghettos and the labor and death camps, and they detail the many ways Jews resisted Hitler—in ghetto and camp uprisings, underground partisan actions, and in individual decisions to "live and die with dignity."

The Holocaust raises questions for us today, as the author says, "of good and evil, of our inner being, of our power to make moral choices." NEVER TO FORGET is an eloquent call to the living, to remember and to examine our own humanity.

TRAVELING LIGHT

*Releasing the Burdens
You Were Never Intended to Bear*

Max Lucado

Bookspan Large Print Edition

WORD PUBLISHING
NASHVILLE
A Thomas Nelson Company

ISBN 0-7394-2001-1

Printed in the United States of America

**This Large Print Book carries the
Seal of Approval of N.A.V.H.**

To my dear friend Joey Paul,
celebrating thirty years of words at Word,
sharing the Word

Contents

Acknowledgments

Here are well-deserved pats on some sturdy backs:

To Liz Heaney and Karen Hill—my editors and my assistant, midwives of the manuscript. Sorry I groaned so much.

To Steve and Cheryl Green—my representative and my friends. Because of you, contracts are read, and bills are paid, and this old boy sleeps well at night.

To Greg Pruett—Bible translator and Hebrew student. Thanks for the great insights.

To Eugene Peterson—Bible translator, author, and hero to many. Thanks for letting me use the title. And, much more, thanks for sharing your heart.

To Steve Halliday—study guide author par excellence.

To my friends at Word Publishing. Once again, you're the best.

To Laura Kendall and Carol Bartley—the great sleuths of the English language. Thanks for making me look smart.

To Jenna, Andrea, and Sara—my delightful daughters. I couldn't be prouder.

To Denalyn—my wife of two decades. Before you were born, where did poets go for inspiration?

To you—the reader. May the real Author speak to you.

And, most of all, to you, Jesus. The only reason we can release a burden is because you are there to take it. All the applause is yours.

1

The Luggage of Life

I've never been one to travel light.

I've tried. Believe me, I've tried. But ever since I stuck three fingers in the air and took the Boy Scout pledge to be prepared, I've been determined to be exactly that—prepared.

Prepared for a bar mitzvah, baby dedication, or costume party. Prepared to parachute behind enemy lines or enter a cricket tournament. And if, perchance, the Dalai Lama might be on my flight and invite me to dine in Tibet, I carry snowshoes. One has to be prepared.

I don't know how to travel light.

Fact is, there's a lot about travel I don't know. I don't know how to interpret the restrictions of a supersaver seat—*half price if you leave on Wednesdays during duck-hunting season and return when the moon is full in a nonelection year.* I don't know why they don't build the whole plane out of the same metal they use to build the little black box. I don't know how to escape the airplane toilet without sacrificing one of my extremities to the jaws of the folding door. And I don't know what to say to guys like the taxi driver in Rio who learned I was an American and asked me if I knew his cousin Eddie who lives in the U.S.

There's a lot about traveling I don't know.

I don't know why we men would rather floss a crocodile than ask for directions. I don't know why vacation slides aren't used to treat insomnia, and I don't know when I'll learn not to eat food whose names I can't pronounce.

But most of all, I don't know how to travel light.

I don't know how to travel without granola bars, sodas, and rain gear. I don't know how to travel without flashlights and a generator and a global tracking system. I don't know how to travel without an ice chest of wieners. What if I stumble upon a backyard barbecue? To bring nothing to the party would be rude.

Every travel-catalog company in the world has my credit-card number. I've got an iron that doubles as a paperweight, a hair dryer the size of a coach's whistle, a Swiss Army knife that expands into a pup tent, and a pair of pants that inflate upon impact. (On one flight my wife, Denalyn, gave me a swat on the leg, and I couldn't get out of my seat.)

I don't know how to travel light. But I need to learn. Denalyn refuses to give birth to any more children even though the airlines allow each passenger three checked bags and two carry-ons.

I need to learn to travel light.

You're wondering why I can't. *Loosen up!* you're thinking. *You can't enjoy a journey carrying so much stuff. Why don't you just drop all that luggage?*

Funny you should ask. I'd like to inquire the same of you. Haven't you been known to pick up a few bags?

Odds are, you did this morning. Somewhere between the first step on the floor and the last step out the door, you grabbed some luggage. You stepped over to the baggage carousel and loaded up. Don't remember doing so? That's because you did it without thinking. Don't remember seeing a baggage terminal? That's because the carousel is not the one in the airport; it's the one in the mind. And the bags we grab are not made of leather; they're made of burdens.

The suitcase of guilt. A sack of discontent. You drape a duffel bag of weariness on one shoulder and a hanging bag of grief on the other. Add on a backpack of doubt, an overnight bag of loneliness, and a trunk of fear. Pretty soon you're pulling more stuff than a skycap. No wonder you're so tired at the end of the day. Lugging luggage is exhausting.

What you were saying to me, God is saying to you, "Set that stuff down! You're carrying burdens you don't need to bear."

"Come to me," he invites, "all of you who are weary and carry heavy burdens, and I will give you rest" (Matt. 11:28 NLT).

If we let him, God will lighten our loads . . . but how do we let him? May I invite an old friend to show us? The Twenty-third Psalm.

> The LORD is my shepherd;
> I shall not want.

He makes me to lie down in green
    pastures;
He leads me beside the still waters.
He restores my soul;
He leads me in the paths of
    righteousness
For His name's sake.

Yea, though I walk through the valley of
    the shadow of death,
I will fear no evil;
For You are with me;
Your rod and Your staff, they comfort me.

You prepare a table before me in the
    presence of my enemies;
You anoint my head with oil.
My cup runs over.
Surely goodness and mercy shall follow
    me
All the days of my life;
And I will dwell in the house of the LORD
Forever. (NKJV)

Do more beloved words exist? Framed and
hung in hospital halls, scratched on prison
walls, quoted by the young, and whispered
by the dying. In these lines sailors have found

a harbor, the frightened have found a father, and strugglers have found a friend.

And because the passage is so deeply loved, it is widely known. Can you find ears on which these words have never fallen? Set to music in a hundred songs, translated into a thousand tongues, domiciled in a million hearts.

One of those hearts might be yours. What kinship do you feel with these words? Where do the verses transport you? To a fireside? Bedside? Graveside?

Hardly a week passes that I don't turn to them. This passage is to the minister what balm is to the physician. I recently applied them to the heart of a dear friend. Summoned to his house with the words "The doctors aren't giving him more than a few days," I looked at him and understood. Face pale. Lips stretched and parched. Skin draping between bones like old umbrella cloth between spokes. The cancer had taken so much: his appetite, his strength, his days. But the cancer hadn't touched his faith. Pulling a chair to his bed and squeezing his hand, I whispered, "Bill, 'The Lord is my shepherd; I shall not want.'" He rolled his head toward me as if to welcome the words.

"He makes me to lie down in green pastures; He leads me beside the still waters. He restores my soul; He leads me in the paths of righteousness for His name's sake."

Reaching the fourth verse, fearful that he might not hear, I leaned forward until I was a couple of inches from his ear and said, "Though I walk through the valley of the shadow of death, I will fear no evil; for You are with me; Your rod and Your staff, they comfort me."

He didn't open his eyes, but he arched his brows. He didn't speak, but his thin fingers curled around mine, and I wondered if the Lord was helping him set down some luggage, the fear of dying.

Do you have some luggage of your own? Do you think God might use David's psalm to lighten your load? *Traveling light means trusting God with the burdens you were never intended to bear.*

Why don't you try traveling light? Try it for the sake of those you love. Have you ever considered the impact that excess baggage has on relationships? We've made this point at our church by virtue of a drama. A wedding is reenacted in which we hear the thoughts of the bride and groom. The groom enters, laden with luggage. A bag dangles from every appendage. And each bag is labeled: guilt, anger, arrogance, insecurities. This fellow is loaded. As he stands at the altar, the audience hears him thinking, *Finally, a woman who will help me carry all my burdens. She's so strong, so stable, so . . .*

As his thoughts continue, hers begin. She enters, wearing a wedding gown but, like her fiancé, covered with luggage. Pulling a hanging bag, shouldering a carry-on, hauling a makeup kit, paper sack—everything you could imagine and everything labeled. She has her own bags: prejudice, loneliness, disappointments. And her expectations? Listen to what she is thinking: *Just a few more minutes and I've got me a man. No more counselors. No more group sessions. So long, discouragement and worry. I won't be seeing you anymore. He's going to fix me.*

Finally they stand at the altar, lost in a mountain of luggage. They smile their way through the ceremony, but when given the invitation to kiss each other, they can't. How do you embrace someone if your arms are full of bags?

For the sake of those you love, learn to set them down.

And, for the sake of the God you serve, do the same. He wants to use you, you know. But how can he if you are exhausted? This truth came home to me yesterday afternoon on a run. Preparing for a jog, I couldn't decide what to wear. The sun was out, but the wind was chilly. The sky was clear, but the forecast said rain. Jacket or sweatshirt? The Boy Scout within me prevailed. I wore both.

I grabbed my Walkman but couldn't decide which tape to bring. A sermon or music? You guessed it, I took both. Needing to stay in touch with my kids, I carried a cell phone. So no one would steal my car, I pocketed my keys. As a precaution against thirst, I brought along some drink money in a pouch. I looked more like a pack mule than a runner! Within half a mile I was peeling off the jacket and hiding it in a bush. That kind of weight will slow you down.

What's true in jogging is true in faith. God has a great race for you to run. Under his care you will go where you've never been and serve in ways you've never dreamed. But you have to drop some stuff. How can you share grace if you are full of guilt? How can you offer comfort if you are disheartened? How can you lift someone else's load if your arms are full with your own?

For the sake of those you love, travel light.

For the sake of the God you serve, travel light.

For the sake of your own joy, travel light.

There are certain weights in life you simply cannot carry. Your Lord is asking you to set them down and trust him. He is the father at the baggage claim. When a dad sees his five-year-old son trying to drag the family trunk off the carousel, what does he say? The father will say to his son what God is saying to you.

"Set it down, child. I'll carry that one."

What do you say we take God up on his offer? We just might find ourselves traveling a little lighter.

By the way, I may have overstated my packing problems. (I don't usually take snowshoes.) But I can't overstate God's promise: "Unload all your worries onto him, since he is looking after you" (1 Pet. 5:7 JB).

2

The Middle C of Life

The Burden of a Lesser God

The LORD . . .
PSALM 23:1

I'm only five feet from an eagle. His wings are spread, and his talons are lifted above the branch. White feathers cap his head, and black eyes peer at me from both sides of a golden beak. He is so close I could touch him. So near I could stroke him. With only a lean and a stretch of my right arm, I could cover the eagle's crown with my hand.

But I don't. I don't reach. Why not? Am I afraid of him?

Hardly. He hasn't budged in two years. When I first opened the box, he impressed me. When I first set him on the shelf, I admired him. Man-made eagles are nice for a while, but you quickly get used to them.

David is concerned that you and I don't make the same mistake with God. His pen has scarcely touched papyrus, and he's urging us to avoid gods of our own making. With his very first words in this psalm, David sets out to deliver us from the burden of a lesser deity.

One might argue that he seeks to do nothing else. For though he will speak of green pastures, his thesis is not rest. He will describe death's somber valley, but this poem is not an ode to dying. He will tell of the Lord's forever house, but his theme is not heaven. Why did David write the Twenty-third Psalm? To build our trust in God . . . to remind us of who he is.

In this psalm David devotes one hundred and fifteen words to explaining the first two:[1] "The LORD." In the arena of unnecessary luggage, the psalmist begins with the weightiest: the refashioned god. One who looks nice but does little. God as . . .

A genie in a bottle. Convenient. Congenial. Need a parking place, date, field goal made or missed? All you do is rub the bottle

and *poof*—it's yours. And, what's even better, this god goes back into the bottle after
he's done.

A sweet grandpa. So soft hearted. So
wise. So kind. But very, very, very old.
Grandpas are great when they are awake,
but they tend to doze off when you need
them.

A busy dad. Leaves on Mondays, returns
on Saturdays. Lots of road trips and business meetings. He'll show up on Sunday,
however, so clean up and look spiritual. On
Monday, be yourself again. He'll never know.

Ever held these views of God? If so, you
know the problems they cause. A busy dad
doesn't have time for your questions. A kind
grandpa is too weak to carry your load. And
if your god is a genie in a bottle, then you are
greater than he is. He comes and goes at
your command.

A god who looks nice but does little.

Reminds me of a briefcase I own. Though
I'd like to fault the salesman, I can't. The purchase was my decision. But he certainly
made it easy. I didn't need a new satchel.
The one I had was fine. Scarred and
scratched but fine. The paint was worn off

the zippers, and the edges were scuffed, but the bag was fine.

Oh, but this new one, to use the words of the college-age boy in the leather store, was "really fine." Loaded with features: copper covers on the corners, smooth leather from Spain, and, most of all, an Italian name near the handle. The salesman gave his line and handed me the bag, and I bought them both.

I left the store with a briefcase that I have used maybe twice. What was I thinking? It carries so little. My old bag had no copper-covered corners, but it had a belly like a beluga. This new one reminds me of a high-fashion model: slim, stiff, and tight-lipped. A book and a newspaper, and this Italian satchel is *"fullisimo."*

The bag looks nice but does nothing.

Is that the kind of God you want? Is that the kind of God we have?

David's answer is a resounding no. "You want to know who God really is?" he asks. "Then read this." And he writes the name *Yahweh.* "Yahweh is my shepherd."

Though foreign to us, the name was rich to David. So rich, in fact, that David chose

Yahweh over *El Shaddai* (God Almighty), *El Elyon* (God Most High), and *El Olam* (God the Everlasting). These and many other titles for God were at David's disposal. But when he considered all the options, David chose *Yahweh.*

Why *Yahweh?* Because *Yahweh* is God's name. You can call me preacher or writer or half-baked golfer—these are accurate descriptions, but these aren't my names. I might call you dad, mom, doctor, or student, and those terms may describe you, but they aren't your name. If you want to call me by my name, say *Max.* If I call you by your name, I say it. And if you want to call God by his name, say *Yahweh.*

God has told us his name. (How he must long to be close to us.)

Moses was the first to learn it. Seven centuries prior to David, the eighty-year-old shepherd was tending sheep when the bush began to blaze and his life began to change. Moses was told to return to Egypt and rescue the enslaved Hebrews. He raised more excuses than a kid at bedtime, but God trumped each one. Finally Moses asked,

"When I go to the Israelites, I will say to them, 'The God of your fathers sent me to you.' What if the people say, 'What is his name?' What should I tell them?"

Then God said to Moses, "I AM WHO I AM. When you go to the people of Israel, tell them, 'I AM sent me to you.'" (Exod. 3:13–14)

God would later remind Moses: "I am Yahweh. To Abraham and Isaac and Jacob I appeared as El Shaddai; I did not make myself known to them by my name Yahweh" (Exod. 6:2–3 JB).

The Israelites considered the name too holy to be spoken by human lips. Whenever they needed to say *Yahweh,* they substituted the word *Adonai,* which means "Lord." If the name needed to be written, the scribes would take a bath before they wrote it and destroy the pen afterward.[2]

God never gives a definition of the word *Yahweh,* and Moses never requests one. Many scholars wish he had, for the study of the name has raised some healthy discussions.

The name I AM sounds strikingly close to the Hebrew verb *to be—havah.* It's quite possibly a combination of the present tense form (I am) and the causative tense (I cause to be). *Yahweh,* then, seems to mean "I AM" and "I cause." God is the "One who is" and the "One who causes."

Why is that important? Because we need a big God. And if God is the "One who is," then he is an unchanging God.

Think about it. Do you know anyone who goes around saying, "I am"? Neither do I. When we say "I am," we always add another word. "I am *happy.*" "I am *sad.*" "I am *strong.*" "I am *Max.*" God, however, starkly states, "I AM" and adds nothing else.

"You are what?" we want to ask. "I AM," he replies. God needs no descriptive word because he never changes. God is what he is. He is what he has always been. His immutability motivated the psalmist to declare, "But thou art the same" (Ps. 102:27 KJV). The writer is saying, "You are the One who is. You never change."[3] Yahweh is an unchanging God.

He is also an uncaused God.

Though he creates, God was never created. Though he makes, he was never made. Though he causes, he was never caused. Hence the psalmist's proclamation:

"Before the mountains were born or you brought forth the earth and the world, from everlasting to everlasting you are God" (Ps. 90:2 NIV).

⁓ God is Yahweh—an unchanging God, an uncaused God, and an ungoverned God.

You and I are governed. The weather dictates what we wear. The terrain tells us how to travel. Gravity dictates our speed, and health determines our strength. We may challenge these forces and alter them slightly, but we never remove them.

God—our Shepherd—doesn't check the weather; he makes it. He doesn't defy gravity; he created it. He isn't affected by health; he has no body. Jesus said, "God is spirit" (John 4:24). Since he has no body, he has no limitations—equally active in Cambodia as he is in Connecticut. "Where can I go to get away from your Spirit?" asked David. "Where can I run from you? If I go up to the heavens, you are there. If I lie down in the grave, you are there" (Ps. 139:7–8).

Unchanging. Uncaused. Ungoverned. These are only a fraction of God's qualities, but aren't they enough to give you a glimpse of your Father? Don't we need this kind of shepherd? Don't we need an unchanging shepherd?

When Lloyd Douglas, author of *The Robe* and other novels, attended college, he lived in a boardinghouse. A retired, wheelchair-bound music professor resided on the first floor. Each morning Douglas would stick his head in the door of the teacher's apartment and ask the same question, "Well, what's the good news?" The old man would pick up his tuning fork, tap it on the side of the wheelchair, and say, "That's middle C! It was middle C yesterday; it will be middle C tomorrow; it will be middle C a thousand years from now. The tenor upstairs sings flat. The piano across the hall is out of tune, but, my friend, that is middle C."[4]

You and I need a middle C. Haven't you had enough change in your life? Relationships change. Health changes. The weather changes. But the Yahweh who ruled the earth last night is the same Yahweh who rules it today. Same convictions. Same plan. Same mood. Same love. He never changes. You can no more alter God than a pebble can alter the rhythm of the Pacific. Yahweh is our middle C. A still point in a turning world.

Don't we need a still point? Don't we need an un-changing shepherd?

We equally need an uncaused shepherd. No one breathed life into Yahweh. No one sired him. No one gave birth to him. No one caused him. No act brought him forth.

And since no act brought him forth, no act can take him out. Does he fear an earthquake? Does he tremble at a tornado? Hardly. Yahweh sleeps through storms and calms the winds with a word. Cancer does not trouble him, and cemeteries do not disturb him. He was here before they came. He'll be here after they are gone. He is uncaused.

And he is ungoverned. Counselors can comfort you *in* the storm, but you need a God who can *still* the storm. Friends can hold your hand at your deathbed, but you need a Yahweh who has defeated the grave. Philosophers can debate the meaning of life, but you need a Lord who can declare the meaning of life.

You need a Yahweh.

You don't need what Dorothy found. Remember her discovery in *The Wonderful Wizard of Oz*? She and her trio followed the yellow-brick road only to discover that the wizard was a wimp! Nothing but smoke and mirrors and tin-drum thunder. Is that the kind of god you need?

You don't need to carry the burden of a lesser god . . . a god on a shelf, a god in a box, or a god in a bottle. No, you need a God who can place 100 billion stars in our galaxy and 100 billion galaxies in the universe. You need a God who can shape two fists of flesh into 75 to 100 billion nerve cells, each with as many as 10,000 connections to other nerve cells, place it in a skull, and call it a brain.[5]

And you need a God who, while so mind-numbingly mighty, can come in the soft of night and touch you with the tenderness of an April snow.

You need a Yahweh.

And, according to David, you have one. He is your shepherd.

3

I'll Do It My Way

The Burden of Self-Reliance

The LORD is my shepherd.
PSALM 23:1 NKJV

You say you can swing a club like Tiger Woods? That's saying a lot.

You hope to score touchdowns like Joe Montana? You'll have to work hard.

And you, young lady? You aspire to be the next Mia Hamm? Good for you.

And me? Well, actually there is one fellow who's caught my attention. He reminds me of me. You've probably never heard of him. Did you see the British Open in '99? Yeah, the one in Carnoustie, Scotland? Remember the player who had a seven-stroke lead with one hole to go?

That's right, the Frenchman. Jean Van de

Velde. He was six strokes and 480 yards away from a major championship, a wad of cash, and a place in history. All he needed to do was score a six on a par four.

I could shoot a six on a par four. My mother could make a six on a par four. This guy could shoot a six with a waffle iron and a banana. Tell the trophy engraver to warm up the pen and practice his *Vs*. He'll need two to write "Jean Van de Velde."

Granted the hole was not easy. Bisected three times by a "wee burn," the Scottish term for a marshy creek. No sweat. Hit three short shots . . . putt three times if you have to. Just take a six, win the hole, and smile for the cameras. Besides it's windy, and the "wee burn" is wee deep. Don't flirt with it.

Oh, but the French love to flirt. Van de Velde pulls out his driver, and somewhere in Des Moines an armchair duffer who'd been lured to sleep by the seven-stroke lead opens one eye. *He's holding a driver?*

Van de Velde's caddie was a thirty-year-old Parisian named Christopher with untidy English and a paintbrush on his chin and bleached hair under his hat. "I think he and I—we want too much show," he later confessed.

Van de Velde pushes his drive halfway to the Eiffel Tower. Now he has 240 yards to the green with nothing but deep grass and heartache in between. Surely he will hit a short shot back in the fairway.

Logic says, "Don't go for the green."

Golf 101 says, "Don't go for the green."

Every Scot in the gallery says, "Aye, laddie. Don't go for the green."

Van de Velde says, "I'm going for the green."

He pulls out a two iron, and the armchair golfer in Des Moines opens the other eye. *A two iron!? Maybe if you're teed up on the beach, trying to hit into the Caribbean!* The spectators are silent. Most out of respect. A few in prayer. Van de Velde's two iron becomes a FORE! iron. *Whack. Clang. Plop.* The ball caroms off the bleachers and disappears into marsh tall enough to hide a lawn gnome.

His lie would've made Pinocchio's nose grow. The next shot lands in the water and the next in the sand. Tally the damage, and you've got four strokes plus a penalty. He's lying five and not on the green. So much for winning the hole. By now he's praying for a seven and a tie. To the great relief of the civilized world, Van de Velde makes the seven. You've got to wonder if he ever recovered from the "wee burn." He lost the play-off.

Golf, like nylon running shorts, reveals a lot about a person. What the eighteenth hole revealed about Van de Velde reminds me of me.

I've done the same thing. The same blasted thing. All he needed was a five iron, but he had to go and pull out the driver. Or, in my case:

All I needed to do was apologize, but I had to argue.

All I needed to do was listen, but I had to open my big mouth.

All I needed to do was be patient, but I had to take control.

All I had to do was give it to God, but I tried to fix it myself.

Why don't I leave the driver in the bag? I know how Christopher the caddie would answer: "I think he and I and Max—we want too much show."

Too much stubbornness. Too much independence. Too much self-reliance.

I don't need advice—*Whack.*

I can handle this myself—*Clang.*

I don't need a shepherd, thank you—*Plop.*

Can you relate? Are Jean and I the only ones to make an anthem out of Sinatra's song "I Did It My Way"? Are we the only two dragging around the cast-iron chest of self-reliance? I don't think so.

We humans want to do things our way. Forget the easy way. Forget the common way. Forget the best way. Forget God's way. We want to do things *our* way.

And, according to the Bible, that's precisely our problem. "We all have wandered away like sheep; each of us has gone his own way" (Isa. 53:6).

You wouldn't think sheep would be obstinate. Of all God's animals, the sheep is the least able to take care of himself.

Sheep are dumb! Have you ever met a sheep trainer? Ever seen sheep tricks? Know anyone who has taught his sheep to roll over? Ever witnessed a circus sideshow featuring "Mazadon and his jumping sheep"? No. Sheep are just too dumb.

And defenseless. They have no fangs or claws. They can't bite you or outrun you. That's why you never see sheep as team mascots. We've heard of the St. Louis Rams

and the Chicago Bulls and the Seattle Sea-
hawks, but the New York Lambs? Who wants
to be a lamb? You couldn't even stir up a decent yell for the cheerleaders.

> We are the sheep.
> We don't make a peep.
> Victory is yours to keep.
> But count us if you want to sleep.

What's more, sheep are dirty. A cat can
clean itself. So can a dog. We see a bird in a
birdbath or a bear in a river. But sheep?
They get dirty and stay that way.

Couldn't David have thought of a better
metaphor? Surely he could have. After all,
he outran Saul and outgunned Goliath. Why
didn't he choose something other than
sheep?

How about:

"The Lord is my commander in chief, and I
am his warrior." There. We like that better. A
warrior gets a uniform and a weapon, maybe
even a medal.

Or, "The Lord is my inspiration, and I am
his singer." We are in God's choir; what a
flattering assignment.

Or, "The Lord is my king, and I am his ambassador." Who wouldn't like to be a spokesperson for God?

Everyone stops when the ambassador speaks. Everyone listens when God's minstrel sings. Everyone applauds when God's warrior passes.

But who notices when God's sheep show up? Who notices when the sheep sing or speak or act? Only one person notices. The shepherd. And that is precisely David's point.

When David, who was a warrior, minstrel, and ambassador for God, searched for an illustration of God, he remembered his days as a shepherd. He remembered how he lavished attention on the sheep day and night. How he slept with them and watched over them.

And the way he cared for the sheep reminded him of the way God cares for us. David rejoiced to say, "The LORD is my shepherd," and in so doing he proudly implied, "I am his sheep."

Still uncomfortable with being considered a sheep? Will you humor me and take a simple quiz? See if you succeed in self-reliance. Raise your hand if any of the following describe you.

You can control your moods. You're never grumpy or sullen. You can't relate to Jekyll and Hyde. You're always upbeat and upright. Does that describe you? No? Well, let's try another.

You are at peace with everyone. Every relationship as sweet as fudge. Even your old flames speak highly of you. Love all and are loved by all. Is that you? If not, how about this description?

You have no fears. Call you the Teflon toughie. Wall Street plummets—no problem. Heart condition discovered—yawn. World War III starts—what's for dinner? Does this describe you?

You need no forgiveness. Never made a mistake. As square as a game of checkers. As clean as grandma's kitchen. Never cheated, never lied, never lied about cheating. Is that you? No?

Let's evaluate this. You can't control your moods. A few of your relationships are shaky. You have fears and faults. Hmmm. Do you really want to hang on to your chest of self-reliance? Sounds to me as if you could use a shepherd. Otherwise, you might end up with a Twenty-third Psalm like this:

I am my own shepherd. I am always in need.

I stumble from mall to mall and shrink to shrink, seeking relief but never finding it.

I creep through the valley of the shadow of death and fall apart.

I fear everything from pesticides to power lines, and I'm starting to act like my mother.

I go down to the weekly staff meeting and am surrounded by enemies. I go home, and even my goldfish scowls at me.

I anoint my headache with extra-strength Tylenol.

My Jack Daniel's runneth over.

Surely misery and misfortune will follow me, and I will live in self-doubt for the rest of my lonely life.

Why is it that the ones who most need a shepherd resist him so?

Ah, now there is a question for the Van de Veldes of life. Scripture says, "Do it God's way." Experience says, "Do it God's way." Every Scot in heaven begs, "Aye, laddie, do it God's way."

And, every so often, we do. And when we do, when we follow the lead of *Notre Dieu* and keep the driver in the bag, somehow the ball stays in the fairway.

Yes, Van de Velde reminds me of me.

After losing the play-off hole, he kept his composure for the crowds. But once he sat in the scorer's tent, he buried his face in his hands. "Next time I'll hit zee wedge," he sobbed. "You'll say I'm a coward, but next time I'll hit zee wedge."

You and me both, Jean.[1]

4

The Prison of Want

The Burden of Discontent

The LORD is my shepherd; I shall not want.
PSALM 23:1 NKJV

Come with me to the most populated prison in the world. The facility has more inmates than bunks. More prisoners than plates. More residents than resources.

Come with me to the world's most oppressive prison. Just ask the inmates; they will tell you. They are overworked and underfed. Their walls are bare and bunks are hard.

No prison is so populated, no prison so oppressive, and, what's more, no prison is so permanent. Most inmates never leave. They never escape. They never get released. They serve a life sentence in this overcrowded, underprovisioned facility.

The name of the prison? You'll see it over the entrance. Rainbowed over the gate are four cast-iron letters that spell out its name:

W-A-N-T

The prison of want. You've seen her prisoners. They are "in want." They want something. They want something bigger. Nicer. Faster. Thinner. They want.

They don't want much, mind you. They want just one thing. One new job. One new car. One new house. One new spouse. They don't want much. They want just one.

And when they have "one," they will be happy. And they are right—they will be happy. When they have "one," they will leave the prison. But then it happens. The new-car smell passes. The new job gets old. The neighbors buy a larger television set. The new spouse has bad habits. The sizzle fizzles, and before you know it, another ex-con breaks parole and returns to jail.

Are you in prison? You are if you feel better when you have more and worse when you have less. You are if joy is one delivery away, one transfer away, one award away, or one makeover away. If your happiness comes from something you deposit, drive, drink, or digest, then face it—you are in prison, the prison of want.

That's the bad news. The good news is, you have a visitor. And your visitor has a message that can get you paroled. Make your way to the receiving room. Take your seat in the chair, and look across the table at the psalmist David. He motions for you to lean forward. "I have a secret to tell you," he whispers, "the secret of satisfaction. 'The LORD is my shepherd; I shall not want'" (Ps. 23:1 NKJV).

David has found the pasture where discontent goes to die. It's as if he is saying, "What I have in God is greater than what I don't have in life."

You think you and I could learn to say the same?

Think for just a moment about the things you own. Think about the house you have, the car you drive, the money you've saved. Think about the jewelry you've inherited and the stocks you've traded and the clothes you've purchased. Envision all your stuff, and let me remind you of two biblical truths.

Your stuff isn't yours. Ask any coroner. Ask any embalmer. Ask any funeral-home director. No one takes anything with him. When one of the wealthiest men in history, John D. Rockefeller, died, his accountant was asked, "How much did John D. leave?" The accountant's reply? "All of it."[1]

"Naked a man comes from his mother's womb, and as he comes, so he departs. He takes nothing from his labor that he can carry in his hand" (Eccles. 5:15 NIV).

All that stuff—it's not yours. And you know what else about all that stuff? *It's not you.* Who you are has nothing to do with the clothes you wear or the car you drive. Jesus said, "Life is not defined by what you have, even when you have a lot" (Luke 12:15 MSG). Heaven does not know you as the fellow with the nice suit or the woman with the big house or the kid with the new bike. Heaven knows your heart. "The LORD does not look at the things man looks at. Man looks at the outward appearance, but the LORD looks at the heart" (1 Sam. 16:7 NIV). When God thinks of you, he may see your compassion, your devotion, your tenderness or quick mind, but he doesn't think of your things.

And when you think of you, you shouldn't either. Define yourself by your stuff, and you'll feel good when you have a lot and bad when you don't. Contentment comes when we can honestly say with Paul: "I have learned to be satisfied with the things I have. . . . I know how to live when I am poor, and I know how to live when I have plenty" (Phil. 4:11–12).

Doug McKnight could say those words. At the age of thirty-two he was diagnosed with multiple sclerosis. Over the next sixteen years it would cost him his career, his mobility, and eventually his life. Because of MS, he couldn't feed himself or walk; he battled depression and fear. But through it all, Doug never lost his sense of gratitude. Evidence of this was seen in his prayer list. Friends in his congregation asked him to compile a list of requests so they could intercede for him. His response included eighteen blessings for which to be grateful and six concerns for which to be prayerful. His blessings outweighed his needs by three times. Doug McKnight had learned to be content.[2]

So had the leper on the island of Tobago. A short-term missionary met her on a mission trip. On the final day, he was leading worship in a leper colony. He asked if anyone had a favorite song. When he did, a woman turned around, and he saw the most disfigured face he'd ever seen. She had no ears and no nose. Her lips were gone. But she raised a fingerless hand and asked, "Could we sing 'Count Your Many Blessings'?"

The missionary started the song but couldn't finish. Someone later commented, "I suppose you'll never be able to sing the song again." He answered, "No, I'll sing it again. Just never in the same way."[3]

Are you hoping that a change in circumstances will bring a change in your attitude? If so, you are in prison, and you need to learn a secret of traveling light. *What you have in your Shepherd is greater than what you don't have in life.*

May I meddle for a moment? What is the one thing separating you from joy? How do you fill in this blank: "I will be happy when _____"? When I am healed. When I am promoted. When I am married. When I am single. When I am rich. How would you finish that statement?

Now, with your answer firmly in mind, answer this. If your ship never comes in, if your dream never comes true, if the situation never changes, could you be happy? If not, then you are sleeping in the cold cell of discontent. You are in prison. And you need to know what you have in your Shepherd.

You have a God who hears you, the power of love behind you, the Holy Spirit within you, and all of heaven ahead of you. If you have the Shepherd, you have grace for every sin, direction for every turn, a candle for every corner, and an anchor for every storm. You have everything you need.

And who can take it from you? Can leukemia infect your salvation? Can bankruptcy impoverish your prayers? A tornado might take your earthly house, but will it touch your heavenly home?

And look at your position. Why clamor for prestige and power? Are you not already privileged to be part of the greatest work in history?

According to Russ Blowers, we are. He is a minister in Indianapolis. Knowing he would be asked about his profession at a Rotary Club meeting, he resolved to say more than "I'm a preacher."

Instead he explained, "Hi, I'm Russ Blowers. I'm with a global enterprise. We have branches in every country in the world. We have representatives in nearly every parliament and boardroom on earth. We're into motivation and behavior alteration.We run hospitals, feeding stations, crisis-pregnancy centers, universities, publishing houses, and nursing homes. We care for our clients from birth to death. We are into life insurance and fire insurance. We perform spiritual heart transplants. Our original Organizer owns all the real estate on earth plus an assortment of galaxies and constellations. He knows everything and lives everywhere. Our product is free for the asking. (There's not enough money to buy it.) Our CEO was born in a hick town, worked as a carpenter, didn't own a home, was misunderstood by his family and hated by his enemies, walked on water, was condemned to death without a trial, and arose from the dead. I talk with him every day."4

If you can say the same, don't you have reason to be content?

A man once went to a minister for counseling. He was in the midst of a financial collapse. "I've lost everything," he bemoaned.

"Oh, I'm so sorry to hear that you've lost your faith."

"No," the man corrected him, "I haven't lost my faith."

"Well, then I'm sad to hear that you've lost your character."

"I didn't say that," he corrected. "I still have my character."

"I'm so sorry to hear that you've lost your salvation."

"That's not what I said," the man objected. "I haven't lost my salvation."

"You have your faith, your character, your salvation. Seems to me," the minister observed, "that you've lost none of the things that really matter."

We haven't either. You and I could pray like the Puritan. He sat down to a meal of bread and water. He bowed his head and declared, "All this and Jesus too?"

Can't we be equally content? Paul says that "godliness with contentment is great gain" (1 Tim. 6:6 NIV). When we surrender to God the cumbersome sack of discontent, we don't just give up something; we gain something. God replaces it with a lightweight, tailor-made, sorrow-resistant attaché of gratitude.

What will you gain with contentment? You may gain your marriage. You may gain precious hours with your children. You may gain your self-respect. You may gain joy. You may gain the faith to say, "The LORD is my shepherd; I shall not want."

Try saying it slowly. "The LORD is my shepherd; I shall not want."

Again, "The LORD is my shepherd; I shall not want."

Again, "The LORD is my shepherd; I shall not want."

Shhhhhhh. Did you hear something? I think I did. I'm not sure . . . but I think I heard the opening of a jail door.

5

I Will Give You Rest

The Burden of Weariness

He makes me to lie down in green pastures.
PSALM 23:2 NKJV

I'll give you the consequences of the burden;
you guess the cause.

- It afflicts 70 million Americans and is
  faulted for 38,000 deaths each year.
- The condition annually costs the U.S.
  $70 billion worth of productivity.
- Teenagers suffer from it. Studies show
  that 64 percent of teens blame it for poor
  school performance.
- Middle agers face it. Researchers say
  the most severe cases occur between
  ages thirty and forty.

- Senior citizens are afflicted by it. One study suggests that the condition impacts 50 percent of the over-sixty-five population.
- Treatments involve everything from mouth guards to herbal teas to medication.[1]

Any idea what's being described?

Chemical abuse? Divorce? Long sermons? None of those answers are correct, though the last one was a good hunch. The answer may surprise you. Insomnia. America can't get to sleep.

For most of my life I secretly snickered at the thought of sleep difficulties. My problem was not in going to sleep. My problem was staying awake. But a few years ago I went to bed one night, closed my eyes, and nothing happened. I didn't fall asleep. Rather than slow to a halt, my mind kicked into high gear. A thousand and one obligations rushed at me. Midnight passed, and I was still awake. I drank some milk, returned to bed. I was still awake. I woke up Denalyn, using the blue ribbon of dumb questions, "Are you awake?" She told me to quit thinking about things. So

I did. I quit thinking about things and started thinking about people. But as I thought of people, I thought of what those people were doing. They were sleeping. That made me mad and kept me awake. Finally, somewhere in the early hours of the morning, having been initiated into the fraternity of 70 million sleepless Americans, I dozed off.

I don't snicker at the thought of sleep difficulties anymore. Nor do I question the inclusion of the verse about rest in the Twenty-third Psalm.

People with too much work and too little sleep step over to the baggage claim of life and grab the duffel bag of weariness. You don't carry this one. You don't hoist it onto your shoulder and stride down the street. You drag it as you would a stubborn St. Bernard. Weariness wearies.

Why are we so tired? Have you read a newspaper lately? We long to have the life of Huck and Tom on the Mississippi, but look at us riding the white waters of the Rio Grande. Forks in the river. Rocks in the water. Heart attacks, betrayal, credit-card debt, and custody battles. Huck and Tom didn't have to face these kinds of things. We do, however, and they keep us awake. And since we can't sleep, we have a second problem.

Our bodies are tired. Think about it. If 70 million Americans aren't sleeping enough, what does that mean? That means one-third of our country is dozing off at work, napping through class, or sleeping at the wheel. (Fifteen hundred road deaths per year are blamed on heavy-eyed truckdrivers.) Some even snooze while reading Lucado books. (Hard to fathom, I know.) Thirty tons of aspirins, sleeping pills, and tranquilizers are consumed every day![2] The energy gauge on the dashboard of our forehead says empty.

Were we to invite an alien to solve our problem, he'd suggest a simple solution—everybody go to sleep. We'd laugh at him. He doesn't understand the way we work. Literally. He doesn't understand *the way* we work. We work hard. There is money to be made. Degrees to be earned. Ladders to be climbed. In our book, busyness is next to godliness. We idolize Thomas Edison, who claimed he could live on fifteen-minute naps. Somehow we forget to mention Albert Einstein, who averaged eleven hours of sleep a night.[3] In 1910 Americans slept nine hours a night; today we sleep seven and are proud of

it. And we are tired because of it. Our minds
are tired. Our bodies are tired. But much
more important, our souls are tired.

We are eternal creatures, and we ask
eternal questions: Where did I come from?
Where am I going? What is the meaning of
life? What is right? What is wrong? Is there
life after death? These are the primal questions of the soul. And left unanswered, such
questions will steal our rest.

Only one other living creature has as
much trouble resting as we do. Not dogs.
They doze. Not bears. They hibernate. Cats
invented the catnap, and the sloths slumber
twenty hours a day. (So that's what I was
rooming with my sophomore year in college.) Most animals know how to rest. There
is one exception. These creatures are
woolly, simpleminded, and slow. No, not hus-
bands on Saturday—sheep! Sheep can't
sleep.

For sheep to sleep, everything must be
just right. No predators. No tension in the
flock. No bugs in the air. No hunger in the
belly.[4] Everything has to be just so.

Unfortunately, sheep cannot find safe pasture, nor can they spray insecticide, deal
with the frictions, or find food. They need

help. They need a shepherd to "lead them" and help them "lie down in green pastures." Without a shepherd, they can't rest.

Without a shepherd, neither can we.

In the second verse of the Twenty-third Psalm, David the poet becomes David the artist. His quill becomes a brush, his parchment a canvas, and his words paint a picture. A flock of sheep on folded legs, encircling a shepherd. Bellies nestled deep in the long shoots of grass. A still pond on one side, the watching shepherd on the other. "He makes me to lie down in green pastures; He leads me beside the still waters" (Ps. 23:2 NKJV).

Note the two pronouns preceding the two verbs. *He* makes me . . . *He* leads me . . .

Who is the active one? Who is in charge? The shepherd. The shepherd selects the trail and prepares the pasture. The sheep's job—our job—is to watch the shepherd. With our eyes on our Shepherd, we'll be able to get some sleep. "You will keep him in perfect peace, whose mind is stayed on You" (Isa. 26:3 NKJV).

May I show you something? Flip to the back of this book, and look at an empty page. When you look at it, what do you see? What you see is a white piece of paper. Now place a dot in the center of the sheet. Look at it again. Now what do you see? You see the dot, don't you? And isn't that our problem? We let the dark marks eclipse the white space.

We see the waves of the water rather than the Savior walking through them. We focus on our paltry provisions rather than on the One who can feed five thousand hungry people. We concentrate on the dark Fridays of crucifixion and miss the bright Sundays of resurrection.

Change your focus and relax.

And while you are at it, change your schedule and rest!

The other day my wife met a friend at a restaurant for coffee. The two entered the parking lot at the same time. When Denalyn stepped out of her car, she saw her friend waving her over. Denalyn thought she was saying something, but she couldn't hear a word. A jack-hammer was pounding pavement only a few feet away. She walked toward her friend, who, as it turned out, was just saying hello, and the two entered the restaurant.

When it came time to leave, my wife couldn't find her keys. She looked in her purse, on the floor, in her friend's car. Finally when she went to her car, there they were. Not only were the keys in the ignition, the car was running. It had been running the entire time she and her friend were in the café.

Denalyn blames the oversight on the noise. "Everything was so loud, I forgot to turn it off."

The world gets that way. Life can get so loud we forget to shut it down. Maybe that's why God made such a big deal about rest in the Ten Commandments.

Since you did so well on the dot exercise, let me give you another. Of the ten declarations carved in the tablets, which one occupies the most space? Murder? Adultery? Stealing? You'd think so. Certainly each is worthy of ample coverage. But curiously, these commands are tributes to brevity. God needed only five English words to condemn adultery and four to denounce thievery and murder.

But when he came to the topic of rest, one sentence would not suffice.

Remember the Sabbath day, to keep it holy. Six days you shall labor and do all your work, but the seventh day is the Sabbath of the LORD your God. In it you shall do no work: you, nor your son, nor your daughter, nor your manservant, nor your maidservant, nor your cattle, nor your stranger who is within your gates. For in six days the LORD made the heavens and the earth, the sea, and all that is in them, and rested the seventh day. Therefore the LORD blessed the Sabbath day and hallowed it. (Exod. 20:8–11 NKJV)

God knows us so well. He can see the store owner reading this verse and thinking, "Somebody needs to work that day. If I can't, my son will." So God says, *Nor your son.* "Then my daughter will." *Nor your daughter.* "Then maybe an employee." *Nor them.* "I guess I'll have to send my cow to run the store, or maybe I'll find some stranger to help me." *No,* God says. *One day of the week you will say no to work and yes to worship. You will slow and sit down and lie down and rest.*

Still we object. "But . . . but . . . but . . . who is going to run the store?" "What about my grades?" "I've got my sales quota." We offer up one reason after another, but God silences them all with a poignant reminder: "In six days the LORD made the heavens and the earth, the sea, and all that is in them, and rested the seventh day." God's message is plain: "If creation didn't crash when I rested, it won't crash when you do."

Repeat these words after me: It is not my job to run the world.

A century ago Charles Spurgeon gave this advice to his preaching students:

> Even beasts of burden must be turned out to grass occasionally; the very sea pauses at ebb and flood; earth keeps the Sabbath of the wintry months; and man, even when exalted to God's ambassador, must rest or faint, must trim his lamp or let it burn low; must recruit his vigor or grow prematurely old. . . . In the long run we shall do more by sometimes doing less.[5]

The bow cannot always be bent without fear of breaking. For a field to bear fruit, it must occasionally lie fallow. And for you to be healthy, you must rest. Slow down, and God will heal you. He will bring rest to your mind, to your body, and most of all to your soul. He will lead you to green pastures.

Green pastures were not the natural terrain of Judea. The hills around Bethlehem where David kept his flock were not lush and green. Even today they are white and parched. Any green pasture in Judea is the work of some shepherd. He has cleared the rough, rocky land. Stumps have been torn out, and brush has been burned. Irrigation. Cultivation. Such are the work of a shepherd.

Hence, when David says, "He makes me to lie down in green pastures," he is saying, "My shepherd makes me lie down in his finished work." With his own pierced hands, Jesus created a pasture for the soul. He tore out the thorny underbrush of condemnation. He pried loose the huge boulders of sin. In their place he planted seeds of grace and dug ponds of mercy.

And he invites us to rest there. Can you imagine the satisfaction in the heart of the shepherd when, with work completed, he sees his sheep rest in the tender grass?

Can you imagine the satisfaction in the heart of God when we do the same? His pasture is his gift to us. This is not a pasture that you have made. Nor is it a pasture that you deserve. It is a gift of God. "For it is by grace you have been saved, through faith—

and this not from yourselves, it is the gift of God" (Eph. 2:8 NIV).

In a world rocky with human failure, there is a land lush with divine mercy. Your Shepherd invites you there. He wants you to lie down. Nestle deeply until you are hidden, buried, in the tall shoots of his love, and there you will find rest.

6

Whaddifs and Howells

The Burden of Worry

He leads me beside the still waters.
PSALM 23:2 NKJV

Your ten-year-old is worried. So anxious he can't eat. So worried he can't sleep. "What's wrong?" you inquire. He shakes his head and moans, "I don't even have a pension plan."

Or your four-year-old is crying in bed. "What's wrong, sweetheart?" She whimpers, "I'll never pass college chemistry."

Your eight-year-old's face is stress-struck. "I'll be a rotten parent. What if I set a poor example for my kids?"

How would you respond to such statements? Besides calling a child psychologist, your response would be emphatic: "You're too young to worry about those things. When the time comes, you'll know what to do."

Fortunately, most kids don't have such thoughts.

Unfortunately, we adults have more than our share. Worry is the burlap bag of burdens. It's overflowing with "whaddifs" and "howells." "Whaddif it rains at my wedding?" "Howell I know when to discipline my kids?" "Whaddif I marry a guy who snores?" "Howell we pay our baby's tuition?" "Whaddif, after all my dieting, they learn that lettuce is fattening and chocolate isn't?"

The burlap bag of worry. Cumbersome. Chunky. Unattractive. Scratchy. Hard to get a handle on. Irritating to carry and impossible to give away. No one wants your worries.

The truth be told, you don't want them either. No one has to remind you of the high cost of anxiety. (But I will anyway.) Worry divides the mind. The biblical word for *worry (merimnao)* is a compound of two Greek words, *merizo* ("to divide") and *nous* ("the mind"). Anxiety splits our energy between today's priorities and tomorrow's problems. Part of our mind is on the now; the rest is on the not yet. The result is half-minded living.

That's not the only result. Worrying is not a disease, but it causes diseases. It has been connected to high blood pressure, heart trouble, blindness, migraine headaches, thyroid malfunctions, and a host of stomach disorders.

Anxiety is an expensive habit. Of course, it might be worth the cost if it worked. But it doesn't. Our frets are futile. Jesus said, "You cannot add any time to your life by worrying about it" (Matt. 6:27). Worry has never brightened a day, solved a problem, or cured a disease.

How can a person deal with anxiety? You might try what one fellow did. He worried so much that he decided to hire someone to do his worrying for him. He found a man who agreed to be his hired worrier for a salary of $200,000 per year. After the man accepted the job, his first question to his boss was, "Where are you going to get $200,000 per year?" To which the man responded, "That's your worry."

Sadly, worrying is one job you can't farm out, but you can overcome it. There is no better place to begin than in verse two of the shepherd's psalm.

"He leads me beside the still waters," David declares. And, in case we missed the point, he repeats the phrase in the next verse: "He leads me in the paths of right-eousness."

"He leads me." God isn't behind me, yelling, "Go!" He is ahead of me, bidding, "Come!" He is in front, clearing the path, cutting the brush, showing the way. Just before the curve, he says, "Turn here." Prior to the rise, he motions, "Step up here." Standing next to the rocks, he warns, "Watch your step here."

He leads us. He tells us what we need to know when we need to know it. As a New Testament writer would affirm: "We will find grace to help us *when we need it*" (Heb. 4:16 NLT, emphasis mine).

Listen to a different translation: "Let us therefore boldly approach the throne of our gracious God, where we may receive mercy and in his grace find *timely help*" (Heb. 4:16 NEB, emphasis mine).

God's help is timely. He helps us the same way a father gives plane tickets to his family. When I travel with my kids, I carry all our tickets in my satchel. When the moment comes to board the plane, I stand between the attendant and the child. As each daughter passes, I place a ticket in her hand. She, in turn, gives the ticket to the attendant. Each one receives the ticket in the nick of time.

What I do for my daughters God does for you. He places himself between you and the need. And at the right time, he gives you the ticket. Wasn't this the promise he gave his disciples? "When you are arrested and judged, don't worry ahead of time about what you should say. Say whatever *is given you to say at that time,* because it will not really be you speaking; it will be the Holy Spirit" (Mark 13:11, emphasis mine).

Isn't this the message God gave the children of Israel? He promised to supply them with manna each day. But he told them to collect only one day's supply at a time. Those who disobeyed and collected enough for two days found themselves with rotten manna. The only exception to the rule was the day prior to the Sabbath. On Friday they could gather twice as much. Otherwise, God would give them what they needed, in their time of need.

God leads us. God will do the right thing at the right time. And what a difference that makes.

Since I know his provision is timely, I can enjoy the present.

"Give your entire attention to what God is doing right now, and don't get worked up about what may or may not happen tomorrow. God will help you deal with whatever hard things come up when the time comes" (Matt. 6:34 MSG).

That last phrase is worthy of your highlighter: "when the time comes."

"I don't know what I'll do if my husband dies." You will, *when the time comes.*

"When my children leave the house, I don't think I can take it." It won't be easy, but strength will arrive *when the time comes.*

"I could never lead a church. There is too much I don't know." You may be right. Or you may be wanting to know everything too soon. Could it be that God will reveal answers to you *when the time comes?*

The key is this: Meet today's problems with today's strength. Don't start tackling tomorrow's problems until tomorrow. You do not have tomorrow's strength yet. You simply have enough for today.

More than eighty years ago a great Canadian man of medicine, Sir William Osler, delivered a speech to the students of Yale University entitled "A Way of Life." In the message he related an event that occurred while he was aboard an ocean liner.

One day while he was visiting with the ship's captain, a loud, piercing alarm sounded, followed by strange grinding and crashing sounds below the deck. "Those are our watertight compartments closing," the captain explained. "It's an important part of our safety drill. In case of real trouble, water leaking into one compartment would not affect the rest of the ship. Even if we should collide with an iceberg, as did the *Titanic,* water rushing in will fill only that particular ruptured compartment. The ship, however, will still remain afloat."

When he spoke to the students at Yale, Osler remembered the captain's description of the boat:

Each one of you is certainly a much more marvelous organization than that great liner and bound on a far longer voyage. What I urge is that you learn to master your life by living each day in a day-tight compartment and this will certainly ensure your safety throughout your entire journey of life. Touch a button and hear, at every level of your life, the iron doors shutting out the Past—the dead yesterdays. Touch another and shut off, with a metal curtain, the Future—the unborn tomorrows. Then you are safe—safe for today.

Think not of the amount to be accomplished, the difficulties to be overcome, but set earnestly at the little task near your elbow, letting that be sufficient for the day; for surely our plain duty is not to see what lies dimly at a distance but to do what lies clearly at hand.[1]

Jesus made the same point in fewer words: "So don't worry about tomorrow, because tomorrow will have its own worries. Each day has enough trouble of its own" (Matt. 6:34).

Easy to say. Not always easy to do, right? We are so prone to worry. Just last night I was worrying in my sleep. I dreamed that I was diagnosed with ALS, a degenerative muscle disease, which took the life of my father. I awakened from the dream and, right there in the middle of the night, began to worry. Then Jesus' words came to my mind, "Don't worry about tomorrow." And for once, I decided not to. I dropped the burlap sack. After all, why let tomorrow's imaginary problem rob tonight's rest? Can I prevent the disease by staying awake? Will I postpone the affliction by thinking about it? Of course not. So I did the most spiritual thing I could have done. I went back to sleep.

Why don't you do the same? God is leading you. Leave tomorrow's problems until tomorrow.

Arthur Hays Sulzberger was the publisher of the *New York Times* during the Second World War. Because of the world conflict, he found it almost impossible to sleep. He was never able to banish worries from his mind until he adopted as his motto these five words—"one step enough for me"—taken from the hymn "Lead Kindly Light."[2]

Lead, kindly Light . . .
Keep Thou my feet; I do not ask to see
The distant scene; one step enough for me.

God isn't going to let you see the distant scene either. So you might as well quit looking for it. He promises a lamp unto our feet not a crystal ball into the future.[3] We do not need to know what will happen tomorrow. We only need to know he leads us and "we will find grace to help us when we need it" (Heb. 4:16 NLT).

7

It's a Jungle Out There

The Burden of Hopelessness

He restores my soul.
PSALM 23:3 NKJV

I wonder if you could imagine yourself in a jungle. A dense jungle. A dark jungle. Your friends convinced you it was time for a once-in-a-lifetime trip, and here you are. You paid the fare. You crossed the ocean. You hired the guide and joined the group. And you ventured where you had never ventured before—into the thick, strange world of the jungle.

Sound interesting? Let's take it a step farther. Imagine that you are in the jungle, lost and alone. You paused to lace your boot, and when you looked up, no one was near. You took a chance and went to the right; now you're wondering if the others went to the left. (Or did you go left and they go right?)

Whatever, you are alone. And you have been alone for, well, you don't know how long it has been. Your watch was attached to your pack, and your pack is on the shoulder of the nice guy from New Jersey who volunteered to hold it while you tied your boots. You didn't intend for him to walk off with it. But he did. And here you are, stuck in the middle of nowhere.

You have a problem. First, you were not made for this place. Drop you in the center of avenues and buildings, and you could sniff your way home. But here in sky-blocking foliage? Here in trail-hiding thickets? You are out of your element. You weren't made for this jungle.

What's worse, you aren't equipped. You have no machete. No knife. No matches. No flares. No food. You aren't equipped, but now you are trapped—and you haven't a clue how to get out.

Sound like fun to you? Me either. Before moving on, let's pause and ask how you would feel. Given such circumstances, what emotions would surface? With what thoughts would you wrestle?

Fear? Of course you would.

Anxiety? To say the least.

Anger? I could understand that. (You'd like to get your hands on those folks who convinced you to take this trip.)

But most of all, what about hopelessness? No idea where to turn. No hunch what to do. Who could blame you for sitting on a log (better check for snakes first), burying your face in your hands, and thinking, *I'll never get out of here.* You have no direction, no equipment, no hope.

Can you freeze frame that emotion for a moment? Can you sense, for just a second, how it feels to be out of your element? Out of solutions? Out of ideas and energy? Can you imagine, just for a moment, how it feels to be out of hope?

If you can, you can relate to many people in this world.

For many people, life is—well, life is a jungle. Not a jungle of trees and beasts. Would that it were so simple. Would that our jungles could be cut with a machete or our adversaries trapped in a cage. But our jungles are comprised of the thicker thickets of failing health, broken hearts, and empty wallets. Our forests are framed with hospital walls and divorce courts. We don't hear the screeching of birds or the roaring of lions, but we do hear the complaints of neighbors and the demands of bosses. Our predators are our creditors, and the brush that surrounds us is the rush that exhausts us.

It's a jungle out there.

And for some, even for many, hope is in short supply. Hopelessness is an odd bag. Unlike the others, it isn't full. It is empty, and its emptiness creates the burden. Unzip the top and examine all the pockets. Turn it upside down and shake it hard. The bag of hopelessness is painfully empty.

Not a very pretty picture, is it? Let's see if we can brighten it up. We've imagined the emotions of being lost; you think we can do the same with being rescued? What would it take to restore your hope? What would you need to reenergize your journey?

Though the answers are abundant, three come quickly to mind.

The first would be a person. Not just any person. You don't need someone equally confused. You need someone who knows the way out.

And from him you need some vision. You need someone to lift your spirits. You need someone to look you in the face and say, "This isn't the end. Don't give up. There is a better place than this. And I'll lead you there."

And, perhaps most important, you need direction. If you have only a person but no renewed vision, all you have is company. If he has a vision but no direction, you have a dreamer for company. But if you have a person with direction—who can take you from this place to the right place—ah, then you have one who can restore your hope.

Or, to use David's words, "He restores my soul."

Our Shepherd majors in restoring hope to the soul. Whether you are a lamb lost on a craggy ledge or a city slicker alone in a deep jungle, everything changes when your rescuer appears.

Your loneliness diminishes, because you have fellowship.

Your despair decreases, because you have vision.

Your confusion begins to lift, because you have direction.

Please note: You haven't left the jungle. The trees still eclipse the sky, and the thorns still cut the skin. Animals lurk and rodents scurry. The jungle is still a jungle. It hasn't changed, but you have. You have changed because you have hope. And you have hope because you have met someone who can lead you out.

Your Shepherd knows that you were not made for this place. He knows you are not equipped for this place. So he has come to guide you out.

He has come to restore your soul. He is the perfect one to do so.

He has the right vision. He reminds you that "you are like foreigners and strangers in this world" (1 Pet. 2:11). And he urges you to lift your eyes from the jungle around you to the heaven above you. "Don't shuffle along, eyes to the ground, absorbed with the things right in front of you. Look up, and be alert to what is going on around Christ. . . . See things from his perspective" (Col. 3:2 MSG).

David said it this way, "I lift up my eyes to the hills—where does my help come from? My help comes from the LORD, the Maker of heaven and earth. He will not let your foot slip—he who watches over you will not slumber. . . . The LORD watches over you . . . the sun will not harm you by day, nor the moon by night. The LORD will keep you from all harm—he will watch over your life" (Ps. 121:1–7 NIV).

God, your rescuer, has the right vision. He also has the right direction. He made the boldest claim in the history of man when he declared, "I am the way" (John 14:6). People wondered if the claim was accurate. He answered their questions by cutting a path through the underbrush of sin and death . . . and escaping alive. He's the only One who ever did. And he is the only One who can help you and me do the same.

He has the right vision: He has seen the homeland. He has the right directions: He has cut the path. But most of all, he is the right person, for he is our God. Who knows the jungle better than the One who made it? And who knows the pitfalls of the path better than the One who has walked it?

The story is told of a man on an African safari deep in the jungle. The guide before him had a machete and was whacking away the tall weeds and thick underbrush. The traveler, wearied and hot, asked in frustration, "Where are we? Do you know where you are taking me? Where is the path?!" The seasoned guide stopped and looked back at the man and replied, "I am the path."

We ask the same questions, don't we? We ask God, "Where are you taking me? Where is the path?" And he, like the guide, doesn't tell us. Oh, he may give us a hint or two, but that's all. If he did, would we understand? Would we comprehend our location? No, like the traveler, we are unacquainted with this jungle. So rather than give us an answer, Jesus gives us a far greater gift. He gives us himself.

Does he remove the jungle? No, the vegetation is still thick.

Does he purge the predators? No, danger still lurks.

Jesus doesn't give hope by changing the jungle; he restores our hope by giving us himself. And he has promised to stay until the very end. "I am with you always, to the very end of the age" (Matt. 28:20 NIV).

We need that reminder. We all need that reminder. For all of us need hope.

Some of you don't need it right now. Your jungle has become a meadow and your journey a delight. If such is the case, congratulations. But remember—we do not know what tomorrow holds. We do not know where this road will lead. You may be one turn from a cemetery, from a hospital bed, from an empty house. You may be a bend in the road from a jungle.

And though you don't need your hope restored today, you may tomorrow. And you need to know to whom to turn.

Or perhaps you do need hope today. You know you were not made for this place. You know you are not equipped. You want someone to lead you out.

If so, call out for your Shepherd. He knows your voice. And he's just waiting for your request.

8

A Heavenly Exchange

The Burden of Guilt

*He leads me in the paths of
righteousness for His name's sake.*
PSALM 23:3 NKJV

A friend organized a Christmas cookie swap
for our church office staff. The plan was simple. Price of admission was a tray of cookies.
Your tray entitled you to pick cookies from
the other trays. You could leave with as many
cookies as you brought.

Sounds simple, if you know how to cook.
But what if you can't? What if you can't tell a
pan from a pot? What if, like me, you are
culinarily challenged? What if you're as comfortable in an apron as a bodybuilder in a
tutu? If such is the case, you've got a problem.

Such was the case, and I had a problem. I

had no cookies to bring; hence I would have no place at the party. I would be left out, turned away, shunned, eschewed, and dismissed. (Are you feeling sorry for me yet?)

This was my plight.

And, forgive me for bringing it up, but your plight's even worse.

God is planning a party . . . a party to end all parties. Not a cookie party, but a feast. Not giggles and chitchat in the conference room, but wide-eyed wonder in the throne room of God.

Yes, the guestlist is impressive. Your question to Jonah about undergoing a gut check in a fish gut? You'll be able to ask him. But more impressive than the names of the guests is the nature of the guests. No egos, no power plays. Guilt, shame, and sorrow will be checked at the gate. Disease, death, and depression will be the Black Plagues of a distant past. What we now see daily, there we will never see.

And what we now see vaguely, there we will see clearly. We will see God. Not by faith. Not through the eyes of Moses or Abraham or David. Not via Scripture or sunsets or summer rains. We will see not God's work or words, but we will see him! For he is not the host of the party; he is the party. His goodness is the banquet. His voice is the music. His radiance is the light, and his love is the endless topic of discussion.

There is only one hitch. The price of admission is somewhat steep. In order to come to the party, you need to be righteous. Not good. Not decent. Not a taxpayer or churchgoer.

Citizens of heaven are righteous. R-i-g-h-t.

All of us *occasionally* do what is right. A few *predominantly* do what is right. But do any of us *always* do what is right? According to Paul we don't. "There is none righteous, no, not one" (Rom. 3:10 NKJV).

Paul is adamant about this. He goes on to say, "No one anywhere has kept on doing what is right; not one" (Rom. 3:12 TLB).

Some may beg to differ. "I'm not perfect, Max, but I'm better than most folks. I've led a good life. I don't break the rules. I don't break hearts. I help people. I like people. Compared to others, I think I could say I'm a righteous person."

I used to try that one on my mother. She'd tell me my room wasn't clean, and I'd ask her to go with me to my brother's room. His was always messier than mine. "See, my room is clean; just look at his."

Never worked. She'd walk me down the hall to her room. When it came to tidy rooms, my mom was righteous. Her closet was just right. Her bed was just right. Her bathroom was just right. Compared to hers, my room was, well, just wrong. She would show me her room and say, "This is what I mean by clean."

God does the same. He points to himself and says, "This is what I mean by righteousness."

Righteousness is who God is.

"Our God and Savior Jesus Christ does what is right" (2 Pet. 1:1).

"God is a righteous judge" (Ps. 7:11 NIV).

"The LORD is righteous, he loves justice" (Ps. 11:7 NIV).

God's righteousness "endures forever" (Ps. 112:3 NIV) and "reaches to the skies" (Ps. 71:19 NIV).

Isaiah described God as "a righteous God and a Savior" (Isa. 45:21 NIV).

On the eve of his death, Jesus began his prayer with the words "Righteous Father" (John 17:25 NIV).

Get the point? God is righteous. His decrees are righteous (Rom. 1:32). His judgment is righteous (Rom. 2:5). His requirements are righteous (Rom. 8:4). His acts are righteous (Dan. 9:16). Daniel declared, "Our God is right in everything he does" (Dan. 9:14).

God is never wrong. He has never rendered a wrong decision, experienced the wrong attitude, taken the wrong path, said the wrong thing, or acted the wrong way. He is never too late or too early, too loud or too soft, too fast or too slow. He has always been and always will be right. He is righteous.

When it comes to righteousness, God runs the table without so much as a bank shot. And when it comes to righteousness, we don't know which end of the cue stick to hold. Hence, our plight.

Will God, who is righteous, spend eternity with those who are not? Would Harvard admit a third-grade dropout? If it did, the act might be benevolent, but it wouldn't be right. If God accepted the unrighteous, the invitation would be even nicer, but would he be right? Would he be right to overlook our sins? Lower his standards?

No. He wouldn't be right. And if God is anything, he is right.

He told Isaiah that righteousness would be his plumb line, the standard by which his house is measured (Isa. 28:17). If we are unrighteous, then, we are left in the hallway with no cookies. Or to use Paul's analogy, "we're sinners, every one of us, in the same sinking boat with everybody else" (Rom. 3:19 MSG). Then what are we to do?

Carry a load of guilt? Many do. So many do.

What if our spiritual baggage were visible? Suppose the luggage in our hearts was literal luggage on the street. You know what you'd see most of all? Suitcases of guilt. Bags bulging with binges, blowups, and compromises. Look around you. The fellow in the gray-flannel suit? He's dragging a decade of regrets. The kid with the baggy jeans and nose ring? He'd give anything to retract the words he said to his mother. But he can't. So he tows them along. The woman in the business suit? Looks as if she could run for senator? She'd rather run for help, but she can't run at all. Not hauling that carpetbag of cagmag everywhere she goes.

Listen. The weight of weariness pulls you down. Self-reliance misleads you. Disappointments discourage you. Anxiety plagues you. But guilt? Guilt consumes you.

So what do we do? Our Lord is right, and we are wrong. His party is for the guiltless, and we are anything but. What do we do?

I can tell you what I did. I confessed my need. Remember my cookie dilemma? This is the e-mail I sent to the whole staff. "I can't cook, so I can't be at the party."

Did any of the assistants have mercy on me? No.

Did any of the staff have mercy on me? No.

Did any of the Supreme Court justices have mercy upon me? No.

But a saintly sister in the church did have mercy on me. How she heard of my problem, I do not know. Perhaps my name found its way on an emergency prayer list. But I do know this. Only moments before the celebration, I was given a gift, a plate of cookies, twelve circles of kindness.

And by virtue of that gift, I was privileged a place at the party.

Did I go? You bet your cookies I did. Like a prince carrying a crown on a pillow, I carried my gift into the room, set it on the table, and stood tall. And because some good soul heard my plea, I was given a place at the table.

And because God hears your plea, you'll be given the same. Only, he did more—oh, so much more—than bake cookies for you.

It was, at once, history's most beautiful and most horrible moment. Jesus stood in the tribunal of heaven. Sweeping a hand over all creation, he pleaded, "Punish me for their mistakes. See the murderer? Give me his penalty. The adulteress? I'll take her shame. The bigot, the liar, the thief? Do to me what you would do to them. Treat me as you would a sinner."

And God did. "For Christ died for sins once for all, the righteous for the unrighteous, to bring you to God" (1 Pet. 3:18 NIV).

Yes, righteousness is what God is, and, yes, righteousness is what we are not, and, yes, righteousness is what God requires. But "God has a way to make people right with him" (Rom. 3:21).

David said it like this: "He leads me in the paths of righteousness" (Ps. 23:3 NKJV).

The path of righteousness is a narrow, winding trail up a steep hill. At the top of the hill is a cross. At the base of the cross are bags. Countless bags full of innumerable sins. Calvary is the compost pile for guilt. Would you like to leave yours there as well?

One final thought about the Christmas cookie party. Did everyone know I didn't cook the cookies? If they didn't, I told them. I told them I was present by virtue of someone else's work. My only contribution was my own confession.

We'll be saying the same for eternity.

9

Get Over Yourself

The Burden of Arrogance

For His name's sake . . .
PSALM 23:3 NKJV

Humility is such an elusive virtue. Once you think you have it, you don't, or you wouldn't think you did. You've heard the story of the boy who received the "Most Humble" badge and had it taken away because he wore it?

Something similar happened to me just the other morning. I had retreated to a nearby town to work on this book. The village is a perfect hideaway; it is quaint, quiet, and has great food.

I'd gone to a café for breakfast when I noticed that people were staring at me. As I parked, two fellows turned and looked in my direction. A woman did a double take as I entered, and several patrons looked up as I passed. When I took my seat, the waitress gave me a menu but not before she'd given me a good study.

Why the attention? Couldn't be my fly; I was wearing sweats. After some thought I took the mature posture and assumed they recognized me from my book jackets. *Why, this must be a town of readers. And,* I shrugged to myself, *they know a good author when they see one.* My appreciation for the village only increased.

Giving a smile to the folks at the other tables, I set about to enjoy my meal. When I walked to the cash register, the heads turned again. *I'm sure Steinbeck had the same problem.* The woman who took my money started to say something but then paused. Overwhelmed, I guessed.

It was only when I stopped in the rest room that I saw the real reason for the attention—a ribbon of dried blood on my chin. My patch job on the shaving nick hadn't worked, and I was left with my own turkey wattle.

So much for feeling famous. They probably thought I was an escapee from a Texas prison.

Oh, the things God does to keep us humble. He does it for our own good, you know. Would you set a saddle on the back of your five-year-old? Would God let you be saddled with arrogance? No way.

This is one piece of luggage God hates. He doesn't dislike arrogance. He doesn't disapprove of arrogance. He's not unfavorably disposed toward arrogance. God hates arrogance. What a meal of maggots does for our stomach, human pride does for God's.

"I hate pride and arrogance" (Prov. 8:13 NIV).

"The LORD despises pride" (Prov. 16:5 NLT).

God says, "Do nothing out of . . . vain conceit" (Phil. 2:3 NIV). And, "Do not let arrogance come out of your mouth" (1 Sam. 2:3 NASB). And, in the same way that he gives grace to the humble, "God opposes the proud" (1 Pet. 5:5 NIV). As humility goes before honor, "pride goes . . . before a fall" (Prov. 16:18 NIV).

Ever wonder why churches are powerful in one generation but empty the next? Perhaps the answer is found in Proverbs 15:25: "The LORD will tear down the house of the proud" (NASB).

God hates arrogance. He hates arrogance

because we haven't done anything to be arrogant about. Do art critics give awards to the canvas? Is there a Pulitzer for ink? Can you imagine a scalpel growing smug after a successful heart transplant? Of course not. They are only tools, so they get no credit for the accomplishments.

And the message of the Twenty-third Psalm is that we have nothing to be proud about either. We have rest, salvation, blessings, and a home in heaven—and we did nothing to earn any of it. Who did? Who did the work? The answer threads through the psalm like a silk thread through pearls.

"He makes me . . ."

"He leads me . . ."

"He restores my soul . . ."

"You are with me . . ."

"Your rod and Your staff . . . comfort me . . ."

"You prepare a table . . ."

"You anoint my head . . ."

We may be the canvas, the paper, or the scalpel, but we are not the ones who deserve the applause. And just to make sure we get the point, right smack-dab in the middle of the poem, David declares who does. The shepherd leads his sheep, not for our names' sake, but "for His name's sake."

Why does God have anything to do with us? *For his name's sake.* No other name on the marquee. No other name up in lights. No other name on the front page. This is all done for God's glory.

Why? What's the big deal? Does God have an ego problem?

No, but we do. We are about as responsible with applause as I was with the cake I won in the first grade. In the grand finale of the musical chairs competition, guess who had a seat? And guess what the little red-headed, freckle-faced boy won? A tender, moist coconut cake. And guess what the boy wanted to do that night in one sitting? Eat the whole thing! Not half of it. Not a piece of it. All of it! After all, I'd won it.

But you know what my folks did? They rationed the cake. They gave me only what I could handle. Knowing that today's binge is tomorrow's bellyache, they made sure I didn't get sick on my success.

God does the same. He takes the cake. He takes the credit, not because he needs it, but because he knows we can't handle it. We aren't content with a bite of adulation; we tend to swallow it all. It messes with our systems. The praise swells our heads and shrinks our brains, and pretty soon we start thinking we had something to do with our survival. Pretty soon we forget we were made out of dirt and rescued from sin.

Pretty soon we start praying like the fellow at the religious caucus: "God, I thank you that the world has people like me. The man on the corner needs welfare—I don't. The prostitute on the street has AIDS—I don't. The drunk at the bar needs alcohol—I don't. The gay caucus needs morality—I don't. I thank you that the world has people like me."

Fortunately, there was a man in the same meeting who had deflected all the applause. Too contrite even to look to the skies, he bowed and prayed, "God, have mercy on me, a sinner. Like my brother on welfare, I'm dependent on your grace. Like my sister with AIDS, I'm infected with mistakes. Like my friend who drinks, I need something to ease my pain. And as you love and give direction to the gay, grant some to me as well. Have mercy on me, a sinner."

After telling a story like that, Jesus said, "I tell you, when this man went home, he was right with God, but the Pharisee was not. All who make themselves great will be made humble, but all who make themselves humble will be made great" (Luke 18:14).

With the same intensity that he hates arrogance, God loves humility. The Jesus who said, "I am gentle and humble in heart" (Matt. 11:29 NASB) loves those who are gentle and humble in heart. "Though the LORD is supreme, he takes care of those who are humble" (Ps. 138:6). God says, "I live with people who are . . . humble" (Isa. 57:15). He also says, "To this one I will look, to him who is humble and contrite" (Isa. 66:2 NASB). And to the humble, God gives great treasures:

He gives honor: "Humility goes before honor" (Prov. 15:33 NRSV).

He gives wisdom: "With the humble is wisdom" (Prov. 11:2 NASB).

He gives direction: "He teaches the humble His way" (Ps. 25:9 NASB).

And most significantly, he gives grace: "God . . . gives grace to the humble" (1 Pet. 5:5).

And this reassurance: "He crowns the humble with salvation" (Ps. 149:4 NIV).

The mightiest of the saints were known for their humility. Though Moses had served as prince of Egypt and emancipator of the slaves, the Bible says, "Moses was . . . more humble than anyone else" (Num. 12:3 NIV).

The apostle Paul was saved through a personal visit from Jesus. He was carried into the heavens and had the ability to raise the dead. But when he introduced himself, he mentioned none of these. He simply said, "I, Paul, am God's slave" (Titus 1:1 MSG).

John the Baptist was a blood relative of Jesus and the first evangelist in history, but he is remembered in Scripture as the one who resolved, "He must increase, but I must decrease" (John 3:30 NKJV).

God loves humility. Could that be the reason he offers so many tips on cultivating it? May I, ahem, humbly articulate a few?

1. Assess yourself honestly. Humility isn't the same as low self-esteem. Being humble doesn't mean you think you have nothing to offer; it means you know exactly what you have to offer and no more. "Don't cherish exaggerated ideas of yourself or your importance, but try to have a sane estimate of your capabilities by the light of the faith that God has given to you" (Rom. 12:3 PHILLIPS).

2. Don't take success too seriously. Scripture gives this warning: "When your . . . silver and gold increase, . . . your heart will become proud" (Deut. 8:13–14). Counteract this pride with reminders of the brevity of life and the frailty of wealth.

Ponder your success and count your money in a cemetery, and remember that neither of the two is buried with you. "People come into this world with nothing, and when they die they leave with nothing" (Eccles. 5:15). I saw a reminder of this in a cemetary. Parked next to the entrance was a nice recreational boat with a For Sale sign. You had to wonder if the fisherman realized he couldn't take it with him.

3. Celebrate the significance of others. "In humility consider others better than your-selves" (Phil. 2:3 NIV). Columnist Rick Reilly gave this advice to rookie professional ath-letes: "Stop thumping your chest. The line blocked, the quarterback threw you a perfect spiral while getting his head knocked off, and the *good* receiver blew the double cov-erage. Get over yourself."[1]

The truth is, every touchdown in life is a team effort. Applaud your teammates. An el-ementary-age boy came home from the try-outs for the school play. "Mommy, Mommy," he announced, "I got a part. I've been cho-sen to sit in the audience and clap and cheer." When you have a chance to clap and cheer, do you take it? If you do, your head is starting to fit your hat size.

4. Don't demand your own parking place. This was the instruction of Jesus to his followers: "Go sit in a seat that is not important. When the host comes to you, he may say, 'Friend, move up here to a more important place.' Then all the other guests will respect you" (Luke 14:10).

Demanding respect is like chasing a butterfly. Chase it, and you'll never catch it. Sit still, and it may light on your shoulder. The French philosopher Blaise Pascal asked, "Do you wish people to speak well of you? Then never speak well of yourself."[2] Maybe that's why the Bible says, "Don't praise yourself. Let someone else do it" (Prov. 27:2).

5. Never announce your success before it occurs. Or as one of the kings of Israel said, "One who puts on his armor should not boast like one who takes it off" (1 Kings 20:11 NIV). Charles Spurgeon trained many young ministers. On one occasion a student stepped up to preach with great confidence but failed miserably. He came down, humbled and meek. Spurgeon told him, "If you had gone up as you came down, you would have come down as you went up."³ If humility precedes an event, then confidence may follow.

6. Speak humbly. "Let no arrogance come from your mouth" (1 Sam. 2:3 NKJV). Don't be cocky. People aren't impressed with your opinions. Take a tip from Benjamin Franklin.

[I developed] the habit of expressing myself in terms of modest diffidence, never using when I advance any thing that may possibly be disputed, the words certainly, undoubtedly, or any others that give the air of positiveness to an opinion; but rather I say, I conceive or I apprehend a thing to be so or so. . . . This habit I believe has been a great advantage to me.⁴

It would be a great advantage to us as well.

One last thought to foster humility.

7. Live at the foot of the cross. Paul said, "The cross of our Lord Jesus Christ is my only reason for bragging" (Gal. 6:14). Do you feel a need for affirmation? Does your self-esteem need attention? You don't need to drop names or show off. You need only pause at the base of the cross and be reminded of this: The maker of the stars would rather die for you than live without you. And that is a fact. So if you need to brag, brag about that.

And check your chin occasionally.

10

I Will Lead You Home

The Burden of the Grave

Yea, though I walk through
the valley of the shadow
of death, I will fear no evil;
for You are with me;
Your rod and Your staff,
they comfort me.
PSALM 23:4 NKJV

Summer in ancient Palestine. A woolly bunch of bobbing heads follow the shepherd out of the gate. The morning sun has scarcely crested the horizon, and he is already leading his flock. Like every other day, he guides them through the gate and out into the fields. But unlike most days, the shepherd will not return home tonight. He will not rest on his bed, and the sheep will not sleep in their fenced-in pasture. This is the day the shepherd takes the sheep to the high country. Today he leads his flock to the mountains.

He has no other choice. Springtime grazing has left his pasture bare, so he must seek new fields. With no companion other than his sheep and no desire other than their welfare, he leads them to the deep grass of the hillsides. The shepherd and his flock will be gone for weeks, perhaps months. They will stay well into the autumn, until the grass is gone and the chill is unbearable.

Not all shepherds make this journey. The trek is long. The path is dangerous. Poisonous plants can infect the flock. Wild animals can attack the flock. There are narrow trails and dark valleys. Some shepherds choose the security of the barren pasture below.

But the good shepherd doesn't. He knows the path. He has walked this trail many times. Besides, he is prepared. Staff in hand and rod attached to his belt. With his staff he will nudge the flock; with his rod he will protect and lead the flock. He will lead them to the mountains.

David understood this annual pilgrimage. Before he led Israel, he led sheep. And could his time as a shepherd be the inspiration behind one of the greatest verses in the Bible? "Yea, though I walk through the valley of the shadow of death, I will fear no evil; for You are with me; Your rod and Your staff, they comfort me" (Ps. 23:4 NKJV).

For what the shepherd does with the flock, our Shepherd will do with us. He will lead us to the high country. When the pasture is bare down here, God will lead us up there. He will guide us through the gate, out of the flatlands, and up the path of the mountain.

But as one shepherd writes:

Every mountain has its valleys. Its sides are scarred by deep ravines and gulches and draws. And the best route to the top is always through these valleys.

Any sheepman familiar with the high country knows this. He leads his flock gently, but persistently up the paths that wind through the dark valleys.[1]

Someday our Shepherd will do the same with us. He will take us to the mountain by way of the valley. He will guide us to his house through the valley of the shadow of death.

Many years ago when I lived in Miami, our church office received a call from a nearby funeral home. A man had identified the body of an indigent as his brother and wanted a

memorial service. He didn't know any ministers in the area. Would we say a few words?
The senior minister and I agreed. When we
arrived, the brother of the deceased had selected a text from a Spanish Bible: "Yea,
though I walk through the valley of the
shadow of death, I will fear no evil; for You
are with me; Your rod and Your staff, they
comfort me" (Ps. 23:4 NKJV).

He needed assurance that, though his
brother had lived alone, he did not die alone.
And for that assurance, he turned to this
verse. You've likely done the same.

If you've attended a memorial service,
you've heard the words. If you've walked
through a cemetery, you've read them.
They're quoted at the gravesides of paupers,
carved on the headstones of kings. Those
who know nothing of the Bible know this part
of the Bible. Those who quote no scripture
can remember this scripture, the one about
the valley and the shadow and the shepherd.

Why? Why are these words so treasured?
Why is this verse so beloved? I can think of a
couple of reasons. By virtue of this psalm,
David grants us two important reminders
that can help us surrender our fear of the
grave.

We all have to face it. In a life marked by doctor appointments, dentist appointments, and school appointments, there is one appointment that none of us will miss, the appointment with death. "Everyone must die once, and after that be judged by God" (Heb. 9:27 TEV). Oh, how we'd like to change that verse. Just a word or two would suffice. "*Nearly* everyone must die . . ." or "*Everyone but me* must die . . ." or "*Everyone who forgets to eat right and take vitamins* must die . . ." But those are not God's words. In his plan everyone must die, even those who eat right and take their vitamins.

I could have gone all day without reminding you of that. We do our best to avoid the topic. One wise man, however, urges us to face it squarely: "We all must die, and everyone living should think about this" (Eccles. 7:2). Solomon isn't promoting a morbid obsession with death. He is reminding us to be honest about the inevitable.

Moses gave the same exhortation. In the only psalm attributed to his pen, he prayed, "Teach us how short our lives really are so that we may be wise" (Ps. 90:12).

The wise remember the brevity of life. Exercise may buy us a few more heartbeats.

Medicine may grant us a few more breaths. But in the end, there is an end. And the best way to face life is to be honest about death.

David was. He may have slain Goliath, but he had no illusions about sidestepping the giant of death. And though his first reminder sobers us, his second reminder encourages us: *We don't have to face death alone.*

Don't miss the shift in David's vocabulary. Up to this point, you and I have been the audience and God has been the topic. "The LORD is my shepherd." "He makes me to lie down." "He leads me beside the still waters." "He restores my soul." "He leads me in the paths of righteousness." For the first three verses, David speaks to us and God listens.

But suddenly in verse four, David speaks to God and we listen. It's as if David's face, which was on us, now lifts toward God. His poem becomes a prayer. Rather than speak to us, he speaks to the Good Shepherd. "You are with me; Your rod and Your staff, they comfort me."

David's implied message is subtle but crucial. Don't face death without facing God. Don't even speak of death without speaking to God. He and he alone can guide you through the valley. Others may speculate or aspire, but only God knows the way to get you home. And only God is committed to getting you there safely.

Years after David wrote these words, another Bethlehem Shepherd would say: "There are many rooms in my Father's house; I would not tell you this if it were not true. I am going there to prepare a place for you. After I go and prepare a place for you, I will come back and take you to be with me so that you may be where I am" (John 14:2–3).

Note the promise of Jesus. "I will come back and take you to be with me." He pledges to take us home. He does not delegate this task. He may send missionaries to teach you, angels to protect you, teachers to guide you, singers to inspire you, and physicians to heal you, but he sends no one to take you. He reserves this job for himself. "I will come back and take you home." He is your personal Shepherd. And he is personally responsible to lead you home. And because he is present when any of his sheep dies, you can say what David said, "I will fear no evil."

When my daughters were younger, we enjoyed many fun afternoons in the swimming pool. Just like all of us, they had to overcome their fears in order to swim. One of the final fears they had to face was the fear of the deep. It's one thing to swim on the surface; it's another to plunge down to the bottom. I mean, who knows what kind of dragons and serpents dwell in the depths of an eight-foot pool? You and I know there is no evil to fear, but a six-year-old doesn't. A child feels the same way about the deep that you and I feel about death. We aren't sure what awaits us down there.

I didn't want my daughters to be afraid of the deep end, so with each I played Shamu the whale. My daughter would be the trainer. I would be Shamu. She would pinch her nose and put her arm around my neck, then down we would go. Deep, deep, deep until we could touch the bottom of the pool. Then up we would explode, breaking the surface. After several plunges they realized they had nothing to fear. They feared no evil. Why? Because I was with them.

And when God calls us into the deep valley of death, he will be with us. Dare we think that he would abandon us in the moment of death? Would a father force his child to swim the deep alone? Would the shepherd require his sheep to journey to the highlands alone? Of course not. Would God require his child to journey to eternity alone? Absolutely not! He is with you!

What God said to Moses, he says to you: "My Presence will go with you, and I will give you rest" (Exod. 33:14 NIV).

What God said to Jacob, he says to you: "I am with you and will watch over you wherever you go" (Gen. 28:15 NIV).

What God said to Joshua, he says to you: "As I was with Moses, so I will be with you; I will never leave you nor forsake you" (Josh. 1:5 NIV).

What God said to the nation of Israel, he says to you: "When you pass through the waters, I will be with you" (Isa. 43:2 NIV).

The Good Shepherd is with you. And because he is with you, you can say what David said: "I will fear no evil; for You are with me; Your rod and Your staff, they comfort me."

Years ago a chaplain in the French army used the Twenty-third Psalm to encourage soldiers before battle. He would urge them to repeat the opening clause of the psalm, ticking it off, one finger at a time. The little finger represented the word *the;* the ring finger represented the word *LORD;* the middle finger, *is;* the index finger, *my;* and the thumb, *shepherd.* Then he asked every soldier to write the words on the palm of his hand and to repeat the verse whenever he needed strength.

The chaplain placed special emphasis on the message of the index finger—*my.* He reminded the soldiers that God is a personal shepherd with a personal mission—to get them home safely.

Did the chaplain's words find their mark? In the life of one man they did. After a battle one of the young soldiers was found dead, his right hand clutching the index finger of the left. "The LORD is my shepherd . . ."[2]

I pray that your final hours will find you clutching the same hope.

11

When Mourning Comes

The Burden of Grief

Though I walk through the valley
of the shadow of death . . .
PSALM 23:4 NKJV

Carlos Andres Baisdon-Niño lay down with his favorite Bible storybook. He began with the first chapter and turned every page until the end. When he finished, he blew his good-night kisses to Mami and Papi, to his three *"niñas,"* and then, as always, he blew one to Papa Dios. He closed his eyes, drifted off to sleep, and awoke in heaven.

Carlos was three years old.

When Tim and Betsa, his parents, and I met to plan the funeral, they wanted me to watch a video of Carlos. "You've got to see him dancing," Tim told me. One look and I could see why. What little Carlos did to the rhythm of a Latin song can't be described with words. He shook from top to bottom. His feet moved, his hands bounced, his head swayed. You got the impression that his heart rate had switched over to his native Colombian beat.

We laughed, the three of us did. And in the laughter, for just a moment, Carlos was with us. For just a moment there was no leukemia, syringes, blankets, or chemotherapy. There was no stone to carve or grave to dig. There was just Carlos. And Carlos was just dancing.

But then the video stopped, and so did the laughter. And this mom and dad resumed their slow walk through the valley of the shadow of death.

Are you passing through the same shadow? Is this book being held by the same hands that touched the cold face of a friend? And the eyes that fall upon this page, have they also fallen upon the breathless figure of a husband, wife, or child? Are you passing through the valley? If not, this chapter may seem unnecessary. Feel free to move on—it will be here when you need it.

If so, however, you know that the black bag of sorrow is hard to bear.

It's hard to bear because not everyone understands your grief. They did at first. They did at the funeral. They did at the graveside. But they don't now; they don't understand. Grief lingers.

As silently as a cloud slides between you and the afternoon sun, memories drift between you and joy, leaving you in a chilly shadow. No warning. No notice. Just a whiff of the cologne he wore or a verse of the song she loved, and you are saying good-bye all over again.

Why won't the sorrow leave you alone?

Because you buried more than a person. You buried some of yourself. Wasn't it John Donne who said, "Any man's death diminishes me"? It's as if the human race resides on a huge trampoline. The movements of one can be felt by all. And the closer the relationship, the more profound the exit. When someone you love dies, it affects you.

It affects your dreams.

Some years ago my wife and I served with other missionaries in Rio de Janeiro, Brazil. Our team consisted of several young couples who, by virtue of being far away from home, became very close. We rejoiced greatly when two of our team members,

Marty and Angela, announced that she was pregnant with their first child.

The pregnancy was difficult, however, and the joy became concern. Angela was told to stay in bed, and we were urged to stay in prayer. We did. And the Lord answered our prayers, though not as we desired. The baby died in the womb.

I've never forgotten Marty's comment. "More than a baby died, Max. A dream died."

Why does grief linger? Because you are dealing with more than memories—you are dealing with unlived tomorrows. You're not just battling sorrow—you're battling disappointment. You're also battling anger.

It may be on the surface. It may subterranean. It may be a flame. It may be a blowtorch. But anger lives in sorrow's house. Anger at self. Anger at life. Anger at the military or the hospital or the highway system. But most of all, anger at God. Anger that takes the form of the three-letter question—why? Why him? Why her? Why now? Why us?

You and I both know I can't answer that question. Only God knows the reasons behind his actions. But here is a key truth on which we can stand.

Our God is a good God.

"You are good, LORD. The LORD is good and right" (Ps. 25:7–8).

"Taste and see that the LORD is good" (Ps. 34:8 NIV).

God is a good God. We must begin here. Though we don't understand his actions, we can trust his heart.

God does only what is good. But how can death be good? Some mourners don't ask this question. When the quantity of years has outstripped the quality of years, we don't ask how death can be good.

But the father of the dead teenager does. The thirty-year-old widow does. The parents of Carlos did. My friends in Rio did. How could death be good?

Part of the answer may be found in Isaiah 57:1–2: "Good people are taken away, but no one understands. Those who do right are being taken away from evil and are given peace. Those who live as God wants find rest in death."

Death is God's way of taking people away from evil. From what kind of evil? An extended disease? An addiction? A dark season of rebellion? We don't know. But we know that no person lives one day more or less than God intends. "All the days planned for me were written in your book before I was one day old" (Ps. 139:16).

But her days here were so few . . .

His life was so brief . . .

To us it seems that way. We speak of a short life, but compared to eternity, who has a long one? A person's days on earth may appear as a drop in the ocean. Yours and mine may seem like a thimbleful. But compared to the Pacific of eternity, even the years of Methuselah filled no more than a glass. James was not speaking just to the young when he said, "Your life is like a mist. You can see it for a short time, but then it goes away" (James 4:14).

In God's plan every life is long enough and every death is timely. And though you and I might wish for a longer life, God knows better.

And—this is important—though you and I may wish a longer life for our loved ones, they don't. Ironically, the first to accept God's decision of death is the one who dies.

While we are shaking heads in disbelief, they are lifting hands in worship. While we are mourning at a grave, they are marveling at heaven. While we are questioning God, they are praising God.

But, Max, what of those who die with no faith? My husband never prayed. My grandpa never worshiped. My mother never opened a Bible, much less her heart. What about the one who never believed?

How do we know he didn't?

Who among us is privy to a person's final thoughts? Who among us knows what transpires in those final moments? Are you sure no prayer was offered? Eternity can bend the proudest knees. Could a person stare into the yawning canyon of death without whispering a plea for mercy? And could our God, who is partial to the humble, resist it?

He couldn't on Calvary. The confession of the thief on the cross was both a first and final one. But Christ heard it. Christ received it. Maybe you never heard your loved one confess Christ, but who's to say Christ didn't?

We don't know the final thoughts of a dying soul, but we know this. We know our God is a good God. He is "not willing that any should perish but that all should come to repentance" (2 Pet. 3:9 NKJV). He wants your loved one in heaven more than you do. And he usually gets what he wants.

You know what else God wants? He wants you to face your sorrow. Denial and dismissal are not a part of God's grief therapy.

David faced his. When he learned of the death of Saul and Jonathan, David and the entire army tore their clothing, wept aloud, and fasted until sunset. His lament was intense and public. "May there be no dew or rain on the mountains of Gilboa," he mourned, "and may their fields produce no grain. . . . We loved Saul and Jonathan and enjoyed them while they lived. They are together even in death. They were faster than eagles. They were stronger than lions" (2 Sam. 1:21–23).

David not only sang this dirge, he "ordered that the people of Judah be taught this song" (v. 18). Death was not soft-pedaled or passed over. Face it, fight it, question it, or condemn it, but don't deny it. As his son Solomon explained, "There is . . . a time to mourn" (Eccles. 3:1, 4 NIV). Don't heed, but do forgive, those who urge you not to.

God will lead you *through,* not around, the valley of the shadow of death. And, by the way, aren't you glad it's just a shadow?

Dr. Donald Grey Barnhouse told of the occasion of his first wife's death. He and his children were driving home from the burial, overcome with grief. He searched for a word of comfort to offer but could think of nothing. Just then, a large moving van drove by. As it passed, the shadow of the truck swept over the car. An inspiration came to Dr. Barnhouse. He turned to his family and asked, "Children, would you rather be run over by a truck or by its shadow?"

The children said, "Well, of course, Dad, we'd rather be run over by the shadow. That can't hurt us at all."

Dr. Barnhouse explained, "Did you know that two thousand years ago the truck of death ran over the Lord Jesus . . . in order that only its shadow might run over us?"[1]

We face death, but thanks to Jesus, we only face its shadow. And thanks to Jesus, we believe that our loved ones are happy and that the little Carloses of the world are dancing as never before.

12

From Panic to Peace

The Burden of Fear

I will fear no evil.
PSALM 23:4 NKJV

It's the expression of Jesus that puzzles us. We've never seen his face like this.

Jesus smiling, yes.

Jesus weeping, absolutely.

Jesus stern, even that.

But Jesus anguished? Cheeks streaked with tears? Face flooded in sweat? Rivulets of blood dripping from his chin? You remember the night.

Jesus left the city and went to the Mount of Olives, as he often did, and his followers went with him. When he reached the place, he said to them, "Pray for strength against temptation."

Then Jesus went about a stone's throw away from them. He kneeled down and prayed, "Father, if you are willing, take away this cup of suffering. But do what you want, not what I want." Then an angel from heaven appeared to him to strengthen him. Being full of pain, Jesus prayed even harder. His sweat was like drops of blood falling to the ground. (Luke 22:39–44)

The Bible I carried as a child contained a picture of Jesus in the Garden of Gethsemane. His face was soft, hands calmly folded as he knelt beside a rock and prayed. Jesus seemed peaceful. One reading of the Gospels disrupts that image. Mark says, "Jesus fell to the ground" (Mark 14:35). Matthew tells us Jesus was "very sad and troubled . . . to the point of death" (Matt. 26:37–38). According to Luke, Jesus was "full of pain" (Luke 22:44).

Equipped with those passages, how would you paint this scene? Jesus flat on the ground? Face in the dirt? Extended hands gripping grass? Body rising and falling with sobs? Face as twisted as the olive trees that surround him?

What do we do with this image of Jesus?

Simple. We turn to it when we look the same. We read it when we feel the same; we read it when we feel afraid. For isn't it likely that fear is one of the emotions Jesus felt? One might even argue that fear was the primary emotion. He saw something in the future so fierce, so foreboding that he begged for a change of plans. "Father, if you are willing, take away this cup of suffering" (Luke 22:42).

What causes you to pray the same prayer? Boarding an airplane? Facing a crowd? Public speaking? Taking a job? Taking a spouse? Driving on a highway? The source of your fear may seem small to others. But to you, it freezes your feet, makes your heart pound, and brings blood to your face. That's what happened to Jesus.

He was so afraid that he bled. Doctors describe this condition as hematidrosis. Severe anxiety causes the release of chemicals that break down the capillaries in the sweat glands. When this occurs, sweat comes out tinged with blood.

Jesus was more than anxious; he was

afraid. Fear is worry's big brother. If worry is a burlap bag, fear is a trunk of concrete. It wouldn't budge.

How remarkable that Jesus felt such fear. But how kind that he told us about it. We tend to do the opposite. Gloss over our fears. Cover them up. Keep our sweaty palms in our pockets, our nausea and dry mouths a secret. Not so with Jesus. We see no mask of strength. But we do hear a request for strength.

"Father, if you are willing, take away this cup of suffering." The first one to hear his fear is his Father. He could have gone to his mother. He could have confided in his disciples. He could have assembled a prayer meeting. All would have been appropriate, but none were his priority. He went first to his Father.

Oh, how we tend to go everywhere else. First to the bar, to the counselor, to the self-help book or the friend next door. Not Jesus. The first one to hear his fear was his Father in heaven.

A millennium earlier David was urging the fear-filled to do the same. "I will fear no evil." How could David make such a claim? Because he knew where to look. "You are with me; Your rod and Your staff, they comfort me."

Rather than turn to the other sheep, David turned to the Shepherd. Rather than stare at the problems, he stared at the rod and staff. Because he knew where to look, David was able to say, "I will fear no evil."

I know a fellow who has a fear of crowds. When encircled by large groups, his breath grows short, panic surfaces, and he begins to sweat like a sumo wrestler in a sauna. He received some help, curiously, from a golfing buddy.

The two were at a movie theatre, waiting their turn to enter, when fear struck again. The crowd closed in like a forest. He wanted out and out fast. His buddy told him to take a few deep breaths. Then he helped manage the crisis by reminding him of the golf course.

"When you are hitting your ball out of the rough, and you are surrounded by trees, what do you do?"

"I look for an opening."

"You don't stare at the trees?"

"Of course not. I find an opening and focus on hitting the ball through it."

"Do the same in the crowd. When you feel

the panic, don't focus on the people; focus on the opening."

Good counsel in golf. Good counsel in life. Rather than focus on the fear, focus on the solution.

That's what Jesus did.

That's what David did.

And that's what the writer of Hebrews urges us to do. "Let us run with endurance the race that is set before us, looking unto Jesus, the author and finisher of our faith" (Heb. 12:1–2 NKJV).

The writer of Hebrews was not a golfer, but he could have been a jogger, for he speaks of a runner and a forerunner. The forerunner is Jesus, the "author and finisher of our faith." He is the author—that is to say he wrote the book on salvation. And he is the finisher—he not only charted the map, he blazed the trail. He is the forerunner, and we are the runners. And we runners are urged to keep our eyes on Jesus.

I'm a runner. More mornings than not I drag myself out of bed and onto the street. I don't run fast. And compared to marathoners, I don't run far. But I run. I run because I don't like cardiologists. Nothing personal, mind you. It's just that I come from a family that keeps them in business. One told my dad he needed to retire. Another opened the chests of both my mom and brother. I'd like to be the one family member who doesn't keep a heart surgeon's number on speed dial.

Since heart disease runs in our family, I run in our neighborhood. As the sun is rising, I am running. And as I am running, my body is groaning. It doesn't want to cooperate. My knee hurts. My hip is stiff. My ankles complain. Sometimes a passerby laughs at my legs, and my ego hurts.

Things hurt. And as things hurt, I've learned that I have three options. Go home. (Denalyn would laugh at me.) Meditate on my hurts until I start imagining I'm having chest pains. (Pleasant thought.) Or I can keep running and watch the sun come up. My trail has just enough easterly bend to give me a front-row seat for God's morning miracle. If I watch God's world go from dark to golden, guess what? The same happens to my attitude. The pain passes and the joints loosen, and before I know it, the run is half over and life ain't half bad. Everything improves as I fix my eyes on the sun.

Wasn't that the counsel of the Hebrew

epistle—"looking unto Jesus"? What was the focus of David? "You are with me; Your rod and Your staff, they comfort me."

How did Jesus endure the terror of the crucifixion? He went first to the Father with his fears. He modeled the words of Psalm 56:3: "When I am afraid, I put my trust in you" (NLT).

Do the same with yours. Don't avoid life's Gardens of Gethsemane. Enter them. Just don't enter them alone. And while there, be honest. Pounding the ground is permitted. Tears are allowed. And if you sweat blood, you won't be the first. Do what Jesus did; open your heart.

And be specific. Jesus was. "Take *this* cup," he prayed. Give God the number of the flight. Tell him the length of the speech. Share the details of the job transfer. He has plenty of time. He also has plenty of compassion.

He doesn't think your fears are foolish or silly. He won't tell you to "buck up" or "get tough." He's been where you are. He knows how you feel.

And he knows what you need. That's why we punctuate our prayers as Jesus did. "If you are willing . . ."

Was God willing? Yes and no. He didn't take away the cross, but he took the fear. God didn't still the storm, but he calmed the sailor.

Who's to say he won't do the same for you?

"Do not be anxious about anything, but in everything, by prayer and petition, with thanksgiving, present your requests to God" (Phil. 4:6 NIV).

Don't measure the size of the mountain; talk to the One who can move it. Instead of carrying the world on your shoulders, talk to the One who holds the universe on his. Hope is a look away.

Now, what were you looking at?

13

Silent Nights and Solitary Days

The Burden of Loneliness

You are with me.
PSALM 23:4 NKJV

A friend of mine worked at a pharmacy while attending the University of Texas. Steve's primary job was to deliver supplies to nursing homes in the Austin area. An additional task, however, involved a short trip next door.

Every four days he shouldered a large jug of water and carried it fifty or so feet to a building behind the pharmacy. The customer was an older woman, perhaps in her seventies, who lived alone in a dark, sparse, and tarnished apartment. A single light bulb hung from the ceiling. The wallpaper was stained and peeling. The shades were drawn, and the room was shadowy. Steve would deliver the jug, receive the payment, thank the woman, and leave.

Over the weeks he grew puzzled by her purchase. He learned that the woman had no other source of water. She would rely on his delivery for four days of washing, bathing, and drinking. Odd choice. Municipal water was cheaper. The city would have charged her twelve to fifteen dollars a month; her expense at the pharmacy added up to fifty dollars a month. Why didn't she choose the less expensive source?

The answer was in the delivery system. Yes, the city water cost less. But the city sent only the water; they didn't send a person. She preferred to pay more and see a human being than pay less and see no one.

Could anyone be that lonely?

It seems that David was. Some of his psalms have the feel of a lone oak on a winter prairie.

He wrote:

Turn to me and be gracious to me,
    for I am lonely and afflicted. (Ps. 25:16 NIV)

I'm tired of all this—so tired. My bed
    has been floating forty days and nights

On the flood of my tears.
My mattress is soaked, soggy with tears.
The sockets of my eyes are black holes;
Nearly blind, I squint and grope. (Ps. 6:6–7
MSG)

David knew what it feels like to be lonely . . .
betrayed.

When they were sick, I dressed in black;
instead of eating, I prayed.
My prayers were like lead in my gut,
like I'd lost my best friend, my brother.
I paced, distraught as a motherless child,
hunched and heavyhearted.

But when I was down
they threw a party!
All the nameless riffraff of the town came
chanting insults about me.
Like barbarians desecrating a shrine,
they destroyed my reputation.

YAHWEH, how long are you going
to stand there doing nothing? (Ps. 35:13–17
MSG)

David knew the feeling of loneliness.
He knew it in his family. He was one of

eight sons of Jesse. But when Samuel the prophet asked to see Jesse's boys, David was overlooked. The prophet counted and asked if there wasn't another child somewhere. Jesse snapped his fingers as if he'd forgotten his keys. "I still have the youngest son. He is out taking care of the sheep" (1 Sam. 16:11).

Jesse's term for "youngest son" was not complimentary. He literally said, "I still have the runt." Some of you were the runt in your family. The runt is the one the others have to put up with and keep an eye on. And on this day the runt was left out. How would you feel if a family meeting was called and your name wasn't?

Things didn't improve when he changed households.

His inclusion in the royal family was King Saul's idea. His exclusion was Saul's idea as well. Had David not ducked, he would have been pinned to the wall by the spear of the jealous king. But David did duck, and David did run. For ten years he ran. Into the wilderness he ran. Sleeping in caves, surviving on wild animals. He was hated and hunted like a jackal.

David was no stranger to loneliness.

You aren't either. By now you've learned that you don't have to be alone to feel lonely. Two thousand years ago 250 million people populated the earth. Now there are more than 5 billion. If loneliness could be cured by the presence of people, then surely there would be less loneliness today. But loneliness lingers.

Very early in my ministry I offered this Sunday morning prayer: "Thank you, Lord, for all our friends. We have so many we can't spend time with them all." After the service a successful businessman corrected me, "You may have more friends than you can see. Not me. I have none." A person can be surrounded by a church and still be lonely.

Loneliness is not the absence of faces. It is the absence of intimacy. Loneliness doesn't come from being alone; it comes from feeling alone. Feeling as if you are

facing death alone,

facing disease alone,

facing the future alone.

Whether it strikes you in your bed at night or on your drive to the hospital, in the silence of an empty house or the noise of a crowded bar, loneliness is when you think, *I feel so alone. Does anyone care?*

Bags of loneliness show up everywhere. They litter the floors of boardrooms and clubs. We drag them into parties and usually drag them back out. You'll spot them near the desk of the overworker, beside the table of the overeater, and on the nightstand of the one-night stand. We'll try anything to unload our loneliness. This is one bag we want to drop quickly.

But should we? Should we be so quick to drop it? Rather than turn from loneliness, what if we turned toward it? Could it be that loneliness is not a curse but a gift? A gift from God?

Wait a minute, Max. That can't be. Loneliness heavies my heart. Loneliness leaves me empty and depressed. Loneliness is anything but a gift.

You may be right, but work with me for a moment. I wonder if loneliness is God's way of getting our attention.

Here's what I mean. Suppose you borrow a friend's car. His radio doesn't work, but his CD player does. You rummage through his collection, looking for your style of music—

let's say, country-western. But you find nothing. He has nothing but his style of music—let's say, classical.

It's a long trip. And you can talk to yourself for only so long. So eventually you reach for a CD. You'd prefer some steel guitar, but you're stuck with soaring tenors. Initially it's tolerable. At least it fills the air. But eventually it's enjoyable. Your heart picks up the pattern of the kettledrums, your head rolls with the cellos, and you even catch yourself attempting a little Italian concerto. "Hey, this isn't so bad."

Now, let me ask you. Would you have made this discovery on your own? No. What led to it? What caused you to hear music you'd never heard before? Simple. You had no other choice, no other option. You had nowhere else to go. Finally, when the silence was too loud, you took a chance on a song you'd never heard.

Oh, how God wants you to hear his music.

He has a rhythm that will race your heart and lyrics that will stir your tears. You want to journey to the stars? He can take you there. You want to lie down in peace? His music can soothe your soul.

But first, he's got to get rid of that country-western stuff. (Forgive me, Nashville. Only an example.)

And so he begins tossing the CDs. A friend turns away. The job goes bad. Your spouse doesn't understand. The church is dull. One by one he removes the options until all you have left is God.

He would do that? Absolutely. "The Lord disciplines those he loves" (Heb. 12:6). If he must silence every voice, he will. He wants you to hear his music. He wants you to discover what David discovered and to be able to say what David said.

"You are with me."

Yes, you, Lord, are in heaven. Yes, you rule the universe. Yes, you sit upon the stars and make your home in the deep. But yes, yes, yes, you are with me.

The Lord is with me. The Creator is with me. Yahweh is with me.

Moses proclaimed it: "What great nation has a god as near to them as the Lord our God is near to us" (Deut. 4:7 NLT).

Paul announced it: "He is not far from each one of us" (Acts 17:27 NIV).

And David discovered it: "You are with me."

Somewhere in the pasture, wilderness, or

palace, David discovered that God meant business when he said:

"I will not leave you" (Gen. 28:15).

"I will . . . not forsake My people" (1 Kings 6:13 NKJV).

"The LORD will not abandon His people" (Ps. 94:14 NASB).

"God . . . will never leave you nor forsake you" (Deut. 31:6 NIV).

The discovery of David is indeed the message of Scripture—*the Lord is with us.* And, since the Lord is near, everything is different. Everything!

You may be facing death, but you aren't facing death alone; the Lord is with you. You may be facing unemployment, but you aren't facing unemployment alone; the Lord is with you. You may be facing marital struggles, but you aren't facing them alone; the Lord is with you. You may be facing debt, but you aren't facing debt alone; the Lord is with you.

Underline these words: You are not alone.

Your family may turn against you, but God won't. Your friends may betray you, but God won't. You may feel alone in the wilderness, but you are not. He is with you. And because he is, everything is different. *You* are different.

God changes your *n* into a *v.* You go from *lonely* to *lovely.*

When you know God loves you, you won't be desperate for the love of others.

You'll no longer be a hungry shopper at the market. Have you ever gone to the grocery on an empty stomach? You're a sitting duck. You buy everything you don't need. Doesn't matter if it is good for you—you just want to fill your tummy. When you're lonely, you do the same in life, pulling stuff off the shelf, not because you need it, but because you are hungry for love.

Why do we do it? Because we fear facing life alone. For fear of not fitting in, we take the drugs. For fear of standing out, we wear the clothes. For fear of appearing small, we go into debt and buy the house. For fear of going unnoticed, we dress to seduce or to impress. For fear of sleeping alone, we sleep with anyone. For fear of not being loved, we search for love in all the wrong places.

But all that changes when we discover God's perfect love. And "perfect love casts out fear" (1 John 4:18 NKJV).

Loneliness. Could it be one of God's finest gifts? If a season of solitude is his way to teach you to hear his song, don't you think it's worth it?

So do I.

14

The Crowing
Rooster and Me

The Burden of Shame

*You prepare a table before me
in the presence of my enemies.*
PSALM 23:5 NKJV

See the fellow in the shadows? That's Peter. Peter the apostle. Peter the impetuous. Peter the passionate. He once walked on water. Stepped right out of the boat onto the lake. He'll soon preach to thousands. Fearless before friends and foes alike. But tonight the one who stepped on the water has hurried into hiding. The one who will speak with power is weeping in pain.

Not sniffling or whimpering, but weeping. Bawling. Bearded face buried in thick hands. His howl echoing in the Jerusalem night. What hurts more? The fact that he did it? Or the fact that he swore he never would?

"Lord, I am ready to go with you to prison and even to die with you!" he pledged only hours earlier. "But Jesus said, 'Peter, before the rooster crows this day, you will say three times that you don't know me'" (Luke 22:33–34).

Denying Christ on the night of his betrayal was bad enough, but did he have to boast that he wouldn't? And one denial was pitiful, but three? Three denials were horrific, but did he have to curse? "Peter began to place a curse on himself and swear, 'I don't know the man'" (Matt. 26:74).

And now, awash in a whirlpool of sorrow, Peter is hiding. Peter is weeping. And soon Peter will be fishing.

We wonder why he goes fishing. We know why he goes to Galilee. He had been told that the risen Christ would meet the disciples there. The arranged meeting place is not the sea, however, but a mountain (Matt. 28:16). If the followers were to meet Jesus on a mountain, what are they doing in a boat? No one told them to fish, but that's what they did. "Simon Peter said, 'I am going out to fish.' The others said, 'We will go with you'" (John 21:3). Besides, didn't Peter quit fishing? Two years earlier, when Jesus called him to fish for men, didn't he drop his net and follow? We haven't seen him fish since. We never see him fish again. Why is he fishing now? Especially now! Jesus has risen from the dead. Peter has seen the empty tomb. Who could fish at a time like this?

Were they hungry? Perhaps that's the sum of it. Maybe the expedition was born out of growling stomachs.

Or then again, maybe it was born out of a broken heart.

You see, Peter could not deny his denial. The empty tomb did not erase the crowing rooster. Christ had returned, but Peter wondered, he must have wondered, "After what I did, would he return for someone like me?"

We've wondered the same. Is Peter the only person to do the very thing he swore he'd never do?

"Infidelity is behind me!"

"From now on, I'm going to bridle my tongue."

"No more shady deals. I've learned my lesson."

Oh, the volume of our boasting. And, oh, the heartbreak of our shame.

Rather than resist the flirting, we return it.

Rather than ignore the gossip, we share it. Rather than stick to the truth, we shade it.

And the rooster crows, and conviction pierces, and Peter has a partner in the shadows. We weep as Peter wept, and we do what Peter did. We go fishing. We go back to our old lives. We return to our pre-Jesus practices. We do what comes naturally, rather than what comes spiritually. And we question whether Jesus has a place for folks like us.

Jesus answers that question. He answers it for you and me and all who tend to "Peter out" on Christ. His answer came on the shore of the sea in a gift to Peter. You know what Jesus did? Split the waters? Turn the boat to gold and the nets to silver? No, Jesus did something much more meaningful. He invited Peter to breakfast. Jesus prepared a meal.

Of course, the breakfast was one special moment among several that morning. There was the great catch of fish and the recognition of Jesus. The plunge of Peter and the paddling of the disciples. And there was the moment they reached the shore and found Jesus next to a fire of coals. The fish were sizzling, and the bread was waiting, and the defeater of hell and the ruler of heaven invited his friends to sit down and have a bite to eat.

No one could have been more grateful than Peter. The one Satan had sifted like wheat was eating bread at the hand of God. Peter was welcomed to the meal of Christ. Right there for the devil and his tempters to see, Jesus "prepared a table in the presence of his enemies."

OK, so maybe Peter didn't say it that way. But David did. "You prepare a table before me in the presence of my enemies" (Ps. 23:5 NKJV). What the shepherd did for the sheep sounds a lot like what Jesus did for Peter.

At this point in the psalm, David's mind seems to be lingering in the high country with the sheep. Having guided the flock through the valley to the alp lands for greener grass, he remembers the shepherd's added responsibility. He must prepare the pasture.

This is new land, so the shepherd must be careful. Ideally, the grazing area will be flat, a mesa or tableland. The shepherd searches for poisonous plants and ample water. He looks for signs of wolves, coyotes, and bears.

Of special concern to the shepherd is the adder, a small brown snake that lives underground. Adders are known to pop out of their holes and nip the sheep on the nose. The bite often infects and can even kill. As defense against the snake, the shepherd pours a circle of oil at the top of each adder's hole. He also applies the oil to the noses of the animals. The oil on the snake's hole lubricates the exit, preventing the snake from climbing out. The smell of the oil on the sheep's nose drives the serpent away. The shepherd, in a very real sense, has prepared the table.[1]

What if your Shepherd did for you what the shepherd did for his flock? Suppose he dealt with your enemy, the devil, and prepared for you a safe place of nourishment? What if Jesus did for you what he did for Peter? Suppose he, in the hour of your failure, invited you to a meal?

What would you say if I told you he has done exactly that?

On the night before his death, Jesus prepared a table for his followers.

On the first day of the Festival of Unleavened Bread, the day the lambs for the Passover meal were killed, Jesus' disciples asked him, "Where do you want us to go and get the Passover meal ready for you?"

Then Jesus sent two of them with these instructions: "Go into the city, and a man carrying a jar of water will meet you. Follow him to the house he enters, and say to the owner of the house: 'The Teacher says, Where is the room where my disciples and I will eat the Passover meal?' Then he will show you a large, upstairs room, fixed up and furnished, where you will get everything ready for us." (Mark 14:12–15 TEV)

Look who did the "preparing" here. Jesus reserved a large room and arranged for the guide to lead the disciples. Jesus made certain the room was furnished and the food set out. What did the disciples do? They faithfully complied and were fed.

The Shepherd prepared the table.

Not only that, he dealt with the snakes.

You'll remember that only one of the disciples didn't complete the meal that night. "The devil had already persuaded Judas Iscariot, the son of Simon, to turn against Jesus" (John 13:2). Judas started to eat, but Jesus didn't let him finish. On the command of Jesus, Judas left the room. "'The thing that you will do—do it quickly.' . . . Judas took the bread Jesus gave him and immediately went out. It was night" (John 13:27, 30).

There is something dynamic in this dismissal. Jesus prepared a table in the presence of the enemy. Judas was allowed to see the supper, but he wasn't allowed to stay there.

You are not welcome here. This table is for my children. You may tempt them. You may trip them. But you will never sit with them. This is how much he loves us.

And if any doubt remains, lest there be any "Peters" who wonder if there is a place at the table for them, Jesus issues a tender reminder as he passes the cup. "Every one of you drink this. This is my blood which is the new agreement that God makes with his people. This blood is poured out for many to forgive their sins" (Matt. 26:27–28).

"*Every one* of you drink this." Those who feel unworthy, drink this. Those who feel ashamed, drink this. Those who feel embarrassed, drink this.

May I share a time when I felt all three?

By the age of eighteen I was well on my way to a drinking problem. My system had become so resistant to alcohol that a six-pack of beer had little or no impact on me. At the age of twenty, God not only saved me from hell after this life, he saved me from hell during it. Only he knows where I was headed, but I have a pretty good idea.

For that reason, part of my decision to follow Christ included no more beer. So I quit. But, curiously, the thirst for beer never left. It hasn't hounded me or consumed me, but two or three times a week the thought of a good beer sure entices me. Proof to me that I have to be careful is this—nonalcoholic beers have no appeal. It's not the flavor of the drink; it's the buzz. But for more than twenty years, drinking has never been a major issue.

A couple of years ago, however, it nearly became one. I lowered my guard a bit. *One beer with barbecue won't hurt.* Then another time with Mexican food. Then a time or two with no food at all. Over a period of two months I went from no beers to maybe one or two a week. Again, for most people, no problem, but for me it could become one.

You know when I began to smell trouble? One hot Friday afternoon I was on my way to speak at our annual men's retreat. Did I say the day was hot? Brutally hot. I was thirsty. Soda wouldn't do. So I began to plot. Where could I buy a beer and not be seen by anyone I knew?

With that thought, I crossed a line. What's done in secret is best not done at all. But I did it anyway. I drove to an out-of-the-way convenience store, parked, and waited until all patrons had left. I entered, bought my beer, held it close to my side, and hurried to the car.

That's when the rooster crowed.

It crowed because I was sneaking around. It crowed because I knew better. It crowed because, and this really hurt, the night before I'd scolded one of my daughters for keeping secrets from me. And now, what was I doing?

I threw the beer in the trash and asked God to forgive me. A few days later I shared my struggle with the elders and some members of the congregation and was happy to chalk up the matter to experience and move on.

But I couldn't. The shame plagued me. Of all the people to do such a thing. So many could be hurt by my stupidity. And of all the times to do such a thing. En route to minister at a retreat. What hypocrisy!

I felt like a bum. Forgiveness found its way into my head, but the elevator designed to lower it eighteen inches to my heart was out of order.

And, to make matters worse, Sunday rolled around. I found myself on the front row of the church, awaiting my turn to speak. Again, I had been honest with God, honest with the elders, honest with myself. But still, I struggled. Would God want a guy like me to preach?

The answer came in the Supper. The Lord's Supper. The same Jesus who'd prepared a meal for Peter had prepared one for me. The same Shepherd who had trumped the devil trumped him again. The same Savior who had built a fire on the shore stirred a few embers in my heart.

"*Every one* of you drink this." And so I did. It felt good to be back at the table.

15

Slippery Sheep and Healed Hurts

The Burden of Disappointment

You anoint my head with oil.
PSALM 23:5 NKJV

Dis changes everything. With *dis*, "obey" becomes "*dis*obey." "Respect" is changed to "*dis*respect." "Regard" is suddenly "*dis*regard." What was an "ability" becomes a "*dis*ability." "Engage" is now "*dis*engage," and "grace" is transformed into "*dis*grace." All because of *dis*.

We'd be hard pressed to find a more potent trio of letters. And we'd be hard pressed to find a better example of their power than the word *appointment*.

Most of us like appointments. Even the organizationally inept like appointments. Appointments create a sense of predictability in an unpredictable world. Down deep we know we control the future as much as a caboose controls the train, yet our Day-Timers give us the illusion that we do.

A disappointment reminds us that we don't. A disappointment is a missed appointment. What we hoped would happen, didn't. We wanted health; we got disease. We wanted retirement; we got reassignment. Divorce instead of family. Dismissal instead of promotion. Now what? What do we do with our disappointments?

We could do what Miss Havisham did. Remember her in Charles Dickens's *Great Expectations*? Jilted by her fiancé just prior to the wedding, her appointment became a missed appointment and a disappointment. How did she respond? Not too well. She closed all the blinds in the house, stopped every clock, left the wedding cake on the table to gather cobwebs, and continued to wear her wedding dress until it hung in yellow decay around her shrunken form. Her wounded heart consumed her life.

We can follow the same course.

Or we can follow the example of the apostle Paul. His goal was to be a missionary in Spain. Rather than send Paul to Spain, however, God sent him to prison. Sitting in a Roman jail, Paul could have made the same choice as Miss Havisham, but he didn't. Instead he said, "As long as I'm here, I might as well write a few letters." Hence your Bible has the Epistles to Philemon, the Philippians, the Colossians, and the Ephesians.[1] No doubt Paul would have done a great work in Spain. But would it have compared with the work of those four letters?

You've sat where Paul sat. I know you have. You were hotter than a two-dollar pistol on the trail to Spain or college or marriage or independence . . . but then came the layoff or the pregnancy or the sick parent. And you ended up in prison. So long, Spain. Hello, Rome. So long, appointment. Hello, disappointment. Hello, pain.

How did you handle it? Better asked, how are you handling it? Could you use some help? I've got just what you need. Six words in the fifth verse of the Twenty-third Psalm: "You anoint my head with oil."

Don't see the connection? What does a verse on oil have to do with the hurts that come from the disappointments of life?

A little livestock lesson might help. In ancient Israel shepherds used oil for three purposes: to repel insects, to prevent conflicts, and to heal wounds.

Bugs bug people, but they can kill sheep. Flies, mosquitoes, and gnats can turn the summer into a time of torture for the livestock. Consider nose flies, for example. If they succeed in depositing their eggs into the soft membrane of the sheep's nose, the eggs become wormlike larvae, which drive the sheep insane. One shepherd explains: "For relief from this agonizing annoyance sheep will deliberately beat their heads against trees, rocks, posts, or brush. . . . In extreme cases of intense infestation a sheep may even kill itself in a frenzied endeavor to gain respite from the aggravation."[2]

When a swarm of nose flies appears, sheep panic. They run. They hide. They toss their heads up and down for hours. They forget to eat. They aren't able to sleep. Ewes stop milking, and lambs stop growing. The entire flock can be disrupted, even destroyed by the presence of a few flies.

For this reason, the shepherd anoints the sheep. He covers their heads with an oil-like repellent. The fragrance keeps the insects at bay and the flock at peace.

At peace, that is, until mating season.

Most of the year, sheep are calm, passive animals. But during mating season, everything changes. The rams put the "ram" in *rambunctious.* They strut around the pasture and flex their necks, trying to win the attention of the new gal on the block. When a ram catches her eye, he tosses his head back and says, "I want ewe, baby." About that time her boyfriend shows up and tells her to go someplace safe. "Ewe better move, sweetie. This could get ugly." The two rams lower their heads and POW! An old-fashioned head butt breaks out.

To prevent injury, the shepherd anoints the rams. He smears a slippery, greasy substance over the nose and head. This lubricant causes them to glance off rather than crash into each other.

They still tend to get hurt, however. And these wounds are the third reason the shepherd anoints the sheep.

Most of the wounds the shepherd treats are simply the result of living in a pasture. Thorns prick or rocks cut or a sheep rubs its head too hard against a tree. Sheep get hurt. As a result, the shepherd regularly, often daily, inspects the sheep, searching for cuts and abrasions. He doesn't want the cut to worsen. He doesn't want today's wound to become tomorrow's infection.

Neither does God. Just like sheep, we have wounds, but ours are wounds of the heart that come from disappointment after disappointment. If we're not careful, these wounds lead to bitterness. And so just like sheep, we need to be treated. "He made us, and we belong to him; we are his people, the sheep he tends" (Ps. 100:3).

Sheep aren't the only ones who need preventive care, and sheep aren't the only ones who need a healing touch. We also get irritated with each other, butt heads, and then get wounded. Many of our disappointments in life begin as irritations. The large portion of our problems are not lion-sized attacks, but rather the day-to-day swarm of frustrations and mishaps and heartaches. You don't get invited to the dinner party. You don't make the team. You don't get the scholarship. Your boss doesn't notice your hard work. Your husband doesn't notice your new dress. Your neighbor doesn't notice the mess in his yard. You find yourself more irritable, more gloomy, more . . . well, more hurt.

Like the sheep, you don't sleep well, you

don't eat well. You may even hit your head against a tree a few times.

Or you may hit your head against a person. It's amazing how hardheaded we can be with each other. Some of our deepest hurts come from butting heads with people.

Like the sheep, the rest of our wounds come just from living in the pasture. The pasture of the sheep, however, is much more appealing. The sheep have to face wounds from thorns and thistles. We have to face aging, loss, and illness. Some of us face betrayal and injustice. Live long enough in this world, and most of us will face deep, deep hurts of some kind or another.

So we, like the sheep, get wounded. And we, like the sheep, have a shepherd. Remember the words we read? "We belong to him; we are his people, the sheep he tends" (Ps. 100:3). He will do for you what the shepherd does for the sheep. He will tend to you.

If the Gospels teach us anything, they teach us that Jesus is a Good Shepherd. "I am the good shepherd," Jesus announces. "The good shepherd gives his life for the sheep" (John 10:11).

Didn't Jesus spread the oil of prevention

on his disciples? He prayed for them. He equipped them before he sent them out. He revealed to them the secrets of the parables. He interrupted their arguments and calmed their fears. Because he was a good shepherd, he protected them against disappointments.

Not only did Jesus prevent wounds, he healed them. He touched the eyes of the blind man. He touched the disease of the leper. He touched the body of the dead girl. Jesus tends to his sheep. He touched the searching heart of Nicodemus. He touched the open heart of Zacchaeus. He touched the broken heart of Mary Magdalene. He touched the confused heart of Cleopas. And he touched the stubborn heart of Paul and the repentant heart of Peter. Jesus tends to his sheep. And he will tend to you.

If you will let him. How? How do you let him? The steps are so simple.

First, go to him. David would trust his wounds to no other person but God. He said, "*You* anoint my head with oil." Not, "your prophets," "your teachers," or "your counselors." Others may guide us to God. Others may help us understand God. But no one does the work of God, for only God can heal. God "heals the brokenhearted" (Ps. 147:3).

Have you taken your disappointments to God? You've shared them with your neighbor, your relatives, your friends. But have you taken them to God? James says, "Anyone who is having troubles should pray" (James 5:13).

Before you go anywhere else with your disappointments, go to God.

Maybe you don't want to trouble God with your hurts. *After all, he's got famines and pestilence and wars; he won't care about my little struggles,* you think. Why don't you let him decide that? He cared enough about a wedding to provide the wine. He cared enough about Peter's tax payment to give him a coin. He cared enough about the woman at the well to give her answers. "He cares about you" (1 Pet. 5:7).

Your first step is to go to the right person. Go to God. Your second step is to assume the right posture. Bow before God.

In order to be anointed, the sheep must stand still, lower their heads, and let the shepherd do his work. Peter urges us to "be humble under God's powerful hand so he will lift you up when the right time comes" (1 Pet. 5:6).

When we come to God, we make requests; we don't make demands. We come with high hopes and a humble heart. We state what we want, but we pray for what is right. And if God gives us the prison of Rome instead of the mission of Spain, we accept it because we know "God will always give what is right to his people who cry to him night and day, and he will not be slow to answer them" (Luke 18:7).

We go to him. We bow before him, and we *trust in him.*

The sheep doesn't understand why the oil repels the flies. The sheep doesn't understand how the oil heals the wounds. In fact, all the sheep knows is that something happens in the presence of the shepherd. And that's all we need to know as well. "LORD, I give myself to you; my God, I trust you" (Ps. 25:1–2).

Go.

Bow.

Trust.

Worth a try, don't you think?

16

Jam Session

The Burden of Envy

My cup overflows with blessings.
PSALM 23:5 NLT

A member of our church gave me a jar of homemade peach preserves a couple of weeks ago. Few delicacies in life compare with her peach preserves. Should I someday face a firing squad, I'll pass on the cigarette but be the first to perk up if Sarah's peach preserves are offered. Each spoonful is a celestial experience. The only problem with her gift was that it didn't last. I'm sad to report that the bottom of my jar is in sight. I'll soon be shaking out the last drop like a lost cowboy shakes his canteen.

To be quite honest, I'm dreading the moment. Its proximity has affected my behavior.

Anyone who requests a taste of my peach preserves is met with a Clint Eastwood snarl, "Don't even think about it."

If I were Sarah's husband, Keith, I wouldn't have such a problem. He gets all the peach preserves he wants. Does the clinking of the spoon at the bottom of the jar trigger tears for Keith? Hardly, he has an unlimited supply. One might even say that he has more than he deserves. And one might wonder why he has so much and I have so little. Why should he have a pantryful and I just a jarful? Who gave him the key to the jam-and-jelly castle? Who made him the master of marmalades? Who crowned Keith the king of confitures? It's not fair. It's not right. In fact, the more I think about it . . .

Which is exactly what I shouldn't do. I shouldn't think about it. For resting at the end of this trail of thought is the deadly briefcase of envy. If you haven't seen one in real life, you've seen one in the spy movies. The assassin carries it up the back stairs into the vacated room at the top of the building. When he is sure no one can see him, he opens the case. The disassembled rifle sits in cushioned slots. The scope, the barrel, the stock—all await the hand of the marksman. The marksman awaits the arrival of his victim.

Who is his victim? Anyone who has more than he has. More karats, more horsepower, more office space, more church members. Jealousy sets her cross hairs on the one who has more. "You want something you don't have, and you will do anything to get it. You will even kill!" (James 4:2 CEV).

Honestly, Max, I would never do that. I would never kill.

With a rifle, maybe not. But with your tongue? With your glare? Your gossip? "Jealousy," informs Proverbs 6:34, "enrages a man" (NASB). Are your sights set on someone? If so, be careful; "jealousy will rot your bones" (Prov. 14:30).

Need a deterrent for envy? An antidote for jealousy? The psalm we are studying offers one. Rather than bemoan the peach preserves you don't have, rejoice in the abundant cup you do. "My cup overflows with blessings" (Ps. 23:5 NLT).

Is an overflowing cup full? Absolutely. The wine reaches the rim and then tumbles over the edge. The goblet is not large enough to contain the quantity. According to David, our hearts are not large enough to contain the blessings that God wants to give. He pours and pours until they literally flow over the edge and down on the table. You'll like the paragraph penned a century ago by F. B. Meyer:

> Whatever the blessing is in our cup, it is sure to run over. With him the calf is always the fatted calf; the robe is always the best robe; the joy is unspeakable; the peace passeth understanding. . . . There is no grudging in God's benevolence; He does not measure out his goodness as an apothecary counts his drops and measures his drams, slowly and exactly, drop by drop. God's way is always characterized by multitudinous and overflowing bounty.[1]

The last thing we need to worry about is not having enough. Our cup overflows with blessings.

Let me ask a question—a crucial question. If focusing on our diminishing items leads to envy, what would happen if we focused on the unending items? If awareness of what we don't have creates jealousy, is it possible that an awareness of our abundance will lead to contentment? Let's give it a try and see what happens. Let's dedicate a few paragraphs to a couple of blessings that, according to the Bible, are overflowing in our lives.

Abounding grace. "The more we see our sinfulness, the more we see God's *abounding grace* forgiving us" (Rom. 5:20 TLB, emphasis mine). To abound is to have a surplus, an abundance, an extravagant portion. Should the fish in the Pacific worry that it will run out of ocean? No. Why? The ocean abounds with water. Need the lark be anxious about finding room in the sky to fly? No. The sky abounds with space.

Should the Christian worry that the cup of mercy will run empty? He may. For he may not be aware of God's abounding grace. Are you? Are you aware that the cup God gives you *overflows* with mercy? Or are you afraid your cup will run dry? Your warranty will expire? Are you afraid your mistakes are too great for God's grace?

We can't help but wonder if the apostle Paul had the same fear. Before he was Paul the apostle, he was Saul the murderer. Before he encouraged Christians, he murdered Christians. What would it be like to live with such a past? Did he ever meet children whom he had made orphans? Did their faces haunt his sleep? Did Paul ever ask, "Can God forgive a man like me?"

The answer to his and our questions is found in a letter he wrote to Timothy: "The grace of our Lord was poured out on me abundantly, along with the faith and love that are in Christ Jesus" (1 Tim. 1:14 NIV).

God is not a miser with his grace. Your cup may be low on cash or clout, but it is overflowing with mercy. You may not have the prime parking place, but you have sufficient pardon. "He will abundantly pardon" (Isa. 55:7 NKJV). Your cup overflows with grace.

Hope. And because it does, your cup overflows with hope. "God will help you overflow with hope in him through the Holy Spirit's power within you" (Rom. 15:13 TLB).

Heaven's hope does for your world what the sunlight did for my grandmother's cellar. I owe my love of peach preserves to her. She canned her own and stored them in an underground cellar near her West Texas house. It was a deep hole with wooden steps, plywood walls, and a musty smell. As a youngster I used to climb in, close the door, and see how long I could last in the darkness. Not even a slit of light entered that underground hole. I would sit silently, listening to my breath and heartbeats, until I couldn't take it anymore and then would race up the stairs and throw open the door. Light would avalanche into the cellar. What a change! Moments before I couldn't see anything—all of a sudden I could see everything.

Just as light poured into the cellar, God's hope pours into your world. Upon the sick, he shines the ray of healing. To the bereaved, he gives the promise of reunion. For the dying, he lit the flame of resurrection. To the confused, he offers the light of Scripture.

God gives hope. So what if someone was born thinner or stronger, lighter or darker than you? Why count diplomas or compare résumés? What does it matter if they have a place at the head table? You have a place at God's table. And he is filling your cup to overflowing.

The overflowing cup was a powerful symbol in the days of David. Hosts in the ancient East used it to send a message to the guest. As long as the cup was kept full, the guest knew he was welcome. But when the cup sat empty, the host was hinting that the hour was late. On those occasions, however, when the host really enjoyed the company of the person, he filled the cup to overflowing. He didn't stop when the wine reached the rim; he kept pouring until the liquid ran over the edge of the cup and down on the table.[2]

Have you noticed how wet your table is? God wants you to stay. Your cup overflows with joy. Overflows with grace. Shouldn't your heart overflow with gratitude?

The heart of the boy did. Not at first, mind you. Initially he was full of envy. But, in time, he was full of gratitude.

According to the fable, he lived with his father in a valley at the base of a large dam. Every day the father would go to work on the mountain behind their house and return home with a wheelbarrow full of dirt. "Pour the dirt in the sacks, Son," the father would say. "And stack them in front of the house."

And though the boy would obey, he also complained. He was tired of dirt. He was weary of bags. Why didn't his father give him what other fathers gave their sons? They had toys and games; he had dirt. When he saw what the others had, he grew mad at them. "It's not fair," he said to himself.

And when he saw his father, he objected. "They have fun. I have dirt."

The father would smile and place his arm on the boy's shoulders and say, "Trust me, Son. I'm doing what is best."

But it was so hard for the boy to trust. Every day the father would bring the load. Every day the boy would fill bags. "Stack them as high as you can," the father would say as he went for more. And so the boy filled the bags and piled them high. So high he couldn't see over them.

"Work hard, Son," the father said one day. "We're running out of time." As the father spoke, he looked at the darkening sky. The boy stared at the clouds and turned to ask about them, but when he did, the thunder cracked and the sky opened. The rain poured so hard he could scarcely see his father through the water. "Keep stacking, Son!" And as he did, the boy heard a mighty crash.

The water of the river poured through the

dam and toward the little village. In a moment the tide swept everything in its path, but the dike of dirt gave the boy and the father the time they needed. "Hurry, Son. Follow me."

They ran to the side of the mountain behind their house and into a tunnel. In a matter of moments they exited the other side and scampered up the hill and came upon a new cottage.

"We'll be safe here," the father said to the boy.

Only then did the son realize what the father had done. He had burrowed an exit. Rather than give him what he wanted, the father gave his boy what he needed. He gave him a safe passage and a safe place.

Hasn't our Father given us the same? A strong wall of grace to protect us? A sure exit to deliver us? Of whom can we be envious? Who has more than we do? Rather than want what others have, shouldn't we wonder if they have what we do? Instead of being jealous of them, how about zealous for them? For heaven's sake, drop the rifles and hold out the cup. There is enough to go around.

One thing is certain. When the final storm comes and you are safe in your Father's house, you won't regret what he didn't give. You'll be stunned at what he did.

17

God's Loving Pursuit

The Burden of Doubt

Surely goodness and mercy shall follow me all the days of my life.
PSALM 23:6 NKJV

Eric Hill had everything you'd need for a bright future. He was twenty-eight years old and a recent college grad with an athletic frame and a soft smile. His family loved him, girls took notice of him, and companies had contacted him about working for them. Although Eric appeared composed without, he was tormented within. Tormented by voices he could not still. Bothered by images he could not avoid. So, hoping to get away from them all, he got away from it all. On a gray rainy day in February 1982, Eric Hill walked out the back door of his Florida home and never came back.

His sister Debbie remembers seeing him leave, his tall frame ambling down the interstate. She assumed he would return. He didn't. She hoped he would call. He didn't. She thought she could find him. She couldn't. Where Eric journeyed, only God and Eric know, and neither of them has chosen to tell. What we do know is Eric heard a voice. And in that voice was an "assignment." And that assignment was to pick up garbage along a roadside in San Antonio, Texas.

To the commuters on Interstate 10, his lanky form and bearded face became a familiar sight. He made a home out of a hole in a vacant lot. He made a wardrobe out of split trousers and a torn sweatshirt. An old hat deferred the summer sun. A plastic bag on his shoulders softened the winter chill. His weathered skin and stooped shoulders made him look twice his forty-four years. But then, sixteen years on the side of the road would do that to you.

That's how long it had been since Debbie had seen her brother. She might never have seen him again had it not been for two events. The first was the construction of a car dealership on Eric's vacant lot. The second was a severe pain in his abdomen. The dealership took his home. The pain nearly took his life.

EMS found him curled in a ball on the side of the road, clutching his stomach. The hospital ran some tests and found that Eric had cancer. Terminal cancer. Another few months and he would be dead. And with no known family or relatives, he would die alone.

His court-appointed attorney couldn't handle this thought. "Surely someone is looking for Eric," he reasoned. So the lawyer scoured the Internet for anyone in search of a brown-haired, adult male with the last name Hill. That's how he met Debbie.

His description seemed to match her memory, but she had to know for sure.

So Debbie came to Texas. She and her husband and two children rented a hotel room and set out to find Eric. By now he'd been released from the hospital, but the chaplain knew where he was. They found him sitting against a building not far from the interstate. As they approached, he stood. They offered fruit; he refused. They offered juice; he declined. He was polite but unimpressed with this family who claimed to be his own.

His interest perked, however, when Debbie offered him a pin to wear, an angel pin. He said yes. Her first time to touch her brother in sixteen years was the moment he allowed her to pin the angel on his shirt. Debbie intended to spend a week. But a week passed, and she stayed. Her husband returned home, and she stayed. Spring became summer, and Eric improved, and still she stayed. Debbie rented an apartment and began homeschooling her kids and reaching out to her brother.

It wasn't easy. He didn't recognize her. He didn't know her. One day he cursed her. He didn't want to sleep in her apartment. He didn't want her food. He didn't want to talk. He wanted his vacant lot. He wanted his "job." Who was this woman anyway?

But Debbie didn't give up on Eric. She understood that he didn't understand. So she stayed.

I met her one Sunday when she visited our congregation. When she shared her story, I asked what you might want to ask. "How do you keep from giving up?"

"Simple," she said. "He's my brother."

I told her that her pursuit reminded me of another pursuit—that her heart reminded me of another heart. Another kind heart who left home in search of the confused. Another compassionate soul who couldn't bear the thought of a brother or sister in pain. So, like Debbie, he left home. Like Debbie, he found his sibling.

And when Jesus found us, we acted like Eric. Our limitations kept us from recognizing the One who came to save us. We even doubted his presence—and sometimes we still do.

How does he deal with our doubts? He follows us. As Debbie followed Eric, God follows us. He pursues us until we finally see him as our Father, even if it takes *all the days of our lives.*

"Surely goodness and mercy shall follow me all the days of my life; and I will dwell in the house of the LORD forever" (Ps. 23:6 NKJV).

This must be one of the sweetest phrases ever penned. Can we read it from a few other translations?

"Goodness and love unfailing, these will follow me all the days of my life, and I shall dwell in the house of the LORD my whole life long" (NEB).

"I know that your goodness and love will

be with me all my life; and your house will be my home as long as I live" (TEV).

"Your beauty and love chase after me every day of my life. I'm back home in the house of YAHWEH for the rest of my life" (MSG).

To read the verse is to open a box of jewels. Each word sparkles and begs to be examined in the face of our doubts: *goodness, mercy, all the days, dwell in the house of the LORD, forever.* They sweep in on insecurities like a SWAT team on a terrorist.

Look at the first word: *surely.* David didn't say, "*Maybe* goodness and mercy shall follow me." Or "*Possibly* goodness and mercy shall follow me." Or "*I have a hunch* that goodness and mercy shall follow me." David could have used one of those phrases. But he didn't. He believed in a sure God, who makes sure promises and provides a sure foundation. David would have loved the words of one of his great-great-grandsons, the apostle James. He described God as the one "with whom there is never the slightest variation or shadow of inconsistency" (James 1:17 PHILLIPS).

Our moods may shift, but God's doesn't. Our minds may change, but God's doesn't.

Our devotion may falter, but God's never does. Even if we are faithless, he is faithful, for he cannot betray himself (2 Tim. 2:13). He is a sure God. And because he is a sure God, we can state confidently, "Surely goodness and mercy shall follow me all the days of my life."

And what follows the word *surely?* "Goodness and mercy." If the Lord is the shepherd who leads the flock, goodness and mercy are the two sheepdogs that guard the rear of the flock. Goodness *and* mercy. Not goodness alone, for we are sinners in need of mercy. Not mercy alone, for we are fragile, in need of goodness. We need them both. As one man wrote, "Goodness to supply every want. Mercy to forgive every sin. Goodness to provide. Mercy to pardon."[1]

Goodness and mercy—the celestial escort of God's flock. If that duo doesn't reinforce your faith, try this phrase: "all the days of my life."

What a huge statement. Look at the size of it! Goodness and mercy follow the child of God each and every day! Think of the days that lie ahead. What do you see? Days at home with only toddlers? God will be at your side. Days in a dead-end job? He will walk you through. Days of loneliness? He will take your hand. Surely goodness and mercy shall follow me—not some, not most, not nearly all—but all the days of my life.

And what will he do during those days? (Here is my favorite word.) He will "follow" you.

What a surprising way to describe God! We're accustomed to a God who remains in one place. A God who sits enthroned in the heavens and rules and ordains. David, however, envisions a mobile and active God. Dare we do the same? Dare we envision a God who follows us? Who pursues us? Who chases us? Who tracks us down and wins us over? Who follows us with "goodness and mercy" all the days of our lives?

Isn't this the kind of God described in the Bible? A God who follows us? There are many in the Scriptures who would say so. You have to go no farther than the third chapter of the first book before you find God in the role of a seeker. Adam and Eve are hiding in the bushes, partly to cover their bodies, partly to cover their sin. But does God wait for them to come to him? No, the words ring in the garden: "Where are you?" (Gen. 3:9). With those words God began a quest for the heart of humanity that continues up to and through the moment you read these words.

Moses can tell you about it. He was forty years in the desert when he looked over his shoulder and saw a bush blazing. God had followed him into the wilderness.

Jonah can tell you about it. He was a fugitive on a boat when he looked over his shoulder and saw clouds brewing. God had followed him onto the ocean.

The disciples of Jesus knew the feeling of being followed by God. They were rain soaked and shivering when they looked over their shoulders and saw Jesus walking toward them. God had followed them into the storm.

An unnamed Samaritan woman knew the same. She was alone in life and alone at the well when she looked over her shoulder and heard a Messiah speaking. God had followed her through her pain.

John the Apostle was banished on Patmos when he looked over his shoulder and saw the skies begin to open. God had followed him into his exile.

Lazarus was three days dead in a sealed tomb when he heard a voice, lifted his head, and looked over his shoulder and saw Jesus standing. God had followed him into death.

Peter had denied his Lord and gone back to fishing when he heard his name and looked over his shoulder and saw Jesus cooking breakfast. God had followed him in spite of his failure.

God is the God who follows. I wonder . . . have you sensed him following you? We often miss him. Like Eric, we don't know our Helper when he is near. But he comes.

Through the kindness of a stranger. The majesty of a sunset. The mystery of romance. Through the question of a child or the commitment of a spouse. Through a word well spoken or a touch well timed, have you sensed his presence?

If so, then release your doubts. Set them down. Be encumbered by them no longer. You are no candidate for insecurity. You are no longer a client of timidity. You can trust God. He has given his love to you; why don't you give your doubts to him?

Not easy to trust, you say? Maybe not, but neither is it as difficult as you think. Try these ideas:

Trust your faith and not your feelings. You don't feel spiritual each day? Of course you don't. But your feelings have no impact on God's presence. On the days you don't feel close to God, trust your faith and not your feelings. Goodness and mercy shall follow you all the days of your life.

Measure your value through God's eyes, not your own. To everyone else, Eric Hill was a homeless drifter. But to Debbie, he was a brother. There are times in our lives when we are gangrels—homeless, disoriented, hard to help, and hard to love. In those seasons remember this simple fact: God loves you. He follows you. Why? Because you are family, and he will follow you all the days of your life.

See the big picture, not the small. Eric's home was taken. His health was taken. But through the tragedy, his family was returned to him. Perhaps your home and health have been threatened as well. The immediate result might be pain. But the long-term result might be finding a Father you never knew. A Father who will follow you all the days of your life.

By the way, the last chapter in Eric Hill's life is the best one. Days before he died he recognized Debbie as his sister. And, in doing so, he discovered his home.

We will as well. Like Eric, we have doubted our Helper. But like Debbie, God has followed us. Like Eric, we are quick to turn away. But like Debbie, God is slow to anger and determined to stay. Like Eric, we don't accept God's gifts. But like Debbie, God still gives them. He gives us his angels, not just pinned on a lapel, but placed on our path.

And most of all, God gives us himself. Even when we choose our hovel over his house and our trash over his grace, still he follows. Never forcing us. Never leaving us. Patiently persistent. Faithfully present. Using all of his power to convince us that he is who he is and that he can be trusted to lead us home.

His goodness and mercy will follow us all the days of our lives.

18

Almost Heaven

The Burden of Homesickness

I will dwell in the house of the LORD forever.
PSALM 23:6 NKJV

For the last twenty years, I've wanted a dog. A big dog. But there were always problems. The apartment was too small. The budget was too tight. The girls were too young. But most of all, Denalyn was unenthusiastic. Her logic? She'd already married one slobbering, shedding beast, why put up with a second? So we compromised and got a small dog.

I like Salty, but small dogs aren't really dogs. They don't bark; they yelp. They don't eat; they nibble. They don't lick you; they sniff you. I like Salty, but I wanted a real dog. A man's-best-friend type of dog. A fat-pawed, big-eating, slurp-you-on-the-face type of dog you could saddle or wrestle or both.

I was alone in my passion until Sara was born. She loves dogs. And the two of us were able to sway the household vote. Denalyn gave in, and Sara and I began the search. We discovered a woman in South Carolina who breeds golden retrievers in a Christian environment. From birth the dogs are surrounded by inspirational music and prayers. (No, I don't know if they tithe with dog biscuits.) When the trainer told me that she had read my books, I got on board. A woman with such good taste is bound to be a good breeder, right?

So we ordered a pup. We mailed the check, selected the name Molly, and cleared a corner for her dog pillow. The dog hadn't even been born, and she was named, claimed, and given a place in the house.

Can't the same be said about you? Long before your first whimper, your Master claimed you, named you, and hung a reserved sign on your room. You and Molly have more in common than odor and eating habits. (Just teasing.)

You're both being groomed for a trip. We prefer the terms *maturation* and *sanctifica-*

tion to *weaning* and *training,* but it's all the same. You're being prepared for your Master's house. You don't know the departure date or flight number, but you can bet your puppy chow that you'll be seeing your Owner someday. Isn't this the concluding promise of David?

"And I will dwell in the house of the LORD forever" (Ps. 23:6 NKJV).

Where will you live forever? In the house of the Lord. If his house is your "forever house," what does that make this earthly house? You got it! Short-term housing. This is not our home. "Our homeland is in heaven" (Phil. 3:20).

This explains the homesickness we feel.

Have you ever longed to be home? May I share a time when I did? I was spending the summer of my nineteenth year working in northern Georgia. The folks in that region are very nice, but no one is too nice to a door-to-door salesman. There were times that summer when I was so lonely for home I felt my bones would melt.

One of those occasions came on the side of a country road. The hour was late, and I was lost. I'd stopped to pull out a flashlight and a map. To my right was a farmhouse. In the farmhouse was a family. I knew it was a family because I could see them. Right through the big plate-glass window, I could see the mother and father and boy and girl. Norman Rockwell would have placed them on a canvas. The mom was spooning out food, and the dad was telling a story, and the kids were laughing, and it was all I could do to keep from ringing the doorbell and asking for a place at the table. I felt so far from home.

What I felt that night, some of you have felt ever since . . .

your husband died.

your child was buried.

you learned about the lump in your breast or the spot in your lung.

Some of you have felt far from home ever since your home fell apart.

The twists and turns of life have a way of reminding us—we aren't home here. This is not our homeland. We aren't fluent in the languages of disease and death. The culture confuses the heart, the noise disrupts our sleep, and we feel far from home.

And, you know what? That's OK.

Homesickness is one of the burdens God doesn't mind if we carry. We, like Molly, are being prepared for another house. And we, like the parakeet from Green Bay, know we aren't there yet.

Pootsie was her name. She escaped from her owner and came into the keeping of the humane society. When no one else claimed her, Sue Gleason did. They hit it off: They talked and bathed together, becoming fast friends. But one day the little bird did something incredible. It flew over to Mrs. Gleason, put her beak in her ear, and whispered, "Fifteen hundred South Oneida Street, Green Bay."

Gleason was dumbfounded. She researched and found that the address existed. She went to the house and found a seventy-nine-year-old man named John Stroobants.

"Do you have a parakeet?" she asked.

"I used to; I miss him terribly."

When he saw his Pootsie, he was thrilled. "You know, he even knows his phone number."[1]

The story isn't as crazy as you might think. You have an eternal address fixed in your mind as well. God has "set eternity in the hearts of men" (Eccles. 3:11 NIV). Down deep you know you are not home yet.

So be careful not to act like you are. Don't lower the duffel bag too soon. Would you hang pictures on the wall of a Greyhound bus? Do you set up a bedroom at the roadside rest stop? Do you load your king-size bed on a commercial flight?

Would you treat this world like home? It isn't. The greatest calamity is not to feel far from home when you are, but to feel right at home when you are not. Don't quench, but rather, stir this longing for heaven.

God's home is a *forever* home. "And I will dwell in the house of the Lord forever" (Ps. 23:6 NKJV).

My friends Jeff and Carol just adopted two small children. Christopher, the older, is only three, but he knows the difference between Jeff's house and the foster home from which he came. He tells all visitors, "This is my forever home."

Won't it be great when we say the same? Couldn't we use a forever home? This home we're in won't last forever. Birthdays remind us of that.

During the writing of this book I turned forty-six. I'm closer to ninety than I am to infancy. All those things they say about aging are coming true. I'm patting myself less on the back and more under the chin. I have everything I had twenty years ago, except now it's all lower. The other day I tried to straighten out the wrinkles in my socks and found out I wasn't wearing any. I can relate to Dave Barry's description of aging:

> . . . dental problems, intestinal malfunctions, muscle deterioration, emotional instability, memory lapses, hearing and vision loss, impotence, seizures, growths, prostate problems, greatly reduced limb function, massive coronary failure, death, and, of course, painful hemorrhoidal swelling.[2]

With the exception of those things, I'm doing fine.

Aging. It's no fun. The way we try to avoid it, you'd think we could. We paint the body, preserve the body, protect the body. And well we should. These bodies are God's gifts. We should be responsible. But we should also be realistic. This body must die so the new body can live. "Flesh and blood cannot have a part in the kingdom of God. Something that will ruin cannot have a part in something that never ruins" (1 Cor. 15:50).

Aging is God's idea. It's one of the ways he keeps us headed homeward. We can't change the process, but we can change our attitude. Here is a thought. What if we looked at the aging body as we look at the growth of a tulip?

Do you ever see anyone mourning over the passing of the tulip bulb? Do gardeners weep as the bulb begins to weaken? Of course not. We don't purchase tulip girdles or petal wrinkle cream or consult plastic-leaf surgeons. We don't mourn the passing of the bulb; we celebrate it. Tulip lovers rejoice the minute the bulb weakens. "Watch that one," they say. "It's about to blossom."

Could it be heaven does the same? The angels point to our bodies. The more frail we become, the more excited they become. "Watch that lady in the hospital," they say. "She's about to blossom." "Keep an eye on the fellow with the bad heart. He'll be coming home soon."

"We are waiting for God to finish making us his own children, which means our bodies will be made free" (Rom. 8:23).

Are our bodies now free? No. Paul describes them as our "earthy bodies" (Phil. 3:21 MSG). Or as other translations state:

"our lowly body" (NKJV)

"the body of our humble state" (NASB)

"these weak mortal bodies" (NLT)

"our vile body" (KJV)

"our simple bodies" (NCV)

You could add your own adjective, couldn't you? Which word describes your body? My *cancerous* body? My *arthritic* body? My *deformed* body? My *crippled* body? My *addicted* body? My *ever-expanding* body? The word may be different, but the message is the same: These bodies are weak. They began decaying the minute we began breathing.

And, according to God, that's a part of the plan. Every wrinkle and every needle take us one step closer to the last step when Jesus will change our simple bodies into forever bodies. No pain. No depression. No sickness. No end.

This is not our forever house. It will serve for the time being. But there is nothing like the moment we enter his door.

Molly can tell you. After a month in our house she ran away. I came home one night to find the place unusually quiet. Molly was gone.

She'd slipped out unnoticed. The search

began immediately. Within an hour we knew that she was far, far from home. Now, if you don't like pets, what I'm about to say is going to sound strange. If you do like pets, you will understand.

You'll understand why we walked up and down the street, calling her name. You'll understand why I drove around the neighborhood at 10:30 P.M. You'll understand why I put up a poster in the convenience store and convened the family for a prayer. (Honestly, I did.) You'll understand why I sent e-mails to the staff, asking for prayers, and to her breeder, asking for advice. And you'll understand why we were ready to toss the confetti and party when she showed up.

Here is what happened. The next morning Denalyn was on her way home from taking the girls to school when she saw the trash truck. She asked the workers to keep an eye out for Molly and then hurried home to host a moms' prayer group. Soon after the ladies arrived, the trash truck pulled into our driveway, a worker opened the door, and out bounded our dog. She had been found.

When Denalyn called to tell me the news, I could barely hear her voice. It was Mardi

Gras in the kitchen. The ladies were celebrating the return of Molly.

This story pops with symbolism. The master leaving his house, searching for the lost. Victories in the midst of prayer. Great things coming out of trash. But most of all: the celebration at the coming home. That's something else you have in common with Molly—a party at your homecoming.

By that moment only one bag will remain. Not guilt. It was dropped at Calvary. Not the fear of death. It was left at the grave. The only lingering luggage will be this God-given longing for home. And when you see him, you'll set it down. Just as a returning soldier drops his duffel when he sees his wife, you'll drop your longing when you see your Father. Those you love will shout. Those you know will applaud. But all the noise will cease when he cups your chin and says, "Welcome home." And with scarred hand he'll wipe every tear from your eye. And you will dwell in the house of your Lord—forever.

Conclusion

I fell asleep in the Louvre.

The most famous museum in the world. The best-known building in Paris. Tourists are oohing and aahing, and that's me, nodding and snoring. Seated on a bench. Back to the wall. Chin to my chest. Conked out.

The crown jewels are down the hall. Rembrandt is on the wall. Van Gogh is one floor up. The *Venus de Milo* is one floor down. I should have been star struck and wide eyed.

Denalyn was. You'd have thought she was at Foley's Red Apple sale. If there was a tour, she took it. If there was a button to push, she pushed it. If there was a brochure to read, she read it. She didn't even want to stop to eat.

But me? I gave the *Mona Lisa* five minutes.

Shameful, I know.

I should have been more like the fellow next to me. When I dozed off, he was transfixed on a seventeenth-century Dutch artist's rendering of a flower. When I awoke, the guy was still staring. I closed my eyes again. When I opened them, he hadn't moved.

I leaned toward him and tried to sound reflective. "Awesome, eh?" No response. "The shades are masterful." Still no reply. "Do you think it's a number painting?" He sighed and said nothing, but I knew what he was thinking, *Uncultured klutz.*

He's right. I was. But it wasn't my fault. I like seventeenth-century art as much as the next guy . . . well, maybe not that much. But at least I can usually stay awake.

But not that day. Why did I fall asleep at the Louvre?

Blame it on the bags, baby; blame it on the bags. I was worn out from lugging the family luggage. We checked more suitcases than the road show of the *Phantom of the Opera.*

I can't fault my wife and daughters. They

learned it from me. Remember, I'm the one who travels prepared for an underwater wedding and a bowling tournament. It's bad enough for one person to travel like that, but five? It'll wear you out.

You think I'll ever learn to travel light?

I tell you what. Let's make a pact. I'll reduce the leather bags, and we'll both reduce the emotional ones. After all, it's one thing to sleep through the Louvre but quite another to sleep through life.

We can, you know. Do we not dwell in the gallery of our God? Isn't the sky his canvas and humanity his magnum opus? Are we not encircled by artistry? Sunsets burning. Waves billowing.

And isn't the soul his studio? The birthing of love, the bequeathing of grace. All around us miracles pop like fireflies—souls are touched, hearts are changed, and . . .

Yawn. We miss it. We sleep through it. We can't help it. It's hard work carrying yesterday's guilt around. This burlap bag of worry has my neck in a knot. The dread of death is enough to break a back.

It's also enough to make you miss the magic of life. Many miss it every Sunday. Good, well-meaning folks sitting in church, fighting to keep the eyes—if not of their heads at least of their hearts—awake.

And what do we miss? We miss God parting the heavens to hear us sing. Shouldn't we be stretching heavenward, tiptoed on our pews?

What do we miss? God is meeting us in communion! Shouldn't we be distributing, along with the wafers and wine, ammonia sticks so we could awaken each other from our faints of awe?

What do we miss? God's Word. Should we not hold it like nitroglycerin? Shouldn't we be wide-awake? We should, but we dragged that trunk of dissatisfaction all over town last week. And, besides that, we couldn't sleep last night; we kept rolling over on our duffel bag of disappointments.

Then let's get rid of the bags! Once and for all, let's give our luggage to him. Let's take him at his word! "Come to me, all of you who are weary and carry heavy burdens, and I will give you rest" (Matt. 11:28 NLT).

Rest from the burden of a small god. Why? Because I have found **the Lord.**

Rest from doing things my way. Why? Because **the Lord is my Shepherd.**

Rest from endless wants. Why? Because **I shall not want.**

Rest from weariness. Why? Because **he makes me to lie down.**

Rest from worry. Why? Because **he leads me.**

Rest from hopelessness. Why? Because **he restores my soul.**

Rest from guilt. Why? Because **he leads me in the paths of righteousness.**

Rest from arrogance. Why? Because of **his name's sake.**

Rest from the valley of death. Why? Because **he walks me through it.**

Rest from the shadow of grief. Why? Because **he guides me.**

Rest from fear. Why? Because **his presence comforts me.**

Rest from loneliness. Why? Because **he is with me.**

Rest from shame. Why? Because **he has prepared a place for me in the presence of my enemies.**

Rest from my disappointments. Why? Because **he anoints me.**

Rest from envy. Why? Because **my cup overflows.**

Rest from doubt. Why? Because **he follows me.**

Rest from homesickness. Why? Because **I will dwell in the house of my Lord forever.**

And tomorrow, when out of habit you pick your luggage back up, set it down again. Set it down again and again until that sweet day when you find you aren't picking it back up.

And on that day, when you feel the load lifted, when you've taken a step toward traveling light, when you have the energy to ponder the mysteries of life, do me a favor. Walk down the hall and turn to the left. Wait your turn behind the scarlet ropes. Take a good, long look at the *Mona Lisa,* and tell me, what's the big deal about her anyway?

Notes

CHAPTER 2: THE MIDDLE C OF LIFE

1. Or, in Hebrew, fifty-four words describe the first one.

2. Around A.D. 200 Christian scholars began writing the vowels for *Adonai* beneath the Tetragrammaton (YHWH), reminding the reader to say "Adonai." The word was still unpronounceable until German scholars in the middle of the nineteenth century inserted the vowels of Adonai between the Yahweh consonants creating the name *Jehovah*—a name that had never existed in any language.

3. Nathan Stone, *Names of God* (Chicago: Moody Press, 1944), 20.

4. Donald W. McCullough, *The Trivialization of God: The Dangerous Illusion of a Manageable Deity* (Colorado Springs: NavPress, 1995), 66.

5. Ibid., 54.

CHAPTER 3: I'LL DO IT MY WAY
1. With appreciation to Rick Reilly and his chapter on Jean Van de Velde, "*Mon Dieu! Better Safe Than Sorry!*" in *The Life of Reilly* (New York: Total Sports Illustrated, 2000), 175–77.

CHAPTER 4: THE PRISON OF WANT
1. Randy C. Alcorn, *Money, Possessions, and Eternity* (Wheaton, Ill.: Tyndale Publishers, 1989), 55.

2. Chris Seidman, *Little Buddy* (Orange, Calif.: New Leaf Books, 2001), 138. Used with permission.

3. Rick Atchley, "I Have Learned the Secret," audiotape 7 of the 1997 Pepperdine Lectures (Malibu, Calif., 1997). Used with permission.

4. Used with permission.

CHAPTER 5: I WILL GIVE YOU REST

1. Robert Sullivan, "Sleepless in America," *Life,* February 1998, 56–66 and *Prime Time Live,* 2 March 1998.

2. Sullivan, "Sleepless," 63.

3. Ibid.

4. Phillip Keller, *A Shepherd Looks at Psalm 23* (Grand Rapids, Mich.: Zondervan Publishing, 1970; reprint, in *Phillip Keller: The Inspirational Writings,* New York: Inspirational Press, 1993), 28–29 (page citations are to the reprint edition).

5. Helmut Thielicke, *Encounter with Spurgeon,* trans. John W. Doberstein (Philadelphia: Fortress Press, 1963; reprint, Grand Rapids, Mich.: Baker Book House, 1975), 220 (page citation is to the reprint edition).

CHAPTER 6: WHADDIFS AND HOWELLS

1. Og Mandino, *The Spellbinder's Gift* (New York: Fawcett Columbine, 1995), 70–71.

2. From "Worrier and Warrior," a sermon by Ted Schroder, Christ Episcopal Church, San Antonio, Texas, on 10 April 1994.

3. See Psalm 119:105.

CHAPTER 9: GET OVER YOURSELF

1. Rick Reilly, *The Life of Reilly* (New York: Total Sports Illustrated, 2000), 73.

2. Paul Lee Tan, *Encyclopedia of 7700 Illustrations* (Rockville, Md.: Assurance Publishers, 1979), 211.

3. Ibid., 1100.

4. William J. Bennett, ed., *The Spirit of America: Words of Advice from the Founders in Stories, Letters, Poem and Speeches* (New York: Touchstone, 1997), 161.

CHAPTER 10: I WILL LEAD YOU HOME

1. Phillip Keller, *A Shepherd Looks at Psalm 23* (Grand Rapids, Mich.: Zondervan Publishing, 1970; reprint, in *Phillip Keller: The Inspirational Writings,* New York: Inspirational Press, 1993), 70 (page citation is to the reprint edition).

2. F. W. Boreham, *Life Verses: The Bible's Impact on Famous Lives,* vol. 2 (Grand Rapids, Mich.: Kregel Publications, 1994), 211.

CHAPTER 11: WHEN MOURNING COMES

1. Michael P. Green, ed., *Illustrations for Biblical Preaching* (Grand Rapids, Mich.: Baker Book House, 1989), 91.

CHAPTER 14: THE CROWING ROOSTER AND ME
1. Charles W. Slemming, *He Leadeth Me: The Shepherd's Life in Palestine* (Fort Washington, Pa.: Christian Literature Crusade, 1964), quoted in Charles R. Swindoll, *Living Beyond the Daily Grind, Book 1: Reflections on the Songs and Sayings in Scripture* (Dallas: Word Publishing, 1988), 77–78.

CHAPTER 15: SLIPPERY SHEEP AND HEALED HURTS
1. "Paul was in prison several times: Philippi (Acts 16:23); Jerusalem (Acts 23:18); Caesarea (Acts 23:33; 24:27; 25:14); and Rome (Acts 28:16, 20, 30)." Robert B. Hughes and J. Carl Laney, *New Bible Companion* (Wheaton, Ill.: Tyndale House Publishers, 1990), 681.

2. Phillip Keller, *A Shepherd Looks at Psalm 23* (Grand Rapids, Mich.: Zondervan Publishing, 1970; reprint, in *Phillip Keller: The Inspirational Writings,* New York: Inspirational Press, 1993), 99 (page citation is to the reprint edition).

CHAPTER 16: JAM SESSION
1. F. B. Meyer, *The Shepherd Psalm* (Grand Rapids, Mich.: Kregel Publications, 1991), 115.

2. From a sermon entitled "God's Antidote to Your Hurt" by Rick Warren.

CHAPTER 17: GOD'S LOVING PURSUIT
1. F. B. Meyer, *The Shepherd Psalm* (Grand Rapids, Mich.: Kregel Publications, 1991), 125.

2. Though originally written for this book, this story initially appeared in *The Gift for All People.* Thanks to Multnomah Publishing for allowing us to use it in *Traveling Light.*

CHAPTER 18: ALMOST HEAVEN
1. Calvin Miller, *Into the Depths of God: Where Eyes See the Invisible, Ears Hear the Inaudible, and Minds Conceive the Inconceivable* (Minneapolis: Bethany House, 2000),

2. Dave Barry, *Dave Barry Turns 40* (New York: Crown, 1990), quoted in Helen Exley, *A Spread of Over 40s Jokes* (New York: Exley Giftbooks, 1992).

Study Guide

Traveling Light

Prepared by Steve Halliday

1

The Luggage of Life

TRAVELING BACK

1. *The bags we grab are not made of leather; they're made of burdens. The suitcase of guilt. A sack of discontent. You drape a duffel bag of weariness on one shoulder and a hanging bag of grief on the other. Add on a backpack of doubt, an overnight bag of loneliness, and a trunk of fear. Pretty soon you're pulling more stuff than a skycap. No wonder you're so tired at the end of the day. Lugging luggage is exhausting.*

   A. Which of the "bags" listed here trouble you the most? Why?

   B. Have you left any luggage behind? How did it feel to do so?

2. *God is saying to you, "Set that stuff down! You're carrying burdens you don't need to bear."*

A. Why do you think we carry burdens we don't need to bear?

B. What keeps you from setting down burdens you needn't bear?

3. *Traveling light means trusting God with the burdens you were never intended to bear.*

A. What does it mean to trust God with a burden? How does one do this?

B. What have you learned from observing others with their "luggage"?

TRAVELING UP

1. Read Psalm 23.

A. What pictures leap to mind when you read this psalm?

B. What memories does this psalm conjure up for you?

C. What part of this psalm means the most to you? Why?

D. How does this psalm teach us to give up personal burdens?

2. Read Matthew 11:28–30.

A. To whom are these words addressed? Does this include you?

B. What promise does Jesus give to those who respond to his invitation?

C. Are you taking advantage of Jesus' invitation? Why or why not?

3. Read 1 Peter 5:7.

A. What does this verse instruct us to do? (How are we to obey?)

B. What reason does Peter give for obeying this command?

C. What benefit can we expect to receive when we obey?

TRAVELING ON

1. Set aside at least a half-hour for prayer, and ask the Lord to reveal any burdens

you need to lay down. Pray with a piece of paper and a pen in hand, and write down any burdens the Lord brings to mind. Show your completed list to your closest friend, and ask him or her to pray with you that God will show you how to release these burdens.

2. What burdens are your loved ones needlessly bearing? What can you do to help them lay down those unnecessary burdens?

2

The Middle C of Life

The Burden of a Lesser God

TRAVELING BACK

1. *With his very first words in [Psalm 23], David sets out to deliver us from the burden of a lesser deity.*

   A. What lesser deities hold an attraction for your acquaintances?

   B. Why would anyone settle for a lesser deity?

2. Max says that many people settle for one of three lesser deities: God as a genie in a bottle, as a sweet grandpa, or as a busy dad.

   A. Describe in your own words each of these lesser deities. What seems attractive about them?

   B. Have any of these three lesser deities appealed to you? Why or why not?

3. *God is the "One who is" and the "One who causes." Why is that important? Because we need a big God. And if God is the "One who is," then he is an unchanging God.*

   A. Why do we need a big God? Why do we need an unchanging God?

   B. What would be different about your life if God were smaller than he is? How would you feel if he changed capriciously?

4. *Unchanging. Uncaused. Ungoverned. These are only a fraction of God's qualities, but aren't they enough to give you a glimpse of your Father? Don't we need this kind of shepherd? Don't we need an unchanging shepherd?*

   A. How do you answer Max's questions?

   B. Give an example of how God has been an unchanging shepherd in your life.

TRAVELING UP

1. Read Exodus 3:13–17; 6:2–8.

 A. What do you learn about God from his name?

 B. What do you learn about God from his track record?

 C. What do you learn about God's concern for his people?

2. Read Psalm 102:25–27; 139:7–12.

 A. What do you learn about God from these passages? How do these verses affect your view of God?

3. Read 1 Timothy 6:13–16.

 A. What do you learn about God from this text?

 B. How does Paul suggest we respond to this God?

4. Read Isaiah 40:21–31.

A. What does this text reveal about God?

B. What does God think of pretenders to his throne?

C. How does God intend for this majestic picture of him to encourage our weary hearts?

TRAVELING ON

1. Do a study on the false gods described in Scripture. Start with names such as "Chemosh," "Baal," "Asherah," and the generic "gods." Do other research, perhaps in a good Bible dictionary, to discover something about these "lesser gods." How do they compare to the God of Jesus?

2. Spend some time meditating and concentrating on the attributes of the real God of the Bible. Consider using a daily devotional such as *How Great Thou Art* (Sister, Ore.: Multnomah, 1999), which focuses for a full year on the majesty and greatness of God.

3

I'll Do It My Way

The Burden of Self-Reliance

TRAVELING BACK

1. *We humans want to do things our way. Forget the easy way. Forget the common way. Forget the best way. Forget God's way. We want to do things* our *way.*

   A. What is it about us that causes us to desire our own way?

   B. When we rely on ourselves rather than God, what is the result?

2. *When David, who was a warrior, minstrel, and ambassador for God, searched for an illustration of God, he remembered his days as a shepherd. . . . And the way he cared for the sheep reminded him of the way God cares for us. David rejoiced to say, "The LORD is my shepherd," and in so doing he proudly implied, "I am his sheep."*

A. Why do you think David chose to picture God through the image of a shepherd? Why not use another image?

B. Do you proudly think of yourself as a sheep? Explain.

3. *Will you humor me and take a simple quiz? See if you succeed in self-reliance. Raise your hand if any of the following describe you.*

You can control your moods.

You are at peace with everyone.

You have no fears.

You need no forgiveness.

A. Describe someone you know who believes he or she fits one of the previous four statements.

B. Which of these four areas of life cause you the most struggles? Explain.

C. Why is it that the ones who most need a shepherd resist him so?

TRAVELING UP

1. Read Jeremiah 17:5–8.

A. What does the Lord think of someone who relies on himself (v. 5)?

B. What is the result of relying on yourself (v. 6)?

C. How does the Lord feel about those who trust in him (v. 7)?

D. What is the result of trusting in God (v. 8)?

2. Read Deuteronomy 8:10–18.

A. What are we to do in times of prosperity (v. 10)?

B. In what way can prosperity create a spiritual threat (vv. 11–14)?

C. Why is it always foolish to believe that we are self-sufficient (vv. 15–18)?

3. Read 1 Corinthians 4:6–7.

   A. What does it mean to "not go beyond what is written" (v. 6 NIV)? Why does the Bible warn us to "not go beyond what is written"?

   B. How would you answer Paul's three questions in verse 7?

TRAVELING ON

1. Consciously get out of your comfort zone, and do something that requires you to rely on another person. Make it as exotic as a parachute jump or as mundane as asking directions to a place you've never visited.

2. Read the classic *A Shepherd Looks at Psalm 23* by Phillip Keller to gain a better picture of what it means to be a sheep in the fold of God.

4

The Prison of Want

The Burden of Discontent

TRAVELING BACK

1. *The prison of want. You've seen her prisoners. They are "in want." They want something. They want something bigger. Nicer. Faster. Thinner. They want.*

   A. Are you in prison?

   B. What things in life are most likely to send you to this prison? Describe them.

2. *David has found the pasture where discontent goes to die. It's as if he is saying, "What I have in God is greater than what I don't have in life."*

   A. What do you have in God? List the first ten things that come to mind.

   B. Can you say that what you have in God is greater than what you don't have in life? Explain.

3. *Are you hoping that a change in circumstances will bring a change in your attitude? If so, you are in prison, and you need to learn a secret of traveling light.*

   A. Answer the question above and explain your answer.

   B. What is this secret of traveling light? How does one master it?

4. *What is the one thing separating you from joy? How do you fill in this blank: "I will be happy when _____"? When I am healed. When I am promoted. When I am married. When I am single. When I am rich. How would you finish that statement?*

   A. Answer the question above.

   B. How does this thing separate you from joy? How long has it been doing so? How can you deprive it of its power over you?

TRAVELING UP

1. Read Luke 12:13–21.

   A. What warning does Jesus give in verse 15? What declaration does he make?

   B. What error did the rich man make in the parable Jesus told?

   C. What does it mean to be "rich toward God" (v. 21)? Are you rich toward God? Explain.

2. Read Philippians 4:10–13.

   A. Why did Paul "rejoice greatly in the Lord" (v. 10 NIV)?

   B. What secret does Paul describe in verse 12? How did he gain access to this secret? Do you know this secret? Explain.

   C. How does verse 13 relate to the context of the passage? How does it relate specifically to contentment?

3. Read 1 Timothy 6:3–10.

A. How does Paul characterize those who teach that godliness is a means to financial gain (v. 5)?

B. What does Paul say *is* "great gain" (v. 6 NIV)?

C. What reason does Paul give for his statement (vv. 7–8)?

D. What warning does Paul give in verses 9–10? Why do so many people ignore this warning? What do you think of his warning? Explain.

TRAVELING ON

1. Make a list of at least a dozen things you possess, whether spiritual or material, that came to you as a result of your relationship with God.

2. Do a Bible study on contentment. Use a good concordance to look up words such as *content* and *contented,* then study

the verses that you find. Also see what a good Bible dictionary or encyclopedia has to say on the topic. What do you learn?

5

I Will Give You Rest

The Burden of Weariness

TRAVELING BACK

1. *People with too much work and too little sleep step over to the baggage claim of life and grab the duffel bag of weariness. You don't carry this one. You don't hoist it onto your shoulder and stride down the street. You drag it as you would a stubborn St. Bernard.*

   A. What sorts of things tend to make you weary?

   B. How do you normally deal with weariness? What did you do the last time weariness struck hard?

2. *In our book, busyness is next to godliness. We idolize Thomas Edison, who claimed he could live on fifteen-minute naps. Somehow we forget to mention Al-*

bert Einstein, who averaged eleven hours of sleep a night.

A. How often do you tell others, "I'm really busy right now"? What keeps you so busy?

B. How much sleep do you normally get? Is it sufficient for you to function well? Explain.

3. *God's message is plain: "If creation didn't crash when I rested, it won't crash when you do." Repeat these words after me: It is not my job to run the world.*

A. Name some of the reasons you have heard (or used yourself) for not getting adequate rest.

B. Why do you think God so emphasized the fourth commandment, about resting on the Sabbath day?

4. *In a world rocky with human failure, there is a land lush with divine mercy. Your Shepherd invites you there. He wants*

you to lie down. Nestle deeply until you are hidden, buried, in the tall shoots of his love, and there you will find rest.

A. What is your favorite way of nestling deeply "in the tall shoots of his love"? Describe what most refreshes you.

B. What is keeping you from resting in God's love right now?

TRAVELING UP

1. Read Exodus 20:8–11.

A. What does it mean to keep the Sabbath day "holy"?

B. What does God command Israel in verses 9–10?

C. What reason does God give in verse 11 for his command?

D. Why do you think God so highly values our rest?

2. Read Isaiah 30:15–18.

   A. According to verse 15, Israel's salvation consisted in what? How did the nation respond to this direction?

   B. What response is described in verse 16? How do we often respond in a similar way?

   C. What is the result of ignoring God's command to rest (v. 17)?

   D. Despite our foolishness, how does the Lord treat us (v. 18)?

3. Read Hebrews 4:1–11.

   A. What does the writer warn us about in verse 1?

   B. What keeps people from entering God's rest (vv. 2–6)?

   C. When is the best time to obey God's command (v. 7)?

D. What kind of rest is the writer describing in verse 9?

E. How do we "labour" to enter God's rest (v. 11 KJV)?

TRAVELING ON

1. What activities or events keep you busy? Try an experiment to judge the accuracy of your assumptions. Keep a "busyness journal" for one week, recording the things that occupy your time. Write down not only what you did but also how long each took. Then at the end of the week evaluate your journal. Are you busy doing the things that matter most? Or do you need to make some changes?

2. How much sleep do you get? Keep a chart for one month, accurately recording the amount and quality of your sleep. Do the results surprise you? What changes, if any, do you need to make?

6

Whaddifs and Howells

The Burden of Worry

TRAVELING BACK

1. *Worry is the burlap bag of burdens. It's overflowing with "whaddifs" and "howells." "Whaddif it rains at my wedding?" "Howell I know when to discipline my kids?" "Whaddif I marry a guy who snores?" "Howell we pay our baby's tuition?"*

   A. What "whaddifs" trouble you the most?

   B. What "howells" give you the most grief?

   C. How do you typically deal with these "whaddifs" and "howells"?

2. *Worry divides the mind. The biblical word for* worry (merimnao) *is a compound of two Greek words,* merizo *("to divide")* and nous *("the mind"). Anxiety splits our*

energy between today's priorities and to-morrow's problems. Part of our mind is on the now; the rest is on the not yet. The re-sult is half-minded living.

A. What practical things can we do to keep from spending today's energies on tomorrow's problems?

B. What issues are most likely to nudge you toward half-minded living? Why?

3. *God leads us. God will do the right thing at the right time. And what a difference that makes.*

A. How has God led you in the past? De-scribe at least one incident.

B. Do we believe that God will do the right thing at the right time? How would our lives change if we really be-lieved this?

C. What in your life would change *right now* if you believed this fully?

4. *Meet today's problems with today's strength. Don't start tackling tomorrow's problems until tomorrow. You do not have tomorrow's strength yet. You simply have enough for today.*

   A. How many of the things you have worried about actually have come to pass?

   B. What issues that should be dealt with today are you avoiding by trying to tackle tomorrow's problems?

TRAVELING UP

1. Read Matthew 6:25–34.

   A. What reason does Jesus give for refusing to worry (vv. 25–27)?

   B. Why should worry not trouble Christians in the same way it troubles nonbelievers (vv. 31–32)?

   C. If we are not to worry, what are we to do (v. 33)? What does this mean in practical terms?

D. What additional reason for not worrying does Jesus give in verse 34?

2. Read Philippians 4:6–8.

A. How does Paul recommend that we
combat worry?

B. According to Paul, what will we enjoy
when we follow his counsel?

C. Rather than worry, what kinds of
things should fill our minds (v. 8)?

3. Read Hebrews 4:14–16.

A. Describe the high priest pictured in
this passage.

B. How is verse 16 designed to combat
our worry?

TRAVELING ON

1. Make a list of the things in life that worry
you the most. Then, one by one, commit
these items to the Lord in prayer. As you
pray for each concern, tear it off your
sheet of paper and throw it in the trash.

2. Use a good concordance to do a word study on worry. Look up terms such as *worry, worried, anxious,* and *anxiety,* and study the verses that you find. What do you learn about how to combat worry?

7

It's a Jungle Out There

The Burden of Hopelessness

TRAVELING BACK

1. *Hopelessness is an odd bag. Unlike the others, it isn't full. It is empty, and its emptiness creates the burden. Unzip the top and examine all the pockets. Turn it upside down and shake it hard. The bag of hopelessness is painfully empty.*

   A. Describe a time when you felt hopeless. What made you feel that way?

   B. What in your life right now threatens your hope? How will you deal with it?

2. *If you have only a person but no renewed vision, all you have is company. If he has a vision but no direction, you have a dreamer for company. But if you have a person with direction—who can take you from this place to the right place—ah, then you have one who can restore your hope.*

A. Why does it take a competent guide to restore hope?

B. Do you have such a guide? Explain.

3. *God, your rescuer, has the right vision. He also has the right direction. He made the boldest claim in the history of man when he declared, "I am the way."*

A. What did Jesus mean when he said, "I am the way"?

B. Why wasn't it arrogant of Jesus to say that he was *the* way? Then what about Muhammad, the Dalai Lama, or spiritual leaders of other faiths?

4. *We ask God, "Where are you taking me? Where is the path?" And he, like the guide, doesn't tell us. Oh, he may give us a hint or two, but that's all. If he did, would we understand? Would we comprehend our location? No, like the traveler, we are unacquainted with this jungle. So rather than give us an answer, Jesus gives us a far greater gift. He gives us himself.*

A. How does it make you feel that God almost never tells us what lies ahead for us? Do you wish he did things differently? Explain.

B. In what ways has Jesus guided you in the past? How are you depending upon his guidance right now?

TRAVELING UP

1. Read Psalm 121.

A. From where did the psalmist expect his hope to arrive (v. 2)?

B. How much sleep does God get each night (vv. 3–4)? Why is this important?

C. What kinds of things is the Lord said to watch over in verses 5–8? How can this give you hope?

2. Read Psalm 33:16–22.

A. What *cannot* save a king or a warrior (vv. 16–17)? Why are these things vain hopes?

B. On whom does the Lord fix his eyes (v. 18)? What difference does this make?

C. What does it mean to "wait in hope" (v. 20 NIV)? How can you put your hope in the Lord?

3. Read Romans 8:18–25.

A. Why should we avoid attaching too much importance to our present sufferings (v. 18)?

B. Why do we need hope in the first place (vv. 19–23)?

C. How does Paul define real hope (v. 24)?

D. Why is it always too soon to give up hope (v. 25)?

TRAVELING ON

1. Take a guided tour of a place you've never visited. During the tour, consciously remind yourself of how your Savior de-

sires to guide you through life. What un-expected discoveries or parallels do you uncover?

2. Do a Bible study on hope. Use a good concordance to look up the word *hope* and its derivatives, like *hoping, hoped, hopeful,* etc. What do you learn?

8

A Heavenly Exchange

The Burden of Guilt

TRAVELING BACK

1. *God is never wrong. He has never rendered a wrong decision, experienced the wrong attitude, taken the wrong path, said the wrong thing, or acted the wrong way. He is never too late or too early, too loud or too soft, too fast or too slow. He has always been and always will be right. He is righteous.*

   A. Has it ever felt as if God made a mistake with your life? If so, how did you deal with this feeling?

   B. Who is the most "righteous" person you know? What makes you say this about him or her?

2. *The weight of weariness pulls you down. Self-reliance misleads you. Disappointments discourage you. Anxiety plagues you. But guilt? Guilt consumes you. So*

what do we do? Our Lord is right, and we are wrong. His party is for the guiltless, and we are anything but. What do we do?

A. Answer the question above.

B. How do you deal with disappointments? With anxiety? Guilt?

3. *It was, at once, history's most beautiful and most horrible moment. Jesus stood in the tribunal of heaven. Sweeping a hand over all creation, he pleaded, "Punish me for their mistakes. See the murderer? Give me his penalty. The adulteress? I'll take her shame. The bigot, the liar, the thief? Do to me what you would do to them. Treat me as you would a sinner." And God did.*

A. Why did innocent Jesus request to take the punishment due to murderers, adulterers, and other sinners?

B. Have you allowed Jesus to take on himself your own sin? Explain.

4. *The path of righteousness is a narrow, winding trail up a steep hill. At the top of the hill is a cross. At the base of the cross are bags. Countless bags full of innumerable sins. Calvary is the compost pile for guilt.*

    A. In what way is Calvary "the compost pile for guilt"?

    B. If you have set your bag of guilt at the foot of Calvary, describe how this came to be. If you have not already done so, why not?

TRAVELING UP

1. Read Romans 3:9–18.

    A. What does it mean to be "under sin" (NIV)? Who is "under sin" (v. 9)?

    B. List the characteristics of being "under sin" (vv. 10–17).

    C. How does verse 18 summarize all the characteristics you just listed?

2. Read Isaiah 45:21–25.

    A. How does God describe himself in verse 21?

    B. What command does God give in verse 22?

    C. What prediction does God give in verses 23–24?

    D. What promise does God give in verse 25? To whom is he referring?

3. Read Romans 5:6–11 and 1 Peter 3:18.

    A. According to Romans 5:6, for whom did Christ die?

    B. What drove Christ to die for us (v. 8)?

    C. What is the difference between being "justified" and "saved" (v. 9 NIV)?

    D. What is the normal response of one who has been "reconciled" (v. 11 NIV)? Is this your response? Explain.

TRAVELING ON

1. Read a contemporary book by an author who exchanged his or her guilt for the forgiveness of God. How does this remind you of your own need for forgiveness?

2. Is there someone in your life whom you need to forgive but haven't? Remember Jesus' words: "But if you do not forgive men their sins, your Father will not forgive your sins" (Matthew 6:15 NIV). Commit today to forgive this person—and if possible, let him or her know what you've done.

Get Over Yourself

The Burden of Arrogance

Traveling Back

1. *God . . . doesn't dislike arrogance. He doesn't disapprove of arrogance. He's not unfavorably disposed toward arrogance. God hates arrogance. What a meal of maggots does for our stomach, human pride does for God's.*

    A. Why do you think God dislikes human pride?

    B. Would you consider yourself a prideful person? Would others agree with you? Explain.

2. *God . . . hates arrogance because we haven't done anything to be arrogant about. Do art critics give awards to the canvas? Is there a Pulitzer for ink? Can you imagine a scalpel growing smug after a successful heart transplant? Of*

course not. They are only tools, so they get no credit for the accomplishments.

A. In what way are we "tools" in God's hands?

B. Is there any room at all for taking pride in one's accomplishments? Explain.

3. *Why does God have anything to do with us?* For his name's sake. *No other name on the marquee. No other name up in lights. No other name on the front page. This is all done for God's glory.*

A. Why isn't it vain of God to associate with us for *his* name's sake?

B. What is meant by "God's glory"? Why is God's glory so important?

4. Consider several ways to cultivate humility and kill ungodly pride:

- Assess yourself honestly.

- Don't take success too seriously.

- Celebrate the significance of others.

- Don't demand your own parking place.

- Never announce your success before it occurs.

- Speak humbly.

- Live at the foot of the cross.

A. Who can help you assess yourself honestly? What does such an assessment reveal?

B. How can you celebrate the significance of others? Who in your immediate circle do you need to celebrate right now?

C. How can you "live at the foot of the cross"? What does this mean?

TRAVELING UP

1. Read Proverbs 16:5, 18–19.

A. What does the Lord think of the proud (v. 5)? How will he respond to them?

B. What is the outcome of pride (v. 18)?

C. What contrast is made in verse 19? Why is this true?

2. Read Isaiah 57:15–19; 66:2.

A. How does the Lord describe himself in verse 15? With whom is he pleased to live?

B. Why will God not "accuse forever" (v. 16)?

C. How will the Lord respond to those who turn to him in faith (vv. 18–19)?

D. Whom does God esteem, according to Isaiah 66:2? Why does the Lord delight in men and women like this?

3. Read Philippians 2:3–11.

A. What does verse 3 instruct us not to do? What should we do instead?

B. What overall instruction do we receive in verse 5?

C. How did Jesus follow this instruction during his earthly ministry (vv. 6–8)?

D. How will God reward Jesus for his faithfulness (vv. 9–11)?

E. In what way are we to emulate Jesus' example? How are you doing in this regard? Explain.

TRAVELING ON

1. Watch a classic movie such as *Citizen Kane* to see how even Hollywood sometimes recognizes the deadly poison of human pride. How does pride ultimately destroy the person who lets it control him or her?

2. Do a Bible study on how God does everything for the sake of his name. Look up references to "the name," "my name," "his name," etc. What do you discover?

10

I Will Lead You Home

The Burden of the Grave

TRAVELING BACK

1. *Someday our Shepherd . . . will take us to the mountain by way of the valley. He will guide us to his house through the valley of the shadow of death.*

   A. Do you think of your own death, or do you avoid the thought? Explain.

   B. Has a believer you were close to ever died? If so, describe how the Shepherd guided him or her through the valley of the shadow of death.

2. *David grants us two important reminders that can help us surrender our fear of the grave. We all have to face it. . . . And though his first reminder sobers us, his second reminder encourages us:* We don't have to face death alone.

A. If you were to face your own death to-morrow, would you be ready? Explain.

B. Do you feel as though you would be facing death alone? Explain.

3. *Don't face death without facing God. Don't even speak of death without speaking to God. He and he alone can guide you through the valley. Others may speculate or aspire, but only God knows the way to get you home. And only God is committed to getting you there safely.*

A. Name a few ways in which God helps his children face death.

B. How can we be certain God is committed to getting us to heaven safely?

4. *[Jesus] may send missionaries to teach you, angels to protect you, teachers to guide you, singers to inspire you, and physicians to heal you, but he sends no one to take you. He reserves this job for himself.*

A. When Jesus comes to take you home, what do you think you might say to him first?

B. Why do you think Jesus insists on coming in person to get you? How does this make you feel?

TRAVELING UP

1. Read Psalm 116:15; 139:16.

A. What does Psalm 116:15 say is "precious" to God? Why is this so?

B. What claim does Psalm 139:16 make? Does this give you comfort? Explain.

2. Read 1 Thessalonians 4:13–18.

A. What do you learn from this passage about those who die in Christ?

B. How are these words intended to "encourage" us? Why are we instructed to repeat these words to others?

3. Read 2 Corinthians 5:1–10.

   A. What does Paul mean by "earthly tent" (v. 1 NIV)? Why use this picture?

   B. What is life like in this "tent"? How does Paul contrast life in the "heavenly dwelling" (v. 2 NIV)?

   C. What token has God given us to assure us that what he says will one day happen, will actually happen (v. 5)?

   D. How is the information in this passage supposed to make us "confident" (v. 6 NIV)?

   E. What preference does Paul express in verse 8? Why does he prefer this?

   F. How is verse 10 both a promise and a warning?

TRAVELING ON

1. Visit a nearby cemetery, and spend at least an hour reading the gravestones to remind yourself both of death's reality

and of the hope believers can have despite its cold embrace.

2. Read Herbert Lockyer's classic book, *Last Words of Saints and Sinners*. How do the deaths of the two groups compare?

11

When Mourning Comes

The Burden of Grief

TRAVELING BACK

1. *The black bag of sorrow is hard to bear. It's hard to bear because not everyone understands your grief. They did at first. They did at the funeral. They did at the graveside. But they don't now; they don't understand. Grief lingers.*

   A. How do you personally deal with sorrow?

   B. How can we help someone whose grief just won't go away?

2. *Only God knows the reasons behind his actions. But here is a key truth on which we can stand.* Our God is a good God.

   A. Why do you think God seldom "explains" his actions in our lives?

B. How have you personally experienced that God is a good God?

3. *Death is God's way of taking people away from evil. From what kind of evil? An extended disease? An addiction? A dark season of rebellion? We don't know. But we know that no person lives one day more or less than God intends.*

A. Have you ever thought about death in this way? That it's God's way of taking people away from evil? How do you respond to this idea?

B. How can the idea of God's sovereignty bring comfort in a time of death? How can the doctrine be used to increase someone's pain?

4. *God will lead you* through, *not around, the valley of the shadow of death. And, by the way, aren't you glad it's just a shadow?*

A. If God really loves us, why doesn't he lead us *around* the valley of the shadow of death? Why lead us *through* it?

B. Is death merely a shadow for you? Explain.

TRAVELING UP

1. Read Lamentations 3:31–33.

    A. How can verse 31 give you hope when you find yourself engulfed in grief?

    B. What do you learn about God in verse 32?

    C. Why is it important that God does not "willingly" bring us grief (v. 33 NIV)? Why does he bring us grief at all?

2. Read John 16:20–22.

    A. What two promises did Jesus give his disciples in verse 20?

    B. What illustration did Jesus use in verse 21 to picture his promises of verse 20? What can we learn from this illustration?

C. What promise does Jesus give in verse 22? How certain is this promise? On what is it based? How can it continue to help you today when you face grief?

3. Read 1 Peter 1:3–9.

A. What great blessing does Peter describe in verses 3–4? Do you share in this blessing? Explain.

B. What kind of shield are we promised in verse 5?

C. Does genuine faith exempt one from grief (v. 6)? Why or why not?

D. How do trials and the grief they bring fit in with the Christian life (v. 7)?

E. What blessing comes to those who believe in Christ (v. 8)?

F. What blessing does faith ultimately bring to those who exercise it (v. 9)?

TRAVELING ON

1. Interview someone you know to be gifted in the art of comforting the grieving. Look for someone whom others seek out in a time of loss. Ask the person what he or she does at these times. What do you learn?

2. Do a Bible study on the words *tear* and *tears.* What do you learn?

From Panic to Peace

The Burden of Fear

TRAVELING BACK

1. *Jesus flat on the ground? Face in the dirt? Extended hands gripping grass? Body rising and falling with sobs? Face as twisted as the olive trees that surround him? What do we do with this image of Jesus? Simple. We turn to it when we look the same.*

   A. Describe the last time you felt the way Jesus is described above.

   B. How does it help us to know that Jesus felt this way?

2. *When you feel the panic, don't focus on the people; focus on the opening. Good counsel in golf. Good counsel in life. Rather than focus on the fear, focus on the solution.*

A. What kind of situations make you most fearful?

B. When you face one of these frightening events, how can you "focus on the opening"? What "solution" can you call upon?

3. *Don't avoid life's Gardens of Gethsemane. Enter them. Just don't enter them alone. And while there, be honest. Pounding the ground is permitted. Tears are allowed. And if you sweat blood, you won't be the first. Do what Jesus did; open your heart.*

A. How do we try to avoid life's Gardens of Gethsemane? Describe the last time you tried to avoid one.

B. Is it easy or hard for you to express your emotions like this? Explain.

4. *Don't measure the size of the mountain; talk to the One who can move it. Instead of carrying the world on your shoulders, talk to the One who holds the universe on his. Hope is a look away.*

A. How do we often try to "measure the size of the mountain"? Why is this a bad idea?

B. In what way is hope "a look away"? How can prayer help to restore our hope? Does it help restore yours? Explain.

TRAVELING UP

1. Read Psalm 56:3–4.

A. How does the psalmist deal with his own fears? Do you follow his example? Explain.

B. Why is the psalmist unafraid of "mortal man" (v. 4 NIV)? Is this a statement of ignorance or something else? Explain.

2. Read Isaiah 41:10–14.

A. Why does God tell Israel not to fear (v. 10)?

B. What promise does God give in verses 11–12?

C. What reason does God give for his promise in verse 13?

D. What command and promise does God give in verse 14? How can his words encourage you today?

3. Read 1 John 4:16–19.

A. On what should we rely when we are afraid (v. 16)?

B. How does John describe God in verse 16? What difference does this make?

C. How can we have "confidence on the day of judgment" (v. 17 NIV)?

D. What antidote to fear does John give in verse 18? How does this antidote work?

E. How is this antidote to be shared? How does this show that we really have the antidote?

TRAVELING ON

1. In your journal write about a time you had "garden" experiences. Explain what situation took you there, how you felt, what prayers you prayed, and how God ministered to you.

2. Read *Foxe's Book of Martyrs* to see how many of God's choicest saints overcame their fear even as they faced death.

13

Silent Nights and Solitary Days

The Burden of Loneliness

TRAVELING BACK

1. *By now you've learned that you don't have to be alone to feel lonely.*

   A. What's the difference between being alone and feeling lonely?

   B. Do you avoid being alone? Explain.

   C. How often, in a normal week, would you say you feel lonely?

2. *Loneliness is not the absence of faces. It is the absence of intimacy. Loneliness doesn't come from being alone; it comes from feeling alone.*

   A. How would you define nonsexual intimacy? With how many friends can you speak intimately? Are you satisfied with this number? Explain.

B. How do you deal with loneliness? When you feel lonely, what do you do?

3. *Could it be that loneliness is not a curse but a gift? A gift from God? . . . I wonder if loneliness is God's way of getting our attention.*

A. Do you agree that loneliness can be a gift from God? Explain.

B. Why might God want to get your attention through loneliness? To what might he want to call your attention?

4. *God changes your* n *into a* v. *You go from* lonely *to* lovely. *When you know God loves you, you won't be desperate for the love of others.*

A. How does assurance of God's love for you, personally, change everything?

B. Does knowledge of God's love eliminate the need for intimate friends? Explain.

C. What's the difference between desiring the love of others and being desperate for it?

TRAVELING UP

1. Read Psalm 88.

   A. How would you describe the man who wrote this psalm?

   B. Why do you think God included this psalm in the Bible?

   C. Have you ever felt as the psalmist did in verses 13–14? Explain.

   D. Most psalms do not end as this one does (v. 18). Why do you think it ends like this? Is this a comfort to you? Explain.

2. Read Deuteronomy 31:6–8.

   A. What command does God give the Israelites in verse 6? What encouragement does he give them?

B. Why do you suppose that Moses repeats to Joshua both the command and the encouragement in verses 7–8? What does this suggest to you about dealing with your own fears?

3. Read John 14:16–18; Matthew 28:16–20.

A. What request did Jesus say he would make of the Father in John 14:16?

B. What promise did Jesus make in John 14:18? How is he fulfilling this promise today?

C. How can we take courage from Jesus' words in Matthew 28:18?

D. What encouragement can we get from Jesus' final words in Matthew 28:20? Are you relying on this promise? Why or why not?

TRAVELING ON

1. Examine your schedule, and find an entire day when you can plan to get alone,

just you and God. Go to a retreat center, a solitary spot, a place in the woods, any place where you can spend a whole day in solitude. Bring your Bible, and make no other plans than to spend the day alone with God.

2. Get a group of your believing friends together, and spend a few hours visiting some of your church's shut-ins, whether at their homes or in care centers. Relieve their loneliness for a while.

The Crowing Rooster and Me

The Burden of Shame

TRAVELING BACK

1. *Is Peter the only person to do the very thing he swore he'd never do? "Infidelity is behind me!" "From now on, I'm going to bridle my tongue." "No more shady deals. I've learned my lesson." Oh, the volume of our boasting. And, oh, the heartbreak of our shame.*

   A. Describe a time when you followed Peter's example and did the very thing you swore you'd never do. What happened?

   B. Why do you think we engage in such foolish boasting? What do we think we'll gain?

2. *We weep as Peter wept, and we do what Peter did. We go fishing. We go back to*

our old lives. We return to our pre-Jesus practices. We do what comes naturally, rather than what comes spiritually. And we question whether Jesus has a place for folks like us.

A. Have you ever "gone fishing" or returned to your pre-Jesus practices after a spiritual failure? If so, how did you feel at the time?

B. Why do we question whether Jesus has a place for folks like us? Have you ever felt this way? Explain.

3. *Jesus prepared a table in the presence of the enemy. Judas was allowed to see the supper, but he wasn't allowed to stay there.* You are not welcome here. This table is for my children. You may tempt them. You may trip them. But you will never sit with them. *This is how much he loves us.*

A. Why do you think Jesus allowed Judas to see the supper? Why not banish him before the disciples gathered?

B. What does the Lord's Supper mean to you personally? What goes through your mind during the service?

4. *The same Jesus who'd prepared a meal for Peter had prepared one for me. The same Shepherd who had trumped the devil trumped him again. The same Savior who had built a fire on the shore stirred a few embers in my heart. "Every one of you drink this." And so I did. It felt good to be back at the table.*

A. Why do you think Jesus prepared a meal for Peter, who denied him, but not for Judas, who betrayed him? What was the difference?

B. How do the stories of both Peter and Max show true repent-ance? How does Jesus always respond to true repentance? Why is this important to understand?

TRAVELING UP

1. Read Joel 2:25–27.

    A. What promise does God make to his people who repent (v. 25)?

    B. Why do you think God twice says in verses 26–27 that his people will never again be shamed? Why does God care about getting rid of shame?

2. Read 2 Timothy 2:15–16.

    A. What instruction is given in verse 15? How can you comply with this command?

    B. How can we avoid being ashamed, according to verse 15?

    C. How does verse 16 continue to tell us how to avoid being ashamed?

3. Read Hebrews 12:2–3.

    A. What are we instructed to do in verse 2? How can this keep us from being ashamed?

B. How did Jesus react to the shame of the cross? Why was there shame at the cross?

C. How are we to benefit from the example of Jesus on the cross?

TRAVELING ON

1. Think of Max's story and how shame kept him from fellowship with God. Be honest with yourself, and ask if you're dealing with anything similar. If so, follow Max's courageous example, and admit this "shameful thing" to a trusted and godly friend. Break its power over you by confessing and forsaking it—and be glad at the Lord's table once more.

2. If you ever have the opportunity, attend a Seder prepared by someone who can explain the Messianic significance of this ancient Jewish meal. Enrich your appreciation of the Lord's Supper.

15

Slippery Sheep and Healed Hurts

The Burden of Disappointment

TRAVELING BACK

1. *A disappointment is a missed appointment. What we hoped would happen, didn't. We wanted health; we got disease. We wanted retirement; we got reassignment. Divorce instead of family. Dismissal instead of promotion.*

   A. What disappointments have you had to face recently?

   B. What do you do with your disappointments?

2. *Just like sheep, we have wounds, but ours are wounds of the heart that come from disappointment after disappointment. If we're not careful, these wounds lead to bitterness. And so just like sheep, we need to be treated.*

A. How do repeated disappointments lead to bitterness?

B. What kinds of things have made you bitter? How do you deal with bitterness?

3. *The large portion of our problems are not lion-sized attacks, but rather the day-to-day swarm of frustrations and mishaps and heartaches.*

A. What little things in life tend to frustrate you the most?

B. What help can you offer to someone plagued with a swarm of mishaps or heartaches?

4. *Jesus tends to his sheep. And he will tend to you. If you will let him. How? How do you let him? The steps are so simple. First, go to him. Second, assume the right posture. Bow before God. Third, trust in him.*

A. How can you "go to" Jesus? What does it mean to "go to" him?

B. Why is it necessary to "bow" before God? What does this mean?

C. What does it mean to "trust" in God? How do we do this, practically speaking?

TRAVELING UP

1. Read Psalm 22:2–5.

A. What disappointment did David suffer in verse 2? Have you ever felt like this? Explain.

B. How did David combat his disappointment in verses 3–5?

C. What was the result of the ancestors' trust described in verses 4–5? How is this meant to encourage us?

D. Consider that this is the psalm Jesus quoted while hanging on the cross. What do you think the psalm taught him about disappointment?

2. Read Romans 5:1–5.

    A. How do we gain peace with God (v. 1)?

    B. What benefit does this peace gain us (v. 2)? How should this make us feel?

    C. What relationship does sufferings have to hope (vv. 3–5)?

    D. Why does hope not disappoint us (v. 5)? How does this matter to us on a day-to-day level?

3. Read Psalm 147:1–3.

    A. How did the Israelites deal with their disappointments (v. 1)?

    B. What encouragement does God give his people in verse 3?

    C. How do you think God heals the brokenhearted? What has he done in your own life?

TRAVELING ON

1. Make a list of your biggest disappointments in life. Write them down. Then take each one, in order, to God in prayer. Give them to him explicitly, one by one.

2. Make a new commitment to get involved in regular prayer. Set a time. Set a place. Set a specific period. Prepare a list of concerns and thanks to bring to God. Then do it.

16

Jam Session

The Burden of Envy

TRAVELING BACK

1. *Jealousy sets her cross hairs on the one who has more.*

    A. Describe a time when you felt jealous of someone. What prompted your jealousy?

    B. Why do most of us want "more"? What keeps us from being content with what we have?

2. *If focusing on our diminishing items leads to envy, what would happen if we focused on the unending items? If awareness of what we don't have creates jealousy, is it possible that an awareness of our abundance will lead to contentment?*

    A. Answer both of the preceding questions.

B. Try to itemize the "unending items" that you possess. What's on your list?

C. Try to list your "abundance." What does this tell you about God's provision?

3. *God is not a miser with his grace. Your cup may be low on cash or clout, but it is overflowing with mercy. You may not have the prime parking place, but you have sufficient pardon.*

A. How often do you ponder God's grace to you? His mercy?

B. How has God been gracious to you this week? This month? This year?

4. *One thing is certain. When the final storm comes and you are safe in your Father's house, you won't regret what he didn't give. You'll be stunned at what he did.*

A. Try to imagine the day you arrive safe in your Father's house. Look around. What has he given you?

B. How can meditating on your eternal future with God help you to deal with what exists today?

TRAVELING UP

1. Read Proverbs 14:30; 23:17.

A. With what does Proverbs 14:30 contrast envy? How is this significant?

B. In what ways do believers sometimes envy "sinners" (Prov. 23:17)?

C. What does it mean to be "zealous for the fear of the LORD" (NIV)?

2. Read James 3:13–4:5.

A. What in verse 13 does James contrast with "bitter envy" in verse 14?

B. Where does envy come from (v. 15)?

C. What always accompanies envy (v. 16)?

D. What causes fights and quarrels among spiritual brothers (4:1)?

E. God himself is said to "envy" in 4:5 (NIV). How does this differ from human envy?

3. Read Titus 3:3–7.

A. How does Paul describe his pre-Christian life (v. 3)? What do you think he envied?

B. How did God deliver us from envy (vv. 4–5)?

C. To what extent did God pour out his Holy Spirit on us (v. 6)? How is this meant to nip envy in the bud?

D. What was the purpose of God's saving us (v. 7)? How can meditating on this truth destroy envy?

TRAVELING ON

1. Draw a line down a sheet of paper, creating two columns. On the left side, list some of the things you envy in others. On the right side, list what God has supplied you in abundance and, if possible, in-

clude a Scripture reference. For example, in the left column you might say "I wish I had better health," and beside it, in the right column, you might list "God will give me a glorious, eternal body (Phil. 3:20–21)."

2. Make a date to serve dinner at a local rescue mission or homeless shelter. Try not to schedule your visit at Thanksgiving or Christmas (since such service organizations usually have more than enough help during those two holidays). And be thankful for what God has given you.

17

God's Loving Pursuit

The Burden of Doubt

TRAVELING BACK

1. *When Jesus found us, we acted like Eric. Our limitations kept us from recognizing the One who came to save us. We even doubted his presence—and sometimes we still do.*

    A. Do you ever doubt God's presence? If so, why?

    B. How do our limitations keep us from recognizing the One who came to save us? How can we overcome these limitations?

2. *If the Lord is the shepherd who leads the flock, goodness and mercy are the two sheepdogs who guard the rear of the flock.*

    A. How does "goodness" differ from "mercy"? How are they the same?

B. Where in your life do you most need God's goodness and mercy right now? Why don't you take the time to talk to him about your need?

3. *Trust your faith and not your feelings. . . . Measure your value through God's eyes, not your own. . . . See the big picture, not the small.*

A. How do we sometimes trust our feelings and not our faith? How can we stop making this mistake?

B. Take a few minutes to describe your value in God's eyes. What has he said about you in the Bible?

C. How can we see the big picture, not the small?

4. *Most of all, God gives us himself. Even when we choose our hovel over his house and our trash over his grace, still he follows. Never forcing us. Never leaving us. Patiently persistent. Faithfully present. Using all of his power to con-*

vince us that he is who he is and that he can be trusted to lead us home.

A. How do you know God has given you himself? How can you be sure of this?

B. How has God used his power to convince you he is who he is? What most convinces you that God can be trusted to lead you home?

TRAVELING UP

1. Read James 1:5–8.

A. To whom is verse 5 addressed? Do you qualify? Explain.

B. What promise does verse 5 make?

C. What condition is placed in verse 6 on the promise of verse 5?

D. To what does James compare someone who doubts God's promise? Why is this picture appropriate?

E. What warning is given in verses 7 and 8? In what way are these individuals "double-minded" (NIV)? How can one correct such a serious problem?

2. Read Jude 20–22.

A. What instruction is given in verse 20? How is this instruction to be carried out?

B. What instruction is given in verse 21? What future event empowers us to follow this instruction?

C. What instruction is given in verse 22? Why do you think the command was given? How can we comply with this command?

3. Read Romans 14:19–23.

A. Describe the command in verse 19. What is the purpose of this command? How well do you fulfill it? Explain.

B. How is it possible to destroy someone for the sake of food (v. 20)?

C. How does verse 21 relate to doubt?

D. What command is given in verse 22? What blessing is available? What does this blessing mean?

E. How is verse 23 an effective guideline for the entire Christian life? What rule is laid out here?

TRAVELING ON

1. Realize that there is a great difference between doubt and questions. Doubt disbelieves in the promises and good character of God; questions merely wonder how God might pull off some incredible feat. To get a "feel" for the difference between doubt and questions, study the vastly different ways God responded to Zechariah in Luke 1:5–20 and Mary in Luke 1:26–38. They asked similar questions ("How can I be sure of this?" versus "How will this be?" [NIV]) regarding mirac-

ulous pregnancies, but one was judged and the other blessed. Why?

2. Read Os Guinness's book *God in the Dark* for a clear and helpful discussion on doubt.

18

Almost Heaven

The Burden of Homesickness

Traveling Back

1. *The twists and turns of life have a way of reminding us—we aren't home here. This is not our homeland. We aren't fluent in the languages of disease and death. The culture confuses the heart, the noise disrupts our sleep, and we feel far from home. And, you know what? That's OK.*

    A. Why do we often forget that this is not our real home?

    B. In what ways do you feel like a foreigner on this earth? Are you OK with that? Explain.

2. *Homesickness is one of the burdens God doesn't mind if we carry. We ... are being prepared for another house. And we ... know we aren't there yet.*

A. Do you feel "homesick" for heaven? Explain.

B. How is God preparing you for "another house"?

3. *The greatest calamity is not to feel far from home when you are, but to feel right at home when you are not.*

A. Could it be that much of the disappointment we feel in life comes from trying to feel right at home when we're not? Explain.

B. How can we consciously guard against feeling at home in this world? Name several practical things we can do.

4. *Every wrinkle and every needle take us one step closer to the last step when Jesus will change our simple bodies into forever bodies. No pain. No depression. No sickness. No end.*

A. How does your own body remind you that this is not your forever home?

B. How would you respond to someone who says this desire for an eternal, painless body is merely wishful thinking and you'd be better off getting all the gusto while you can?

TRAVELING UP

1. Read Philippians 1:20–23.

   A. Describe Paul's firm expectation in verse 20. What challenge faced him?

   B. In your own words, explain what Paul meant in verse 21.

   C. Describe Paul's dilemma in verse 22. Why was he so torn?

   D. What did Paul mean by "depart" in verse 23 (NIV)? Depart where? Why would this be "better"?

2. Read Philippians 3:17–4:1.

   A. How does Paul describe the enemies of Christ in verses 18–19? What traits characterize them?

B. Describe the main contrast of these people with believers in Christ (v. 20).

C. For whom are Christians waiting (vv. 20–21)? What are they waiting for him to do?

D. What effect should meditating on this truth have on believers (4:1)? Does it have this effect on you? Explain.

3. Read 1 Corinthians 15:50–57.

A. What two contrasts does Paul make in verse 50? Why should this matter to us? Why is it important?

B. What "secret" or "mystery" does Paul describe in verses 51–52?

C. What kind of "clothes" will believers wear in heaven (v. 53)? Why is this important?

D. Restate the message of verses 54–57 in your own words. Imagine that you are describing this situation to an eight-year-old.

E. Are you "homesick"? Why or why not?

TRAVELING ON

1. Do a study in the four Gospels and in the Book of Acts on the Lord Jesus' postresurrection body. Describe it. Then realize that our resurrection bodies will look and act similar to his!

2. Read Joni Eareckson Tada's book titled *Heaven*. Joni has lived in a wheelchair for decades since a diving accident at age seventeen, so she expresses a uniquely powerful vision of heaven.